Josh and Satch

Baseball and American Society
Series ISBN 0-88736-566-3

1. Blackball Stars
   John B. Holway
   ISBN 0-88736-094-7   CIP 1988

2. Baseball History, Premier Edition
   Edited by Peter Levine
   ISBN 0-88736-288-5   1988

3. My 9 Innings: An Autobiography of 50 Years in Baseball
   Lee MacPhail
   ISBN 0-88736-387-3   CIP 1989

4. Black Diamonds: Life in the Negro Leagues from the Men Who Lived It
   John B. Holway
   ISBN 0-88736-334-2   CIP 1989

5. Baseball History 2
   Edited by Peter Levine
   ISBN 0-88736-342-3   1989

6. Josh and Satch: The Life and Times of Josh Gibson and Satchel Paige
   John B. Holway
   ISBN 0-88736-333-4   CIP 1991

7. Encyclopedia of Major League Baseball Team Histories
   Edited by Peter C. Bjarkman
   Volume 1: American League
   ISBN 0-88736-373-3   CIP 1991

8. Encyclopedia of Major League Baseball Team Histories
   Edited by Peter C. Bjarkman
   Volume 2: National League
   ISBN 0-88736-374-1   CIP 1991

9. Baseball History 3
   Edited by Peter Levine
   ISBN 0-88736-577-9   1990

10. The Immortal Diamond: Baseball in American Literature
    Peter C. Bjarkman
    ISBN 0-88736-481-0 (hardcover)   CIP forthcoming, 1991
    ISBN 0-88736-482-9 (softcover)   CIP forthcoming, 1991

11. Total Latin American Baseball
    Peter C. Bjarkman
    ISBN 0-88736-546-9   CIP forthcoming, 1992

12. Baseball Players and Their Times: Oral Histories of the Game, 1920–1940
    Eugene Murdock
    ISBN 0-88736-235-4   CIP 1991

13. The Tropic of Baseball: Baseball in the Dominican Republic
    Rob Ruck
    ISBN 0-88736-707-0   CIP 1991

14. The Cinema of Baseball: Images of America, 1929–1989
    Gary E. Dickerson
    ISBN 0-88736-710-0   CIP 1991

15. Baseball History 4
    Edited by Peter Levine
    ISBN 0-88736-578-7   CIP forthcoming, 1991

16. Baseball and American Society: A Textbook of Baseball History
    Peter C. Bjarkman
    ISBN 0-88736-483-7 (softcover)   CIP forthcoming, 1992

17. Cooperstown Symposium on
    Baseball and the American Culture (1989)
    Edited by Alvin L. Hall
    ISBN 0-88736-719-4   CIP 1991

18. Cooperstown Symposium on
    Baseball and the American Culture (1990)
    Edited by Alvin L. Hall
    ISBN 0-88736-735-6   CIP forthcoming, 1991

Josh and Satch
The Life and Times of
Josh Gibson and Satchel Paige

John B. Holway

Meckler

Westport ▪ London

FIRST EDITION

Library of Congress Cataloging-in-Publication Data

Holway, John.
    Josh and Satch : the life and times of Josh Gibson and Satchel
Paige / John B. Holway.
      p.   cm.
    Includes index.
    ISBN 0-88736-333-4 : $ (alk. paper)
    1. Gibson, Josh, 1911–1947.   2. Paige, Leroy, 1911–
3. Baseball players—United States—Biography.   I. Title.
GV865.G53H65   1991
796.357′092′2—dc20
[B]   91-3242
                                                      CIP

British Library Cataloguing in Publication Data is available.

ISBN 0-88736-333-4

Meckler Publishing, the publishing division of Meckler Corporation,
  11 Ferry Lane West, Westport, CT 06880.
Meckler Ltd., 247-249 Vauxhall Bridge Road, London SW1V 1HQ,
  U.K.

Printed on acid free paper.
Printed and bound in the United States of America.

*To Dick Clark and
the members of SABR*

I really want to read this book, because you're going from man to man. You can say you got the story from the people. That's the first time I ever heard of that. All the books I got, there ain't another book in there can say that. They just stood in one place and wrote the book. Somebody told 'em about so-and-so. Can't tell 'em how he even looked. That's where this book is going to be so different. You talked to all these men. See, this is going to be worth reading.

—Satchel Paige

Josh, if you and Satch played with me n' Paul on the Cardinals, we'd win the pennant by July 4th and go fishin' the rest of the year.

—Dizzy Dean

Contents

Introduction

On a muggy night in May 1944, a 14-year-old boy joined some 30,000 fans at Washington's old Griffith Stadium to watch one of the great matchups of baseball history, the two most famous names in the Negro leagues going against each other head to head—Josh Gibson vs Satchel Paige.

Satch, wearing the brown and white colors of the Kansas City Monarchs, took his pre-game warm-ups in front of the third base dugout, as I crowded at the railing with other scorecard-waving kids to watch. He used a windmill windup made famous by Dizzy Dean and emulated by Joe E. Brown in the 1930s movie, "Elmer the Great."

Across the field, on the first base side, Josh, in the pinstripes of the Washington Homestead Grays, was warming up his own pitcher. I recall him laughing merrily at some joke that tickled his funny bone.

My journey to the park was symbolic—by segregated Virginia bus to Washington, then by integrated trolley to the park. No one in the stands that night guessed it, but baseball, and American society at large, was soon about to make that same journey, from segregation to integration. And, said Eric (Ric) Roberts, who was covering the game for the black Pittsburgh *Courier,* Paige played a great part in bringing about that change.

Gibson would never board that integrated trolley to the majors. He would be dead at the age of 35, just three months before Jackie Robinson trotted out onto the field in his Dodger uniform.

Paige would make the trip. In fact, the next time I saw him was in Cleveland's cavernous Municipal Stadium, pitching in the World Series before what was then the greatest crowd in major league history.

Now, almost half a century later, I have spent 20 years researching the long melancholy chapter in American history that Josh and Satch symbolized. Among other things, I have learned that neither of these mythic gladiators was the only great black player of his age. As Paige himself said on many occasions:

If you want to know the truth, I wasn't the onliest one who could pitch in the Negro leagues. I told them at Cooperstown we had a lot of

Satchels, there were a lot of Joshes. We had top pitchers. We had quite a few men could hit the ball like Babe and Josh. Wasn't any mebbe so.

There were pitchers who were as good as Satch, maybe better, such as the Indian half-breed, Smokey Joe Williams, and the tough ex-soldier, Bullet Joe Rogan, both of whom were in their thirties before they pitched in the black majors. In a 1952 poll of Negro league experts, Williams edged Paige as the best pitcher by a single vote. In the Negro leagues, Paige is second in victories to lefty Big Bill Foster, 137–122.* (If the totals appear low, remember that the Negro leagues averaged 50–80 games a year, compared to 154–162 for the white majors.) However, if Satchel's victories in the white majors and minors, plus Latin America, are added, he totaled 215. (This does not include victories against semipro teams, which may have been another 200.) And as for strikeouts, Paige's total is almost double that of his closest rival, Foster.

Likewise, there were other black sluggers who blasted more home runs than Josh did. Surprisingly, his 141 homers rank only fourth on the all-time list, behind the slender left-hander, Turkey Stearnes, the leader with 185, burly Mule Suttles, and Oscar Charleston. But again, if one adds Latin America, Josh comes out way ahead. And Josh came to bat far less than the others. He averaged 44 homers for every 550 at bats, compared to 30 for Stearnes.

Gibson also came to bat far less often than Babe Ruth or Hank Aaron. Josh had 1812 official at bats, compared to 8399 for Babe and 12,364 for Hank. If Gibson had batted as often as Aaron, he would have slugged 996!

Josh and Satch have burned their names into baseball's consciousness, and its conscience. As other great blacks followed them— Willie Mays, Aaron, Reggie Jackson, Juan Marichal, Dwight Gooden— Gibson and Paige left us all sighing at what they—but also all of us— had missed.

Gibson may have hit the only ball ever to clear the roof of Yankee Stadium, and he swatted several other 500-footers to go with it. And Josh was cursed with two of the worst home run graveyards of the twentieth century—Forbes Field in Pittsburgh and Griffith Stadium in

---

*All Negro League statistics are based on research into original box scores. They are considered to be as complete as possible; however, some games were not reported in the newspapers, black or white.

Washington. Suttles at least had two easy targets to aim at in St. Louis and Newark, though he faced two "death valleys" in Birmingham and Chicago. Stearnes had a good target in Mack Park, Detroit, but his long blasts died in Chicago and Hamtramck. If any of the three had played a full 154-game schedule in, say, cozy Ebbets Field, one faints at how many homers he might have hit. The number of 75 for one season does not seem out of reach.

And this is not against patsy black pitching. Josh hit five homers in 61 at bats against Dizzy Dean, Johnny VanderMeer and other white big leaguers. That's a rate of 45 for 550 at bats. He also hit .426 against them.

The careers of Josh and Satch overlapped for 17 years, 1930–46, which coincided exactly with the last 17 years of baseball segregation. For most of those years they were rivals, and tales of their showdowns became legends. Satchel's Kansas City teammate, Buck O'Neil, remembers Satch and Josh, each at one end of a Pittsburgh bar, "yelling about what they would do to each other the next day."

For five years, 1932–34 and 1936–37, they were teammates on the Pittsburgh Crawfords and formed perhaps the greatest battery in the history of baseball. Certainly only Mickey Cochrane and Lefty Grove of the white leagues could compare with them.

Now both Josh and Satch are in the Hall of Fame, though Foster, Rogan, Suttles, and Stearnes still are not. Cooperstown is baseball's last citadel of the old order, still ruled by the generation that had kept blacks out of the white majors for 60 years. But that citadel will crumble some day, and probably not too far hence.

Today we make the mistake of thinking of Paige as a comedian, which he was, as much as a great athlete, which he also was. Indeed, he was one of America's most quotable humorists, in the tradition of Ben Franklin, Mark Twain, Will Rogers, Dizzy Dean, and Art Buchwald. But he was much more than a Stepinfetchit making white folks chuckle. When the laughs died down, there remained a long record of accomplishments that helped change the face of the country.

In July 1940 the *Saturday Evening Post* had run a picture spread on Satchel. "For the first time," Roberts said, "the white media had burned incense at the foot of a black man outside the prize ring." The *Post* story did what the black press had been unable to do: It elevated Paige from a great but obscure pitcher, toiling in baseball's bushes, onto a pedestal beside the other great athletes of his race, Olympian Jesse Owens and heavyweight champ Joe Louis.

Before the *Post* article, Roberts said, he remembered Satchel pitching for 3,000 people. After it, the crowds were 30,000. "He led us out of the wilderness," Roberts said. "How crucial he was!"

"Satchel was a lot of franchises," nodded Buck O'Neil. "If Memphis needed to make a payroll, Satchel would pitch three innings for them. Babe Ruth made the payroll for a lot of clubs too."

Lefty Grove was the fastest man in the white majors then, but old-timers like Bill Drake of the black leagues said they never saw anyone faster than Paige until Bob Feller came along. Grove won 31 games in 1931; Feller would probably have won 30 if he hadn't missed his peak years in the Navy. Satchel always believed he could have won 30 too, and most black veterans who saw him agree. Another 30-game winner, Dizzy Dean, hooked up with Paige in many a duel in the 1930s. "Paige is the best pitcher I ever seen," he declared, "and I been lookin' in the mirror for a long time."

"I played against Bob Feller and all of them," pitcher-catcher-raconteur Ted "Double Duty" Radcliffe insisted. "I'm not saying this because he's colored now, but Satchel's the greatest pitcher ever lived!"

I began researching an article on Gibson in 1969, a project that soon grew to include all the great, but largely forgotten—or never known—players of the "hidden half" of baseball history.

My hobby took me to Kansas City, where one of Satch's old teammates, Newt Allen, gave me his address, usually a closely guarded secret. A kid was raking leaves when I arrived and asked if this was Satchel Paige's house.

"Satchel who?"

"Satchel Paige. Used to be a baseball pitcher."

The boy shrugged. "I never heard of him," he said. "He doesn't live around here."

Next I tracked Paige to the dressing room of the Atlanta Braves, where he was serving as pitching coach. I was not made to feel welcome. Satch either ignored my questions, preferring to compare colognes with his locker mate, Hank Aaron, or snapped answers at me as if I were nothing but "po' white trash." Uncomprehending, I closed my notebook and gave up.

Later a friend put me in touch with Paige's agent, who said, "Sure, he'll talk" if I sent $250. I did and flew back to Kansas City to the same house I had gone to originally. I rang the bell. The same boy answered. I introduced myself, and he turned and called over his shoulder, "Dad," and Satchel sauntered into the room. We had a nice long talk, about him and about all the players he had known in the black leagues. They could have gone to the majors "by the hundreds" he said.

Like Paige, Ted Williams rode both the segregated bus and the integrated trolley during his career, 1939–60. Ted was one of the first to attack the bastion at Cooperstown with a graceful and eloquent plea at his own induction. While most men in their moments on the Cooperstown stage make long-winded speeches about what "I did" and what "I said," Williams made a short speech, mostly about others. He told the thousands listening that day:

> The other day Willie Mays hit his 522nd home run. He has gone past me, and he's pushing. And I say to him, "Go get 'em, Willie." Baseball gives every American boy a chance to excel. Not just to be as good as someone else, but to be better. This is the nature of man and the name of the game. I hope that some day Satchel Paige and Josh Gibson will be voted into the Hall of Fame as symbols of the great Negro players who are not here only because they weren't given a chance.

1906–1926

Satchel Paige was the first of the great baseball stars to come out of Mobile. He would be followed by Hank Aaron, Billy Williams, and Tommy Agee. Mobile may have hit more major league home runs than any other city in America. In fact, a lot of great athletes came out of Alabama, including Joe Louis, Jesse Owens, Willie Mays, and Mule Suttles.

Leroy "Satchel" Paige was one of 11 children, born in the year "1900-aught." The fuss over his age was showman Bill Veeck's idea after Satch joined the Indians in 1948. In the Negro leagues, Satch hadn't made much out of it. His early rival, Smokey Joe Williams, had been a subject of debate about his age in the early 1930s. Joe's club, the Homestead Grays, claimed he was 56, though actually he was probably ten years younger than that. Satch made a mental note of the publicity Joe got, and Veeck picked up on it.

Another great Mobile player, "Double Duty" Radcliffe, both pitched and caught, and claims to be the only man ever to strike out Josh Gibson and hit a homer off Paige. Duty says he was born in 1904, "and Satch is a few years older than me." At an old-timers' reunion in 1984, Cool Papa Bell settled the question once and for all. "Satchel is two years older than I am," he revealed, "and I'm 101."

The whole matter could have been settled, Paige once said, by an entry in the family bible. Unfortunately, however, his grandfather was reading the Bible under a chinaberry tree one day when a wind came up and blew it out of his hands, and the family goat ate it. Shown another Bible with a date in it, Satchel dismissed it as "the Old Testament." "Man, what you want my birth certificate for anyway?" he mused. "Everybody knows old Satchel was born." All he would say is he was "too old to vote." Age, he said, "is a question of mind over matter. If you don't mind, age don't matter."

Billy Hunter, who played with Paige on the St. Louis Browns in 1953, kept badgering Satch about his age. "Forty-eight," the pitcher said. The next time it was "52." Asked to explain the contradiction, Paige replied that "I'm as old as Mr. Veeck wants me to be."

I myself have no trouble with the date on his birth certificate of

July 7, 1906. That would make Satch 20 when he broke in with Chattanooga, his first pro team, in 1926, and 42 when he joined the Indians in 1948.

In his autobiography, *Maybe I'll Pitch Forever*, Paige wrote of living in a "shotgun" house—it was a straight shot from the front door out the back door. He said he earned pennies, and a nickname, carrying satchels at the train depot. (Another famous Satch, trumpeter Louis Armstrong, got his nickname Satchmo by selling papers in New Orleans and keeping the pennies in his mouth—"Satchel mouth.")

Josh Gibson was five years younger, born December 21, 1911 in Buena Vista, GA, about 100 miles southwest of Atlanta. (If you try to check that date as assiduously as people have checked Paige's birthdate, it would probably be equally hard to verify.)

Josh was one of the unluckiest baseball players ever in the timing of his birthday. His career began with the Great Depression in 1930, covered the last 17 years of baseball apartheid, and ended just three months before integration—and if he hadn't been 4-F, he would have run into World War II as well. Some say his bitterness at being passed over for the unknown Jackie Robinson contributed to his death at the age of 35. If he had been born just one or two years earlier, presumably he would have gotten a bid to the majors, as the older Paige did.

While he was born in a bad year, Gibson was born on a good day for baseball hitters. He's a Sagittarius, the same as Ty Cobb and Joe DiMaggio. The sign has produced more big league batting titles than any other but Taurus and is fourth on the home run titles list. On the other hand, Paige is a Cancer, which has produced few other star pitchers. It's about average among ERA leaders and doesn't appear at all on the list of the top ten strikeout kings of all time. The only other outstanding Cancer pitcher was Carl Hubbell.

At the age of 12, Satchell Paige was caught stealing toys and was sent away to reform school for five years, much as Babe Ruth had been sent away ten years earlier, and, like Babe, emerged, in 1923, with his baseball skills well honed.

In 1923, 11-year-old Josh and his family joined the migration of southern blacks to the North, to Pittsburgh, where his father worked in a steel mill. In later years he told his friend, outfielder Ted Page, that the best thing his father ever did for him was to bring him up north. They lived on "The Hill," which is still a black ghetto, and Josh went to vocational school, dropping out in 1926 to take a variety of odd jobs.

At 15 Josh, already grown to man-size, started playing with the

Crawfords, a semipro club that passed the hat during games and doled out the collection among the players. He was already attracting attention busting long home runs.

In 1926, the Chattanooga Black Lookouts (which was also Willie Mays' first team) were offering Satch $50 a month to pitch. "Fifty dollars was what we were calling money then," so he took it. Mrs. Paige, however, thought it was a sin to play for money and never went to see her son Leroy play. Chattanooga played in the Negro Southern league, which was a step below the two major black leagues, the Negro National league and the Eastern Colored league. He apparently made his debut May 16, beating Birmingham 5–4.

Catcher William "Big C" Johnson played against Paige that year:

> The first time I met him, I struck out on his "pea ball." But we must have beat him pretty bad, because I came up four more times and hit him four times straight. Every time I came up I switched left- and right-handed. That might have confused him; he didn't know if I was the same man or not. He didn't have much curve or experience. Later he developed a little wrinkle. But I don't think I ever hit him again. He learned how to pitch.

Radcliffe claims that he caught Satch in Chattanooga. "Well," he quotes the pitcher as saying, "get Radcliffe up here to catch me."

Paige learned to "read" batters by looking at their knees, as a matador studies a bull. He said he really did call in his outfield and strike out the batter. He slept with the rest of the team in the ballparks, laying his head on his suitcase, and with his first paycheck bought a steak and a shotgun, and went looking for a girl.

1927

S acco and Vanzetti. Lindbergh. The Holland Tunnel. Coolidge deported black leader Marcus Garvey.

"Ol' Man River," "Can't Help Lovin' Dat Man," "Why Do I Love You?," "I'm Looking Over a Four Leaf Clover," "My Heart Stood Still," "My Blue Heaven."

The Jazz Singer, The Way of All Flesh, Flesh and the Devil, Seventh Heaven, Buster Keaton's *The General.*

Broadway: Ziegfeld Follies.

Books: *Elmer Gantry, The Royal Road to Romance, The Bridge of San Luis Rey.*

Ruth hit 60 homers. Walter Johnson retired. The Yanks beat the Pirates 4–0. Gene Tunney beat Jack Dempsey on the "long count." Abe Saperstein organized the Harlem Globetrotters.

In 1927, Birmingham joined the Negro National league, and Satchel joined Birmingham. The Black Barons played in Rickwood Park, a pitcher's paradise with one of the biggest playing fields in the country. It had already frustrated Suttles—who had jumped to St. Louis with a much friendlier park—as, 20 years later, it would frustrate young Willie Mays. It was the home park of the white Barons of the Southern association. Third baseman Pie Traynor, among others, had gotten his minor league training there. Blacks were allowed to attend the white games, and vice versa, though seating was segregated, and the white Birmingham *News Herald* covered the Black Barons as conscientiously as it covered the whites.*

Satch was still so skinny that "if I stood sidewise, you couldn't see me." But on the Black Barons, he was in the big time. The manager,

---

*North–South stereotypes often break down during research of the Negro leagues. The Memphis *Commercial-Appeal,* another southern white paper, covered the black Memphis Red Sox. Pulitzer's liberal St. Louis *Post-Dispatch* ignored Cool Papa Bell and the black St. Louis Stars, but the more conservative *Globe-Democrat* reported every game. And in New York, the *Times* didn't consider news of the Lincoln Giants or Black Yankees fit to print.

Big Bill Gatewood, was a pitcher who had once reputedly killed a man with a pitch. Satch credited Gatewood with polishing the lessons he had learned in Chattanooga. "Satchel liked Bill Gatewood," said little outfielder Jimmie Crutchfield. "Crazy about him. Gatewood would get a bottle and talk all night long."

Paige said Gatewood taught him the hesitation pitch. Cool Papa Bell says Satch had developed the pitch on the streets of Mobile, throwing rocks at rival kids. When they ducked behind a tree, he strode to throw but didn't bring his arm around until after his front foot went down, so that when they thought it was safe to peek out, they got konked. Later, Satch would claim he developed the pitch late in his career, after his fastball had lost a few feet. As Dizzy Dean said after giving reporters contradictory versions of his first name, "Them ain't lies, them's scoops."

Satch writes erroneously that George "Bill" Perkins was his catcher at Birmingham that year. Actually, Poindexter Williams and Spoony Palm shared the catching; Perkins, who would become Paige's favorite receiver, didn't arrive until 1928. At any rate, Paige claims, he told his catcher not to bother with signs, he only had a fastball anyway, or rather two fastballs: his "be ball" ("it be where I want it to be") and his "jump ball." The first he gripped with his fingers along the seams and the second across them.

The first big league game that Satchel ever pitched, as far as we can determine, was on July 3 in Detroit. According to Dick Clark, chairman of SABR's Negro league committee, the fourth-place Detroit Stars rocked him for five runs in 1.2 innings. We don't know how many hits he gave up, but he walked three men.

The next game we know about was two weeks later in Birmingham on July 16. Paige bounced back from his humiliating debut by beating sixth-place Memphis 12–1. The cocky rookie would later write that he began by announcing loudly that he would strike out the first six men. He said after he got five, the enemy waved a white flag of surrender, so he eased up and let the sixth man pop up. Satch said the Birmingham fans went wild, he pulled off his cap and waved it at them, and "I knew I was in around Birmingham."

On July 26, Paige went in in relief against the champion Chicago American Giants. In four innings, he gave up seven hits, two runs, walked one, and whiffed one, as he was tagged with his second loss.

Paige told his ghost that his catcher had only to hold up his mitt, and Satch would hit it. That's not how others remember it; they say he was on the wild side.

Luckily for his future development, the rookie came under the tutelage of two veteran Alabamians, pitchers Sam Streeter and Harry Salmon. Both were products of the Birmingham coal mines, both had savvy and good control. But they were two very different stylists on the mound.

Streeter was a chubby, chunky left-hander with a spitball and a curve. Salmon, a lanky right-hander, threw fastballs with a mean side-arm motion, like Don Drysdale's, that terrified right-handed hitters.

"He pitched from the side like [Ewell] Blackwell," Satchel told me. "I never did see anyone pitch like that. He was hard to hit. Everybody would leave the plate when he went into his act." In later years, Satch also liked to whip the ball from the side, and possibly it was Salmon who provided the model.

At that time Salmon, or "Beans," as he was called, was considered faster than the younger Paige. Whenever the two pitched a doubleheader, Cool Papa Bell said, it was Salmon, not Paige, who drew the tougher opponent. In 1930, when Cum Posey of the Homestead Grays went down to Birmingham to recruit a pitcher, he passed up Satch and selected Salmon instead.

When I met Salmon on a summer evening in 1970, he was living on relief and lounging in a Pittsburgh ghetto taxi stand. He said he beat Satch twice in 1926 when Paige was with Chattanooga, both times by scores of 2–1. According to Salmon, they faced each other again in 1934 and Salmon won that one too. In between times, they were teammates at Birmingham:

> He was my roommate. Well, yes, I taught him some things. When he started, he was real fast. Wasn't much of a curveball man, but he was a good strikeout man. But the thing of it was, the balk part. He'd most always get his foot off the rubber. When he'd go to pitch, his foot would slide off. That beat us a whole lot of times.

The little (5'7") Streeter was the opposite of both Paige and Salmon. John McGraw of the Giants is supposed to have said that Sam had the best control of any lefty he'd seen. "He could throw it in a cup," agreed Crutchfield.

Streeter was "mostly slow on everything," said Vic Harris of the Grays. "He knew how to spot his pitches. You never did get a good one to hit. He'd outsmart you." Josh Gibson would later catch both Satch and Sam and agreed that Sam was the smartest pitcher in the league.

Satchel himself considered Streeter "one of the best left-handers you'd ever want to see . . . Another Sandy Koufax." On his list of the ten greatest pitchers, Paige put Sam second, right behind Bob Feller and ahead of Don Newcombe and Sandy Koufax, (Satch's list: Feller, Streeter, Newcombe, Bertram Hunter of the Crawfords, Koufax, Hilton Smith and Joe Rogan of the Monarchs, Bob Lemon, Allie Reynolds, and Bill Foster of the Chicago American Giants.)

Outfielder Ted Page laughed:

> Streeter kept breaking the curve off right in front of you. You'd walk up on his pitches, and he kept breaking each one off a little shorter. Before you knew it, you were halfway to the pitching mound.
>
> But when Sam got in a tough spot, he'd throw the spitball. He threw strikes with it too.

"The spit would fly everywhere," Grays first baseman Buck Leonard chuckled. "I wouldn't watch the ball, I'd watch the spit."

Streeter had been around since 1920, when he pitched for the great Rube Foster on the Chicago American Giants. Sam was 80 years old, retired from his second career in the steel mills, when I met him in his middle-class Pittsburgh home. He remembered Satchel well, of course.

> He could throw hard, but he didn't have any curveball. I worked with him, taught him a curveball, got him control. See, he'd wind up and wouldn't watch his batter. He'd look around, and when he'd come back, he didn't see *where* he was throwing it.
>
> I told him to kind of keep his eye on the plate, not to turn too far, to glance at the plate before he turned his ball loose. He got to the point where he had *good* control.

Salmon:

> You know, you writers, the more you write, the better you are. That's the way Satchel developed his control: practice, practice. We used to all go out and throw and see how many strikes could we throw. Well, he was a hard thrower, learned how to pitch afterwards. You know, his arm got sore later, and when the years come by, you learn how to pitch with your head more than your arm. That's what he became: a good-headed pitcher.

Gatewood asked Webster McDonald of the Chicago American Giants to show the kid how to hold men on base. But Paige resisted the lesson. "We don't do it that way," he told the patient Mac. "Oooh boy," McDonald sighed, "everything was what *he* wanted to do."

Pitching in the black big leagues was not easy.

The St. Louis Stars boasted Cool Papa Bell (.319 that year), Frog Redus (.357), Willie Wells (.382, with a league-leading 23 homers in the 100-game season), and big Mule Suttles, who was injured for half the year but hit .456. Cleveland had Ed Wesley, .421 for half a season. And the Detroit Stars had Cristobal Torriente (.320), Ed "Huck" Rile (.397), and Turkey Stearnes, at .346 the best all-round hitter in the league, who topped all hitters in doubles and triples and finished second in home runs and steals. Lifetime, Turkey was first in homers and doubles and fourth in steals. Satch remembered Stearnes well:

> Turkey was one of the greatest hitters we ever had. He was as good as Josh. I tried to pitch him on the inside, but he could hit it over the right field fence, he could hit it over the left field fence, or the center field fence.
>
> The thing about those ballplayers, they were a little rough, there wasn't any mebbe so. You just couldn't hardly throw hard enough to get those men out. I could make them hit it one way, like to left field, or right field, but to just throw something to try to get them out, you just stood a hell of a bad chance.

In his book, Paige said he pitched in St. Louis and, to force the hitters to back off the plate, deliberately hit the first three men he faced. The fourth one, Mitch Murray, chased him around the bases with his bat. But the tale doesn't ring true. The first man up would have been Bell, and the third one, Willie Wells, one of the great shortstops of all time. Neither mentioned it when I talked to them. And the cleanup man would have been Suttles, not Murray. The story also doesn't sound like Satch. In later years, he would disdain the beanball, saying, "I don't call that no baseball when I got to cave your ribs out to get you."

Between league games five days a week, the Black Barons barnstormed against semipro teams to meet the payroll. Some of the richer clubs traveled in their own Pullman cars, but the Black Barons traveled in roadsters, six or seven men to a car. At his induction to Cooperstown in 1971, Paige said he had no patience with white big leaguers who complained that the clickety-click of the train's wheels kept them awake. Satch had to sleep, or try to, with his knees against his chest, scrunched between two other players in the back seat. "I played in some towns," he said, where, if I didn't play, they didn't want the team—in *town*—let alone in the ballpark!"

Off the field, Satch helped keep the club loose. Salmon grinned that "Satchel was full of fun all the way. You know how youngsters are. He was our showman. He even played a Jew's harp at times."

In spite of a sensational rookie outfielder, Roy "Red" Parnell, who was hitting over .500 at the midway point, Birmingham started out slowly. They finished fifth in an eight-club league over the first half, losing more than they won.

But with Paige joining the Big Two, Salmon and Streeter, Birmingham took off in the second half. Parnell ended up hitting .426, with a league-leading 18 stolen bases. Catcher Nish Williams, another miner, hit .410—his foster son, Donn Clendennon, would later star with the 1969 Miracle Mets. Palm hit .367, outfielder Sandy Thompson .316, and second baseman "Geechee" Meredith .286.

Satchel's record was 8–3. Three of his wins were consecutive shut-outs in September. He defeated sixth-place Memphis on a seven-inning one-hitter September 5; followed that with a nine-inning one-hitter over the same club three days later; and then four-hit the seventh-place Cubans five days after that.

Salmon finished at 14–6; Streeter was 14–12 and led the league in complete games, and the Black Barons won the second-half pennant.

Paige bested both his two mentors, giving up only 3.27 runs per game (that's total runs; earned runs are not available). He also topped Salmon in strikeouts, 80–74, and almost passed Streeter, who had 89 in more than twice as many innings. Their lessons in control must have paid off: Satch walked only 19 men in 93 innings, or one for every four strikeouts.

If there had been a rookie of the year award in the Negro leagues, it would surely have gone either to Satch or to Parnell. Twenty-two years later, when Paige was named Rookie of the Year in the American league of 1948, "I declined the honor. I wasn't sure which year those gentlemen had in mind."

Next, the upstart Barons met the great American Giants, the defending champs, in the play-off. Playing in cavernous Southside Park, the same field that had made the 1906 White Sox the infamous "Hitless Wonders," the American Giants (like the old White Sox) featured a splendid pitching corps. Little Willie "Piggie" Powell was 9–4, and submariner Webster McDonald 10–5. The ace was lefty Big

Bill Foster, half-brother of pioneer and Hall of Famer Rube Foster. Probably the best black left-hander of all time, Bill that year set a new Negro league record for victories with a 21–3 record.

The Giants swept the Barons in four straight games, as the Chicago pitchers cooled Parnell down to a .125 average. Foster beat Streeter 5–0. Powell, a money pitcher, beat Salmon and Paige 10–5, though Salmon, the starter, drew the loss. In game three, Foster beat Robert Poindexter and Salmon 6–4. And finally, Powell beat Streeter and Paige 6–2, though again Satchel didn't get the loss. He was rushed into the game in the first inning after the Giants had bombed Sam for four runs. Paige gave two more runs and struck out five in a losing cause.

More than 40 years later, Powell had lost both legs and the use of one arm, when Dick Clark, his wife Marilyn, and I interviewed him in his hospital room in Three Rivers, MI. "Satchel Paige? Sure I beat him—name me somebody I didn't beat," the chesty Powell declared. He told us:

> Satchel was the fastest that's ever been in baseball. He was faster than Bob Feller, faster than Lefty Grove. But until he learned a curveball, he was just a thrower.
>
> He didn't know how to field a bunt, and that's how you beat him—bunt and run, bunt and run, bunt and run. [Paige would later claim that the reason he could pitch in the white majors until the age of 48 was that no one bunted on him.]
>
> Back then it just wasn't like it is now, with everybody swinging on the ball. They would do their thing. If they could bunt, they'd bunt. They had men didn't do nothing *but* bunt. And it was so hard to get them out. You didn't know what side he was going to bunt on. If you break to the left and he bunt to the right, and you lose one step, he's on!
>
> Jelly Gardner [of Chicago] was just as fast as this guy Cool Papa—I know you've heard of him. To tell you the truth, it's just like it is now when you play football. You know most all the colored kids that are on there, when they get the ball, they can run. It was the same thing in baseball. Everywhere you go, they had five or six *fast* men on there, could lay the ball down and get away. It wasn't like it is nowadays, everybody swinging. 'Cause they would drag and bunt on you a lot, because everybody could throw hard back there in those times.

1928

Herbert Hoover ("a chicken in every pot") beat Al Smith in a landslide.

"She's Funny That Way," "Lover, Come Back to Me," "Button Up Your Overcoat," "Makin' Whoopie," "Love Me Or Leave Me," "I'll Get By," "I Can't Give You Anything But Love, Baby," "Shortnin' Bread," Benny Goodman's Boogie Woogie.

The Jazz Singer, Mickey Mouse, Charlie Chaplin's *The Circus, Wings* with Clara Bow

Broadway: *The Front Page, Animal Crackers. Abie's Irish Rose* closed after 2,400 performances. Cops closed Mae West in *Diamond Lil* after one performance.

Books: *Lady Chatterley's Lover, Swann's Way,* Robert Frost's *West Running Brook.*

The Yanks beat St Louis 4–0. Johnny Weissmuller won the 400 meters in the Olympics and retired.

In 1928, Cy Perkins arrived in Birmingham to catch Satch. It was to Perkins that Paige was probably referring when he said the catcher just had to hold up a target, and Satch would hit it. Perkins would remain Satch's favorite catcher.

With Cy behind the plate, Satchel exceeded even his splendid rookie year. He won 12 and lost only 4, his 3.07 TRA was second to Powell's 2.94, and his 112 strikeouts were second to Foster's 118, though Bill pitched 87 innings more than Satchel did. The legendary Paige control was asserted, as he walked only 19, or about one for every six K's.

However, the rest of the Barons faded. Streeter was injured and didn't win any games. Salmon was 11–10, Parnell dropped 122 points to .326.

Paige was getting them out with smoke and control, plus a variety of deliveries.

"They say Bob Gibson was fast," Cool Papa said. "But Satchel was faster than all of them." Paige had a lot of names for his heater—"Thoughtful Stuff," the "Bat Dodger," the "Four-Day Rider," the

"Hurry Up Ball," the "Wobbly Ball," the "Nothin' Ball," "Long Tom," and the "Midnight Creeper"—even his catchers laughed that they didn't know what they all meant. But the hitters couldn't hit them.

"What's he throwing?" Monte Irvin once asked a teammate.

"I don't know," came the reply. "I haven't seen it yet."

Once when Satch threw to first, the batter swung, and the umpire called a strike. Another time the batter protested a called strike: "That last one sounded a little low, didn't it, ump?" Hitters agreed that the ball actually did have a buzz or a hum to it.

Catcher Double Duty Radcliffe used to reassure the batters that "I'm having a little trouble seeing it myself."

"He just changed the *size* of the ball," Ric Roberts marveled.

Bill Foster said Satch's fastball "looked like one of these little white 'zuzu' biscuits you can buy in the grocery store. About the size of a fifty-cent piece. Looked just like a streak or something."

Outfielder Ted Page called it "a little white marble." Ted saw both Satch and the legendary Smokey Joe Williams. "Joe's ball looked bigger but always seemed to jump."

Satchel's ball "looked like a white dot," whistled fellow pitcher Bill "Sugar" Cornelius. "He'd show you fastballs at your knee all day."

Quincy Trouppe, who would catch Satch on the prairies of North Dakota and later caught for the Cleveland Indians, said Paige's fastball looked like "a marble." He wrote in his autobiography, *20 Years Too Soon* that Satch had long, wiry arms, a long stride, and long, strong fingers. "He could put such tremendous backspin on his fastball that it would rise two to four inches." If you tried a Ted Williams uppercut on Satchel "you were in trouble."

"He threw *fire*, that's what he threw!" exclaimed Buck Leonard, the "black Gehrig," who says he never got a hit off Satch in 17 years of trying.

And that was in the daytime, gulped the Kansas City Monarchs' Newt Allen, who shuddered at the thought of trying to hit Satch under the lights.

Allen said Satch "kicked his foot way up here like Dizzy Dean, and then he'd throw around that foot. Half the guys were hitting at that foot coming up."

Paige seemed to keep that foot raised for an eternity, sighed one hitter, Clarence "Half a Pint" Israel. "That bat got awful heavy." (Tom Seaver said Sadaharu Oh's habit of raising his leg at bat had the same disconcerting effect on pitchers.)

Since Paige, at that time, had nothing but a fastball, hitters didn't have to look for anything else. And, as Ted Page insisted, "I don't think you can throw a ball faster than you can swing a bat." Bell said he used to stick his bat out and let Satchel hit it.

But most batters admitted that he had "FASTBALL" written on the bottom of his left shoe. "Everybody knew what was coming," Satchel admitted with a smile. "But they didn't know where it was gonna be. If you're looking for it here, and I throw it up there, it's too late—you can't get back up there to hit it. I used to get a little cocky every once in a while; yeah, I would tell 'em where I was gonna throw it. They still couldn't hit it."

Satchel worked on his control until he could warm up with a Coke bottle top for home plate. "I could nip frosting off a cake," he smiled. "If you got control, you're going to be pretty hard to hit, because you find a man's weakness, or your catcher's gonna tell you. You don't need a curveball or a knuckleball."

Satchel also had "a lot of tricky motions," Ted Page said. "If you hit my overhand ball," Satch maintained, "then you'd have to hit my sidearm fast one too. Then I could pitch underhand. I could pitch any kind of way."

The underhand pitch was particularly tough, said Cleveland historian Icabod Flewellen, a former semipro player. "You'd hit it hard, but it wouldn't rise; it had a tendency to sink."

Hall of Famer William "Judy" Johnson said Satch could throw three straight balls and then three straight strikes any time he wanted to. "He would throw the ball on the corner just far enough so if you would swing, you wouldn't get all the bat on it. Control. What you don't see in the big leagues now."

"They say Bob Gibson was fast," says Cool Papa Bell. "But Satchel was faster than all of them."

Paige admired Bell. "He hit me pretty good," Satchel admitted. "He only took a half-swing. "It's hard to throw a ball by a man who only takes a half-swing."

Bell told author Jim Bankes that Paige announced before one game: "I'm not gonna throw any fast ones today. All you're gonna get is slow stuff," his so-called "Little Tom." "Know what?" Bell said. "He shut us out."

Who was faster, Paige or Smokey Joe Williams? "I always say Paige," Bell told Jim Bankes, "because Williams cut the ball."

Satch was fast, Cool Papa agreed, but the Monarchs' Bullet Joe Rogan was a better *pitcher.*

Paige modestly agreed that Rogan (9–3 that year) was "the greatest Negro pitcher anybody ever heard of before I came along." The two men were exact opposites. Where Satchel was tall and gangly, Rogan was almost tiny, about 5′6″, dwarfed by all his teammates. Where Paige relied on speed, Rogan threw everything in the pitchers' repertoire. Where Paige was an automatic out at the plate, Rogan hit clean-up for the Monarchs' murderers' row. Where Satch was comical and droll, the Bullet was dour and private.

Paige said the two faced each other once. "He beat me 1–0 in the eleventh inning. . . . He was a chunky little guy, but he could throw hard. If you want to know the truth, he could throw hard as Smokey Joe Williams—yeah."

At bat "Rogan would stand way back at the plate," Paige said. "That's where he tricked me up, because I had never seen him bat before. But if you throw it outside, he could [still] hit it out of the park."

The Monarchs' Frank Duncan, who caught Rogan, Paige, Williams, and Dean (and later managed Jackie Robinson), maintained that Rogan and Paige threw the fastest balls he ever saw. Rogan also had a curve with a three-foot drop.

Duncan gave Paige the edge in control:

> That Satchel could throw a fastball in a quart cup. Ball just as light, could catch him just as easy, no trouble catching him, just sit down there. But Rogan! One over here, one over there, one up here and one down here. When the day was over you were tired. He'd walk five-six-seven men. But he didn't give any runs.
>
> But if you had to take the two, you'd pick Rogan, because he could hit, you could use him so many places in the field. The pitching, you'd just as soon have Satchel as have Rogan, understand?

In Pittsburgh meanwhile, where the semi-pro Crawfords were beginning to make a reputation, Harold Tinker watched a 16-year old kid playing third base for the Gimbel Brothers team, digging balls out of the rock-strewn playground fields and hitting balls half-way up the hillside. "That boy would be a good boy for the Crawfords," Tinker said to himself. So, Tinker told historian Rob Ruck, "I went to him and, 'Josh,' I said, 'don't you want to play with a real team?' "

"Yes sir," the boy replied, "I guess so."

So Josh Gibson joined the Crawfords, who were impressed by his throwing arm and made him into a catcher. He could also blast balls "out on Bedford Avenue and up on the hospital," says Tinker: "He was the most tremendous hitter I've ever come across in baseball—I'm barring none.

"You could put your hands on him and feel him, and man, he was hard. His muscles were hard. He wasn't big, but he was a sinewy type. He was big muscular. He was built like metal. If you run into him, it was just like you run into a wall."

Against a white semi-pro team, Gibson came up with men on first and second and the Crawfords two runs behind. The pitcher proceeded to walk the boy, even though first base was occupied. After two balls, Josh called time and asked Tinker if it would be all right to swing. "Well, Josh, if you feel you can hit it, you go ahead and hit it." So the kid reached out and whipped the next pitch over the centerfield fence. "Them people went crazy," Tinker said with a laugh and a shake of his head.

1929

S t. Valentine's Day massacre. Teapot Dome convictions. Admiral
Byrd flew over the South Pole. The stock market reached a record
high in September, crashed in October.

"Am I Blue?," "Without a Song," "Singing in the Rain," "Star-
dust," "Tiptoe Through the Tulips."

The Coconuts, with the Marx brothers.

Radio: "The Goldbergs," "Amos 'n Andy."

Books: *The Sound and the Fury, Farewell to Arms, Look Homeward,
Angel; Lady Chatterley's Lover.*

Comics: Popeye.

Babe Ruth hit #500. The A's beat the Cubs 4–1. Bill Tilden won
his seventh U.S. Open.

The Black Barons dropped to sixth in a seven-team league, as
Parnell, Streeter, and perhaps most significantly, Perkins, had moved
on to other teams.

Satchel's record fell to 11–11 with a high 5.28 TRA. He was a
workhorse, though, leading the league in innings, hits, and runs. And
he set a Negro league record in strikeouts with 184 in 196 innings, a
mark that would never be broken. One of Satchel's wins was a two-
hitter over fourth-place Detroit with 17 strikeouts, or one more than
the white big league record at the time.

Satchel and Salmon (9–15) were virtually a two-man staff. Harry
topped Satch with a league-leading 33 games, 21 of them complete,
compared to 30 and 20 for Satch.

In Pittsburgh meanwhile, 17-year-old Josh Gibson was making a
reputation pounding home runs for the Crawfords, a neighborhood
boys' team. Even the Pittsburgh *Courier* was taking note of him. Of
course the paper devoted most of its attention to the city's major black
pro team, the Homestead Grays, which had grown from a steel
workers' recreational club to one of the top black teams in the country,
finishing third in the Negro American league. They were directed by
Cumberland "Cum" Posey, who was also one of the country's better
basketball players and boss of the famous Loendi Big Five.

The Grays starred moody, hard-hitting John Beckwith (.380), outfielder Vic Harris (.371), infielder Walter "Rev" Cannady (.336), and Sam Streeter (9–5).

Their biggest star however was the legendary Joe Williams (12–7), the big half-black half-Commanche Indian, who held an Indian sign on white major leaguers. Often compared to Walter Johnson, Joe had once beaten Johnson in a showdown 1–0. In all, he won 20 games against white stars and lost only seven. One of his losses was reputedly a ten-inning 20-strikeout no-hitter against the 1917 champion New York Giants. Joe lost the game but won his nickname, Smokey.

If white Pittsburgh kids grew up dreaming of playing with Paul Waner on the Pirates, black kids dreamt of joining Joe Williams on the Grays. Homestead manager Vic Harris said the teenaged Gibson actually achieved that dream in 1929:

> My brother was playing on the same team as Josh, the Crawfords, as we called them, up on the Hill. That was '29, the season was almost over. We had a catcher, Buck Ewing, and George Britt was both pitcher and catcher, but both had busted fingers. So I caught until they put my younger brother in the cab and sent him up to the playground there— Ammond Center, that's where they were playing. So Rich went up and got Gibson, and I went back to left field. I think we were playing the Memphis Red Sox, if I'm not mistaken. A twilight game.

We have not yet found the box score of that historic first game, nor do we know how Josh did. Apparently the injuries to the regulars healed, and Gibson went back to the Crawfords with tales to tell the other awestruck kids about what it was like to play with the Homestead Grays.

As for Paige, he told his biographer that he joined the Baltimore Black Sox in October to barnstorm against Babe Ruth and other white all-stars, but that Ruth sat out the games that Paige pitched. Satch's memory is faulty, however. The Babe did not play any games against the Black Sox that year.

Brooklyn outfielder Floyd "Babe" Herman did play against Satch in California, which may be the source of the confusion. Paige claimed that in one of the games in Los Angeles, he whiffed 22 of the all-stars, far surpassing the then big league record of 16, and even the present mark, Roger Clemens' 20. Unfortunately, this game also is suspect. If such a game was played, it has not yet been discovered in the files of the Los Angeles papers, which usually did a good job of covering such autumn exhibitions.

That winter, Cuba "waved plenty of green in my face," so Satchel and Salmon sailed to the island for the winter season. The first thing the Cubans did was put Paige in the best hotel he'd ever stayed in. But when he tried to get a drink in the bar, he was told that ballplayers there never drink and they go to bed early. Thereafter, Paige dutifully went to bed early and did his drinking in his room.

He did not pitch well in Cuba. His record was a mediocre 6–5, far below the league leader, Yoyo Diaz, who was 13–3.

Cuba was the beginning of year-round baseball for Paige. For the next 29 year years he played spring, summer, fall, and winter. Jim Kaat holds the white major league record with 26 years pitched. But, as Satchel pointed out, they were six-month years.

1930

Four million unemployed. Drought in the Midwest. Gandhi demanded independence for India.

"Mood Indigo," "On the Sunny Side of the Street," "Body and Soul," "Georgia on My Mind," "Beyond the Blue Horizon," "What Is This Thing Called Love?," "Walking My Baby Back Home," "I Got Rhythm," "Little White Lies," "Embraceable You."

All Quiet on the Western Front, Animal Crackers, The Blue Angel with Marlene Dietrich, *Hell's Angels* with Jean Harlow, *The Big Trail* with John Wayne, *Little Caesar.*

Broadway: *Green Pastures.*

Grant Wood's *American Gothic.*

Blondie.

Radio: "Lum 'n Abner," "Easy Aces," "The Lone Ranger."

Bill Terry hit .401. Hack Wilson had 56 homers, 190 RBIs. Ruth made $80,000, more than Hoover ("but I had a better year than he did"). The President was booed at the World Series, as the A's beat the Cards 4-3. Gallant Fox won the Triple Crown. Max Schmeling beat Jack Sharkey.

In March, Paige sailed back to the mainland, where a long decade of Depression had settled in. He joined the Baltimore Black Sox, defending champs of the East, apparently hoping, along with several other stars of the West, that the paychecks would be a little steadier out east. (Satchel said in his book that he joined the Nashville Elite—pronounced E-light—Giants, but this is a memory trick.) Among the western stars who jumped to the East that spring were Turkey Stearnes, who went to New York, and Mule Suttles, who joined Paige in Baltimore. There was no eastern league any more, the Depression had killed it, but the teams struggled on as independents, playing each other and anyone else who could draw a few fans. They passed the hat, took out team expenses, and the players divvied up anything that was left.

The Black Sox had won the eastern pennant in '29, but their million-dollar infield—Jud Wilson, Frank Warfield, Dick Lundy, and

19

Oliver Marcelle—was broken up. The graceful shortstop, Lundy, and the temperamental, olive-skinned third baseman, Marcelle, had played in Cuba the winter before, got in a fight over cards, and Lundy had bitten Marcelle's nose off. In 1930, therefore, Marcelle, wearing a nose patch, jumped the team. First baseman Wilson moved to third, and Suttles replaced him at first, giving the Sox another million-dollar foursome. What they lost in defense, they more than made up in power. Suttles played only 14 games before he jumped back to St. Louis, but he slugged eight home runs. Extrapolated to a normal 550 at-bat season, that works out to 83 home runs. And Baltimore's Westport Park had a deep left field target for the right-handed Suttles.

Mule returned to St. Louis, with an extremely short porch in left field; ironically, he could hit only 12 more homers the rest of the year. The Black Sox replaced him with David "Showboat" Thomas, replacing black ball's hardest-hitting first baseman with its slickest-fielding. They still had almost a million-dollar infield. Fourteen years later, Thomas would be given a tryout before a grudging Branch Rickey. Well past his prime, and never a great hitter, Showboat was not hired.

But Satch complained that he didn't get many chances to pitch in Baltimore. He says, "They had about seven or eight good pitchers on that ball club—I mean starters." This was an exaggeration; the cash-strapped black teams usually carried about four or five pitchers, total.

Satchel's old buddy Streeter was there and could compile only a 1–1 record. The ace of the staff was left-hander Pud Flournoy, a veteran of the Philadelphia champions of 1923–25, who had an 11–1 mark.

Laymon Yokely, perhaps the fastest man in the East, was 4–4 that year but had an 8–0 lifetime record barnstorming against white big leaguers such as Jimmy Foxx, Hack Wilson, and others. (He later lost two games to them after his arm went bad.) "Yokely never did put the ball in his glove," Satch said. "He put it behind him and pitched. And he could pitch, too!"

Paige got a chance to see the best hitters in the East, including Wilson, who hit .372. Wilson "didn't hit the ball out of the park, but he could triple and double by the month, just like he had a contract."

Baltimore's moody, longball-hitting John Beckwith batted .480 and led the league with 19 homers in only 50 games (52 per 550 at bats).

In New York, feisty little Charlie "Chino" Smith (he had "Chinese-looking eyes," the players said) hit .468. Smith owns the highest lifetime average in Negro league history, .423. Paige once said Chino and Jud were the two best batters he had ever faced, though that was before he met Gibson. It was Smitty's second straight .400-year: In 1929 he had hit .454 with 20 homers, and a slugging average of .821—Babe Ruth's best was .847.

The left-handed Smith "was a drag man," Paige said.

He would drag the ball. He would just bunt it all the time, carry it with him down to first base, and it was hard for you to get there and get that ball and throw it down the line, because it was about a foot from the line all the time. I don't care if you pitched it on the outside corner, he'd lay it down the third base line. He was rough to get out, he was *really* rough. He was even rougher than Cool Papa, and Cool Papa was really fast. Yeah, and Chino could hit the ball too, and when I say hit it, I mean *hit* the ball. And the people thought I could throw when I went to Cleveland! I had a fastball back when you was talking about. And those guys could drag it. And they could hit it.

Satchel did well in limited action, ending up with a 3–1 record, before he and Suttles and Stearnes decided that there was no gold for them in the east, packed it in, and went back west to their old teams to see if things had gotten any better there.

They hadn't. But Paige was glad to see his old catcher, Perkins, again. And the Barons had a couple of new players.

One was Herman "Jabbo" (or Jambo) Andrews, who came over in a trade from Memphis and won the batting championship with .394. He was the only rookie to lead a major league, black or white, and one of only two league leaders to be traded midway through the season—the other was Dale Alexander of Boston and Detroit in 1932.

Another newcomer was Terris "The Great" McDuffie, an outfielder who led the league in stolen bases, switched to pitching, and in 1944, along with Showboat Thomas, would win a tryout with Brooklyn.

Overall, the Black Barons finished fifth, but Satch posted a 9–4 record in games that have been confirmed. That gave him 12–5 on the year, counting both East and West. We don't have a breakdown on his eastern statistics, but back at Birmingham he cut his TRA to 3.17 per game, second best in the league behind his old buddy, Radcliffe, who had 2.80 for the champion St. Louis Stars. Paige's bee ball wasn't humming quite so much though; he whiffed only 69 men in 102 innings.

Interestingly, we have box scores for only two Birmingham home games, both from the white Birmingham *Age-Herald*. The black week-lies, such as the Chicago *Defender,* relied on the teams to mail in their box scores, and apparently the Black Barons didn't do that. So all their data comes from road games. Perhaps we could double Satch's won-lost record if the home games are ever found. If so, he might actually have won 20 games total for the year, a feat as rare in the short 100-game Negro league season as winning 30 in the 154-game schedule of the white majors. Also, if all Paige's home games were known, surely his TRA would go down, since Rickwood Field in Birmingham was one of the largest in the country, a pitchers' paradise.

Streeter, who returned with Satch, still had time to lead the league both in games started and complete games, and he finished with a 12–11 mark. Salmon, who went to Memphis in the Andrews deal, was 11–9 overall and finished second in the league in strikeouts.

The year had begun with a historic event—the first professional night game. On April 28, the Kansas City Monarchs and the Independence Kansas white team each turned on their separate lighting systems 100 miles apart. (In 1927, two Massachusetts teams, Salem and Lynn, had played a night game in Lynn; both were members of the New England league, but it is not clear whether or not it was an official league game.) At any rate, the experiments would save both black baseball and the white minors during the long decade of hard times ahead.

The Monarchs' lights were portable, and the team carried them around the country, bringing the first night games to dozens of cities, including St. Louis, Detroit, and Pittsburgh.

While the Monarchs made their way east with their revolutionary "midnight sun," the Memphis Red Sox preceded them to Pittsburgh. They must have remembered the kid who went in to catch against them the year before, because outfielder Nat Rogers recalled:

> We didn't have no catcher and had to use the second baseman. Candy Jim Taylor was managing the Red Sox, picked Josh up and carried him up there to Shannon, Pennsylvania to catch. So Josh played for Memphis. Just for that one game. Candy said he'd never make a catcher.

Rogers is correct; a confirming box score has indeed been found.

A few days later the Monarchs arrived and set up their light poles in Forbes Field, home of the National league Pirates, on July 25, 1930.

One of the fans in the stands was the 18-year-old Gibson, probably in on a free pass. The Grays' William "Judy" Johnson, the Hall of Fame third baseman, said the pitcher was the great Smokey Joe Williams, although this is an error. The hurler was Lefty Claude Williams, who was having a sensational season of his own; he reputedly won 22 games without a loss (undoubtedly including semipro games), and this may very well be true—at least we have found no losses for him yet. In other respects, Johnson's memory was vivid:

> Forbes Field was packed. The Monarchs had this big bus, they took all the seats out and put a big dynamo in to generate the electricity. I couldn't see the outfielders out there. If the ball went up above the lights, you had to watch out it didn't hit you in the head. We were in the clubhouse trying to discuss signals, because we had never played a night game. Buck Ewing was catching. When Buck got down to give the signal, why [Williams] couldn't even see his hand! I guess if we'd had some lime or something to put on it, we'd have been better off. [Williams misunderstood the signal, and] Ewing split his hand right down. My sub catcher was in right field, he wouldn't come in to catch, he was afraid.
>
> Here we are, Forbes Field is packed. Josh Gibson was sitting in the stands, him and a bunch of boys who played sandlot baseball. I asked if he would catch. "Yes sir, Mr. Johnson!" I had to hold up the game, let him go in the clubhouse and put on a suit. When he got back, [Williams] and him got together on the signals.

Josh was not any help at the plate. We don't know how many times he came to bat that night—the hometown Pittsburgh *Courier,* like many other black newspapers in the East, had the maddening habit of giving only runs and hits in its box score, without at bats. But we do know that he didn't get any hits against big Chet Brewer, the Monarchs' great "sandpaper man," who could make the ball do magic tricks by nicking the cover.

With the kid behind the plate, Williams went on to win on Harris' homer in the ninth to keep his perfect victory string alive. But defensively, Young Josh was all thumbs. Johnson recalled:

> I never saw a man get hit so much—in the chest, knee, mask. Josh was back there trying to catch those balls. He was determined! We finished the game, and I felt so sorry for the poor boy. He said, "Mr. Johnson, how did I look?"
>
> I said, "You looked bad. But if you want to continue playing baseball, we'll sign you." We signed him the next day, and he turned out to be one of the best hitters that ever put on a uniform.

Gibson was in the big leagues to stay.

Young Josh's moment of triumph quickly turned tragic. Within a month, his young wife, Helen, died giving birth to twins. Josh put the babies in the care of his in-laws and set out with the Grays on a barnstorming tour against the Monarchs and their lights.

Many experts considered the Grays that year one of the finest black teams of all time. They reportedly ran up a record of 134 wins and only 10 losses against all comers.

In Joe Williams they had the man voted the best pitcher in the history of black baseball—he defeated Paige for the honor in a 1952 Pittsburgh *Courier* poll of experts by a single vote, 20–19. Joe was about 44, nearing the end of his marvelous career then, but he could still whip men almost half his age. In his hey day he had defeated Hall of Famers Walter Johnson, Grover Alexander, Waite Hoyt, Chief Bender, and Rube Marquard. When he tossed a ten-inning no-hitter at the 1917 champion New York Giants, striking out 20, Giant outfielder Ross Youngs slapped him on the butt and told him, "That was a hell of a game, Smokey," giving him his lifelong nickname. Joe could still pitch in 1930. His record was 7–1 against top black teams, and he led all eastern pitchers with a Total Run Average of 2.64 and struck out nine men for every one he walked.

First baseman and manager Oscar Charleston is, by common consent, the best black *player* of his day—manager John McGraw of the New York Giants reportedly said the best player, period. An intense man with smouldering, leonine eyes, Charleston had a grip that could wrench the steering wheel off a car, and the guts to pull the hood off a Ku Klux Klansman. In his prime a decade earlier, Charleston had played center field like Willie Mays, run bases like Ty Cobb, and hit with almost the power of Babe Ruth. Charleston, a lifetime .357 hitter, had batted over .400 six times in the States and Cuba. Thirty-four years old in 1930, he hit .333 and led the league in triples.

At third base, Judy Johnson, another Hall of Famer, hit .275 and is considered one of the four best third sackers in black history, the other three being Wilson, Marcelle, and Ray Dandridge. Charleston, Johnson, and Gibson gave the Grays three future Hall of Famers, and Williams should make it four. (Wilson, who joined them in 1931, would be the fifth.)

Vic Harris in right field was a .324 hitter, plus a slashing base-runner, and would write an unparalleled record as manager—eight pennants in nine years, 1937–45. He would have made it nine except for the war.

As we've seen, Lefty Williams was enjoying a remarkable year.

At second, temperamental George Scales (.303) was one of the finest curveball hitters in black ball annals.

Mischievous, little, light-skinned Paul Stephens—"Country Jake"—was one of the widest-ranging shortstops ever to play, of any race or any era. Usually an automatic out, he enjoyed his best year at bat, .324.

The man who built the team—and a dynasty—was Cumberland "Cum" Posey, who had guided the Grays from their early days as a semipro steel mill team about 1914. The college-educated Posey had also been one of the top basketball players of his generation.

Their foes, the Monarchs, were the best in the West, but they had just suffered a crippling auto accident that put several of their regulars out of action. Missing, most prominently, was Bullet Joe Rogan.

Brewer, who moved up to fill Rogan's shoes, had an 8–8 mark that year, though the year before he had led all Western pitchers with 17 wins and only three losses. Chet would have been a star pitcher on most other teams; on the Monarchs, unfortunately, he had been overshadowed by Rogan in the 1920s and would be again by Paige in the '30s and '40s. "But I beat everyone those other two did," he maintained.

Many old-timers considered Newt "Colt" Allen (.345) the best second baseman they saw.

Frank Duncan was an excellent defensive catcher and, 15 years later, would be Jackie Robinson's first professional manager. Usually a banjo hitter, Dunc swatted .372 that summer.

However, after the accident the Monarchs were no match for the Grays, who won 11 out of the 12 games they played each other.

Gibson was still awkward behind the plate. "He was mostly a blocker, like [Louis] Santop," said outfielder Crush Holloway, comparing Josh to the first great black slugger, who had flourished ten to twenty years earlier.

"Gibson dropped a lot of balls," said Cool Papa Bell. "He didn't have the sure hands Campanella did."

"He couldn't catch a sack of baseballs," another outfielder, Ted Page, said with a smile.

We called him "Boxer," because he'd catch like he was wearing boxing gloves. Biz Mackey [Campanella's tutor] used to say to young catchers, "You drop as many balls as Josh Gibson." On foul balls he was terrible. He said they made him drunk. I credit the man who really helped him on foul balls as Judy Johnson. Johnson was one of the real smart ballplayers in my era. He really helped Josh become a great catcher.

Johnson agreed:

Honestly, he was the greatest hitter I've ever seen, but he wasn't a great catcher. But he wanted to learn. He used to catch batting practice for me and then catch the ball game. A lot of times after the game, I'd have papers I was trying to get straightened out for the next day or something, and he'd come in. "Jing"—he used to call me Jing—"how'd I look today?"

I'd say, "Josh, you caught a real good game, except . . ."

He'd say, "Well, I'll try to freshen up on that tomorrow."

That boy was game. I've seen the time Josh had his finger split and tied a piece of tape around it and played just as though nothing had happened. You think these kids now would do that? He really wanted to learn.

Judy showed the kid how to judge the spin on foul balls; it carries the ball away from the plate going up, then carries it back toward the plate coming down.

He also taught Josh how to handle everything the pitchers threw at him—spitballs, emery balls, and shine balls so laden with vaseline that, says Bell, "it made you blink your eyes in the sun. On a knuckleball, he would just knock it down. He'd hold his right hand back here, behind his back. That's the way a lot of catchers catch that knuckleball."

But nobody had to teach Josh to throw. "Nobody," said Page, "threw better, more accurately, or quicker."

Newt Allen of the Monarchs adds:

When there was nobody on base, he dropped six out of ten pitches. But the pitch you were going to steal on, he caught that one and threw you out. We watched him and watched him. There weren't any passed balls by him. But they'd hit in his glove and he'd drop them, pick them up and throw them. You get ready to steal and out you were. No, he didn't drop that one. It sounds funny, but it's true.

From Bell:

And Gibson was a smart catcher. He was smart and he was fast. Sometimes he just dropped the ball on purpose to get some guy to run.

And he threw a light ball; you could catch it without a glove. Campanella threw a brick. But there were two things Campanella could do better than Gibson—catch pop flies and receive the ball. If I had to have Gibson and Campanella on the same team, I'd rather have Campanella catch and Gibson at some other position.

At bat, the rookie found the Monarch hurlers tough; they held him to an average of just .242. His wife's death, of course, was a factor; his inexperience was another, and the lights were surely a third one. They were far from the candlepower put out by a modern major league lighting plant.

When the two teams reached Kansas City, Joe Williams and Chet Brewer hooked up in one of the greatest pitching battles ever witnessed. For 11 innings they dueled without a score. Chet gave only four hits, Joe only one; Brewer struck out 19 of the Grays, Williams fanned 27 of the Monarchs. We don't have data on walks, but later Josh would maintain that Joe had the best control of any man he ever caught, including Satchel. The Grays finally won on a walk to little Jake Stephens, an error, and a fluke hit that caromed off the third base bag for two bases. Like the rest of the Grays, Josh was powerless against Brewer, who struck out ten men in a row, which of course must have included Gibson, who got no hits in five at bats.

Brewer's opinion of the kid was colored by that first barnstorming tour. In later years, when other pitchers trembled at the sight of Gibson coming to bat, Brewer told them:

> What's wrong with you guys? He's human like anybody else. I always figured him a big old rookie boy, never was afraid of him.
> Josh did something a lot of pitchers didn't pick up on. When he crouched, you couldn't throw him anything low. Josh hit a low ball like some people hit a golf ball. And when he stood up, anything from the belt up, he'd hit that out of sight. Like Pete Rose. I don't think Pete Rose would hit in our colored league, because our guys would throw that right over his letters in the crouch. When he straightened up, it would be by him.

Once, walking together back to the hotel where both teams bathed, Josh told Brewer:

> "See this bat, Chet Brewer? I'm gonna wear it out on you."
> I said, "The first time you get a hit on me, I'm gonna hit you."
> "You poor so-and-so, you can't hurt anyone."

The first time up I got his cap bill, don't know how I missed his head. Down in the dirt he went. I walked halfway to home. "Missed you this time, but I'm gonna get you next time." He got up again flat-footed. Even I was kind of afraid I was going to rack him back.

Gibson hit one home run on the tour, the first big league blast of his life. It came in St. Louis against the St. Louis Stars—Bell, Wells, Suttles, Radcliffe, George Giles—against the ace of the St. Louis staff, Ted "Big Florida" Trent. Trent was 12–2 that year, following 21–2 in 1928. He had a curveball that "could go around a barrel," Radcliffe said—"and I think he could make it go in the barrel." A year later, Trent would strike out the New York Giants' great Bill Terry (.349) four times in one night. "The lights were dim," Terry said, but nobody else struck out four times that night.

The St. Louis park had an extremely short left field foul line. Two trolley car barns abutted left field, one at the foul line and the other in left-center, where the fence slanted back to the flagpole in deep center field. Bell said the foul pole was 269 feet from home. St. Louis historian Normal "Tweed" Webb put it at 250 feet, but added that balls pulled over the fence there were ground rule doubles. It's not clear how high the fence was; St. Louis catcher Quincy Trouppe said 60 feet, though this seems unlikely.

Gibson "hit the ball way over the second shed, 400 and some feet," center fielder Bell said. It was a night game under the park's new permanent lights. Bell marveled: "We said, 'Bring him up close so we can look at him.' He was just a boy!"

Though there was no Eastern league that year, after knocking off the proud Monarchs, the Grays strutted to the top of the hill in the East.

The only club to dispute them was the New York Lincoln Giants. Originally from Lincoln, Nebraska, they were owned by Irishman Jim Keenan, who also owned the legendary New York Renaissance basketball squad, which often beat the famous New York Celtics.

The Lincolns boasted their own Hall of Famer, John Henry "Pop" Lloyd. Old-timers still argue which was the best black shortstop ever—Lloyd, Lundy, or Wells. Philadelphia A's manager Connie Mack compared Lloyd to Honus Wagner, the best of the whites, and Wagner himself was quoted as saying he was proud to be compared to Lloyd.

In Havana in 1909, Lloyd outhit the great Ty Cobb, .500 to .369. Pop wore steel shin guards under his socks to guard against Cobb's spikes and put the Georgia Peach out three straight times stealing. Ty was so mad he stomped off the field vowing never to play blacks again.

Lincoln shortstop light-hitting Bill Yancey also played for the Rens, and both are in basketball's Hall of Fame.*

New York's pitching ace was Bill Holland, who was given the honor of being the first black man to pitch in Yankee Stadium. His league record that year was 12-1, making him the biggest winner in the East, though Holland claimed that he actually won 20, which would presumably include semi-pro games.

Paige described Bill as "a chunky little guy":

> Bill Holland didn't have no fastball, but he had screw balls, knuckle balls, sliders, and sinkers, like that. He could throw any pitch. He looked like you could just tear it up, as far as that's concerned. Yeah, but you just couldn't hardly hit him out of the infield. He was hard for me to beat—he was hard for anyone to beat. He kept you off stride all the time, just like they say when I throwed that hesitation. All his pitches were delayed. He had the right motion. Didn't nobody pick up on that ball.

Light-skinned Luther Farrell compiled an 8-1 record on the mound and a .543 average at the plate. Two years earlier, 1928, he had led the league in home runs and in 1926 had pitched a seven-inning World Series no-hitter, beating Don Larson to it by 30 years.

These were the two teams that squared off for the championship of the East. Given a little more bench strength, especially in the bullpen, they might have challenged the white champions that year, the Athletics and Cardinals.

The play-off, the best six out of 11, opened in Pittsburgh's Forbes Field Saturday, September 20. The Grays' Lefty Williams easily won the opener 9–1, his 28th straight victory without a loss. Charleston weighed in with a homer.

The nightcap was a wild slugfest. Young Gibson swatted a triple against Farrell in the spacious park, which probably saw more three-base hits than any other big league field in the country.

Josh's second contribution was a blast that flew over the center-field fence 457 feet away. No man had ever cleared the spot before, and only three men have done it since—Charleston, Mickey Mantle,

---

*In 1971–72 Yancey served on Cooperstown's special Negro League committee that elected Paige and Gibson to the baseball Hall of Fame.

and Dick Stuart. Frank Howard hit one half-way up the light tower in left-center.

Wrote W. Rollo Wilson of the *Courier:* "Samson Gibson is green but a terrific threat when crouching over the plate with a bat."

The blow gave the Grays a 13-8 lead after four innings. By the seventh the Lincolns had retaken the lead 16–13. The Grays tied it with two in the eighth and one in the ninth, and won it in the tenth on Chaney White's bases-loaded single.

That night the exhausted players piled into their buses for the all-night ride to New York and a Sunday doubleheader at Yankee Stadium.

Some 25,000 fans came out to see Holland try to stop the Grays' bats and the ancient wonder, Joe Williams. Holland spaced six singles, one to Gibson, while Williams gave up a home run to second baseman Walter "Rev" Cannady and a triple into the crowd by Lloyd, as the Lincolns won 6–2.

Farrell came back in the second game and atoned for his disgrace of the day before by locking in a pitching duel with the Crawfords' George "Chippie" Britt. Josh slugged Farrell for a double, and the Grays took a 2–0 lead into the eighth. After two singles, the usually brilliant Stephens muffed a grounder to let one run in, Britt wild-pitched a second one home, and it was all tied up. In the tenth, Stephens walked, swiped second, and when Farrell himself kicked away a ground ball, raced home with the Grays' winning run.

For the next three days the Series went into hiatus, but not the players. The Grays rode back to Pittsburgh, where they had games scheduled every day with semipro teams. Posey may have had the best team in black baseball, maybe in all baseball, but he still had to meet the payroll.

Thursday the Grays and Lincs resumed their business in Philadelphia's Bigler Field, home of the black Philly Hilldales. Holland and Joe Williams squared off against each other once more. Jenkins and Clint Thomas slugged home runs for Lincoln. Vic Harris replied with a long one for Pittsburgh. And Josh walloped an even longer one, in fact, the longest ever hit in that park, over the roof and across the street, and the Grays won 13–7.

The Grays now led four games to one. But Friday New York's fork-balling Mervyn "Red" Ryan tamed the Grays, hit a home run in his own behalf, and beat Britt 6–4. That made it four games to two, the Grays leading, with two final doubleheaders coming up in New

York on the weekend. The Lincolns had to win three out of the four games to stay in the Series.

Saturday, September 27, the scene returned to Yankee Stadium, where the kid Gibson slammed perhaps the longest home run ever hit in the House that Ruth Built.

With a pair of binoculars from a seat behind home, you can get a close-up look at the modernistic circular stairs at the rear of the left field runway that divides the grandstand from the bleachers. The stairs weren't there in 1930; they were built when the stadium was remodeled in 1976, the same year that the roof over the third tier was taken down and the distinctive gingerbread hanging decorations were removed; a few were put along the back of the bleachers as decoration. In 1976 also, the present bull pen was built to shorten the immense distances in "Death Valley." Until then the runway was the bull pen, and it was at the gate to the bull pen, 415 feet away from home, that Al Gionfriddo robbed Joe DiMaggio of a home run in the 1947 World Series with one of the finest catches in baseball history.

If you can imagine the old roof, only a handful of men have reached the gingerbread front of it in the history of the stadium, and no one is definitely known to have cleared it. Mickey Mantle hit the facing in the shorter right field several times, an estimated 376 feet from home and 118 feet above the field. Ted Williams also may have sent balls rocketing against it.

In left field, which is deeper, two men, Doug DeCinces and Dave Winfield, have driven balls deep into the bull pen. In 1932, Jimmie Foxx slammed one into the third tier above the bull pen against Lefty Gomez; it went so far that Gomez said it took him 45 minutes to climb up to the spot afterwards.

Home run historian Mark Gallagher reports that Frank Howard may or may not have driven a monumental shot over the left field roof in the 1970s. The ball was lost in the night haze, and the umpire ruled it foul. Did it go out of the park? At least we know that nobody inside the park ever claimed to have retrieved it. Except for Howard's blast, nobody else in the American league has sent a ball clear over the roof in fair territory—or foul.

But in September 1930, 18-year-old Josh Gibson may have done it, when he walloped the fourth big league home run of his life in the equivalent of a Negro league World Series game.

Before the first game that day, New York catcher Larry Brown said, the Lincolns held a clubhouse skull session to go over each of the

Grays' hitters with Farrell, their starting pitcher. "Don't give Josh nothin' inside," they emphasized. Rookie shortstop Bill Yancey was particularly emphatic on that point. ("He was scared to death of Josh," said center fielder Clint Thomas. "When Josh came to bat, Yancey played left field.") Farrell nodded and obeyed. Four straight times he got Josh out.

But in the ninth, Farrell came out of the game, and Broadway Connie Rector (he didn't get his nickname wearing blue jeans) took the mound. A ten-year veteran, Rector was 3–1 that year with a dangerously high TRA of 7.02. But the year previous, he had been the best hurler in the East—in fact, just about the best black hurler ever—with an amazing 20–2 record. Rector was not overpowering. He walked as many men as he whiffed, which was unusual for a black pitcher back then. He completed only about half his games, also unusual for his day. He pitched as hard as he needed to. When the slugging Lincolns got him 18 runs, he won 18–13; when they got him two runs, he won 2–1. The secret of his success was the most tantalizing slow ball in America. "The first one was slow," first baseman George Giles said. "The second one walked up to the plate. The third one crawled up there." Batters went frantic waiting for the ball to arrive so they could swing. How would the overanxious rookie, Gibson, handle the master teaser?

Like a veteran. Rector must have forgotten the clubhouse meeting, because he got one ball a little too close, and Gibson, with "those arms like sledge hammers," supplied all the power himself and sent the ball whistling toward the bull pen like a golf drive.

I have talked to three eye-witnesses, each of whom had a slightly different version of what he saw, just as the eyewitness accounts of Babe Ruth's "called shot" in 1932 are all different. All three who saw Gibson's blast are deceased and cannot be called back for further questioning. Since each one was at a different point in the park, each saw the blow from a different perspective.

Judy Johnson was presumably in the visitors' dugout. The Yankee front office isn't sure where the visitors sat in 1930, but Mark Koenig, the only surviving member of the 1930 Yankees, says the Yankees sat behind third base and the visitors behind first, just the opposite of the current arrangement. Johnson, on the first base side, therefore would have had a good view of a long drive to left field, and he says emphatically that the ball "went out over the roof, over everything."

Holland, in the third base dugout, said the ball left the park between the roof and the third tier and came down against the back wall of the bull pen, which angles sharply back behind the grandstand. However, Bill's view may have been partially blocked by the stands.

Brown, the catcher, was at home plate, presumably with the best view of anyone in the park. He said the ball went over the roof and hit the back of the bull pen, about two feet below the top of the wall.

Even the Yankees public relations office cannot say how far from home the bull pen wall was. Using a scale diagram of the park circa 1950, the wall was, as close as I can measure it, 505 feet from home.

The newspapers are of little use. The white papers didn't consider the game worthy of their coverage, and the black papers merely spoke of Josh's blow as a long home run. His hometown *Courier* said it went 430 feet into the bleachers, the longest blow in the stadium that year. That would contradict the three players, two of whom agreed that it landed in the bull pen, not the bleachers, and the third who said it went out of the park entirely.

Is it possible for a ball to clear the roof 118 feet high, about 400 feet from home, and come down in the bull pen another 100 feet away? For that answer I went to Francis Mirabelle, an expert on ballistics with the Army's Aberdeen Proving Ground in Maryland. Mirabelle said that, because of air resistance, the highest point of a missile, whether an artillery round or a baseball, is about 60 percent of the distance of its entire flight. If it landed 505 feet away, then, the apogee would have been 300 feet from home, and the ball would have been on its downward flight when it passed the roof, whether over it or under it. It is ballistically possible that an extremely high fly could have cleared the roof and still have landed in the bull pen. Mirabelle drew several possible trajectories, including one for Brown's version that the ball went between the roof and the upper tier. Using Mirabelle's reckoning, if Mantle's hardest blast, in 1963, was still going up when it hit the roof facing, 376 feet away, as eyewitnesses say, then it would have traveled at least 607 feet unimpeded.

As far as is known, Gibson himself gave almost no details of the blow. In a 1938 interview with Cum Posey, he said, "I hit the ball on a line into the bull pen in deep left field." He called it one of the two longest balls he had ever hit. Since Gibson was known as more of a line-drive hitter than a fly-ball hitter, we can assume that the ball probably did not go over the roof but instead went over the corner of the third tier, to the right of where Foxx's drive would bang into the seats two years later. According to Mirabelle, the optimum launch angle for maximum distance is 32–38 degrees. A ball with enough height to clear the roof on its way down would have to be launched at more than the optimum angle.

But whether over the roof or not, it was still a magnificent wallop. "And that was no big league ball," said Johnson. The black leagues used a Wilson ball, while the wealthier white majors used the more expensive Reach and Spalding balls. "If that had been a big league ball, I guess it would have ended up in the Bronx." ("If Josh had hit a big league ball," said Radcliffe, "he might have *killed* somebody.")

The blow gave the Grays an 8–5 lead with the Lincolns coming up for their last at bats. Lefty Williams walked the bases full, and manager Charleston motioned old Joe Williams in from the bull pen. Lloyd countered by lifting the weak-hitting Yancey and sending up Cuban catcher Julio Rojo to pinch-hit. Rojo smacked Williams' first pitch for a triple to right to clear the bases and tie the game, and Rector himself batted in the winner with a single. So Josh's famous homer came anticlimactically in a losing cause.

Rector started the second game, and Gibson pummeled him for three more hits—but no home runs—as the Grays won 7–3 to go two up again.

The Lincs would have to win both games Sunday, or it would all be over. Lloyd decided to go with his ace, Holland, who would attempt the iron man feat of winning both games. Joe Williams was his opponent in game one. Lloyd, Cannady, and Jenkins all cracked out three hits. Holland, meanwhile, was in control. "You done hit Connie in the bull pen," he taunted Gibson. "Let's see you hit me in there now." Josh didn't come close. He got a single in four at bats, and Holland won 6–2.

Holland had a high opinion of Josh however:

> Josh Gibson was my favorite catcher. No question about him, he was a great hitter. If Josh had been in his prime and came along when Roy Campanella did, you'd never have heard of Campanella. If Josh had been in the majors, he'd have set some records up there. They'd have polished him up a little, and he'd have been something! Campanella was strictly a pull hitter, pitchers would pitch outside to him. But Gibson was an all-round great hitter; he could hit the ball where it was pitched, over the right field fence, over center field, or over left field. And he was so much faster than Campanella, although he was a 200-pounder.

Holland came back gamely in the night cap against Britt. He had a 2–0 lead until the Grays put one man on, and Britt hit a Texas leaguer to right. Second baseman Cannady pedaled back, Smith charged in, and the two collided, as the runner scored. Smith lay motionless and had to be carried from the field. The next spring he would be dead. The cause is not clear, but it might possibly have been from complications from that injury.

In the eighth, Holland's world caved in. Farrell, who replaced Smith, committed a two-base error, then misplayed Johnson's fly into a three-base error. (Farrell was an alcoholic; whether or not this contributed to his disastrous fielding is not known.) "Holland went up in the air like an umbrella," Lincoln outfielder Clint Thomas said. A walk, a single, and a double by Gibson brought in four more runs, and the Grays were champs 5–2.

Would you believe? The tired champions climbed into the bus and drove to Newark for a game that night against the International league all-stars! Joe Williams lost 8–2 to Dauntless Dave Danforth, formerly of the St. Louis Browns.

1931

Japan invaded Manchuria. Gandhi went on a hunger strike. American hunger strikers marched on Washington. Al Capone went to prison.

"All of Me," "Between the Devil and the Deep Blue Sea," "Dancing in the Dark," "Lady of Spain," "Where the Blue of the Night Meets the Gold of the Day" by Bing Crosby, "When the Moon Comes Over the Mountain" by Kate Smith.

Public Enemy, City Lights, Dracula, Frankenstein.

Radio: Ed Sullivan, Eddie Cantor, "Little Orphan Annie," "Myrt and Marge."

Broadway: *Of Thee I Sing, George White's Scandals.*

Books: *The Good Earth,* Drew Pearson's *Washington Merry Go-Round,* Ely Culbertson's *Contract Bridge.*

Dick Tracy.

Lefty Grove was 31–4. The Cards beat him and the A's 4–3. Notre Dame coach Knute Rockne died in a plane crash.

The Depression grew grimmer. Men out of work sold apples or pencils on the street or shuffled into "Hoovervilles"—tent cities of the unemployed. Luckier than most, both Gibson and Paige had jobs, even though many of the old teams had broken up.

Paige wrote that he joined the Nashville Elite Giants, though there is no confirmation of that in the newspapers. In fact, there is no record that the Elites even existed that summer, as teams and leagues sank out of sight.

We do know that in '31 Satchel joined the Cleveland Cubs, a nondescript team whose only other player of note was a fancy-fielding first baseman, Shifty Jim West. Their second baseman was distinguished mainly by his nickname, Black Bottom Buford. The Cubs played in a tiny bandbox next to League Park, home of the American league Indians. Paige said he got angry every time he looked at League Park and realized it was closed to him. "All season long it burned me."

Paige's record at Cleveland was 2–2, according to research by

36

Dick Clark and the author. One of his wins was a six-inning shutout, one of his losses was 1–0. Another loss was 8–1, as St. Louis, the champions of the West, beat him with 11 hits.

In June, Satch got one of the biggest breaks of his life: Gus Greenlee, Pittsburgh's big-spending, cigar-chomping numbers king, laid out a reported $250 to bring Paige and Streeter to his new club, the Crawfords (not to be confused with Gibson's former boys' team of the same name), which he hoped would challenge the Grays.

One of the pivotal personalities in black baseball history, Greenlee—"Big Red"—was a racketeer who got his start hijacking beer trucks, according to Judy Johnson. He even hijacked beer belonging to Lucky Luciano and Dutch Schultz of "Murder Inc."—Greenlee had guts. He operated the city's numbers racket, which collected penny bets from the city's poor and paid off 500-to-one on three-digit numbers every day. Then a crime prosecuted by the government, today the numbers is known as the "lottery" and operated by the government in most states. Gus built a stable of fighters, grooming John Henry Lewis for the world lightheavyweight crown, and opened the Crawford Grille on Wylie Avenue on Pittsburgh's black Hill neighborhood. On the second floor, along with some high-priced prostitutes, Gus' henchmen counted the sackfulls of pennies from each day's take. Downstairs in the Grille, Gus held court and brought in top entertainers such as Lena Horne, whose father ran the numbers business upstairs. Gus was a benevolent racketeer, who felt he had the welfare of his people at heart. Jim Bankes reports that ex-fighter Jack Johnson was also a partner, but Greenlee ran the old champ out when Johnson tried to expand into the drug trade. Gus also ran the strong-arm protection racket off the Hill—Judy Johnson told Bankes two of the gangsters ended up "at the bottom of the river."

Greenlee was also determined to build the best baseball team in the world. To catch Satch he picked up Bill Perkins. Ted Page liked to recall the story:

We stole Perkins out from under the sheriff's watch dogs in Dawson, Georgia. Perkins was the idol of the town; they had built a ballpark for him out of old logs and broken down doors. Everybody came to watch the ball games, and the sheriff was the ticket taker. Well, we went down in spring training and saw him and wanted to take him back north, but the sheriff said, "No, he has to stay here, we built a ballpark for him." He said if we left town in the morning and his man—he didn't say "man," I'll let you guess what he said—if his man wasn't there, we better not be in

Georgia. And we weren't. We hid Perkins in the bus and drove right past
the sheriff sitting in front of the store.

Statistics are sketchy, since there was no organized league schedule, and the strapped black newspapers cut way back on their
coverage of games played. But Paige wrote that his first game for Gus
was against the crosstown rivals, the Grays. Paige recalled that Greenlee told him, "Remember, they got Smokey Joe Williams and Lefty
Williams."

Satch just shrugged and remarked "They don't worry old Satch."
He said he struck out 16. That night, Greenlee "locked the door on
his grill, and we went to town."

Again, no box score has yet been discovered, so we don't know
how Satch may have done against Josh, or whether he faced the great
Smokey Joe. Paige said he faced Joe twice in his career:

> It's a funny thing. When I did get in the big league, they wanted to
> ask me did I see crowds like I saw when I was in the big leagues? And I
> told 'em, "Yes," because in fact when we was playing all-star games, like
> when I played against Smokey Joe, like Forbes Field, we used to pack that
> park.
>
> I pitched against him in Pittsburgh and Philadelphia. I beat him the
> first game, he beat me the second. We ended up one-one. It was 3–2 the
> second game. Scores never did get very high back then, I guess because
> they had so many good pitchers. Smokey Joe could throw harder than all
> of them.

It is tantalizing to hope that somewhere, some day, box scores
confirming the games will turn up, but so far, none have been found.
Since the Grays and Crawfords were both Pittsburgh teams, and big
rivals, it is hard to imagine that the Pittsburgh *Courier* did not cover
them.

Of the games we do know about for 1931, Paige pitched six
against top black clubs. He won three and lost three. That left him
with a 5–5 record for the year and a 4.47 TRA. He struck out six men
for every walk.

Meanwhile, on the Grays, Joe Williams slipped to 5–6. But Big
Bill Foster came from Chicago to take over as ace of the pitching staff
with a 7–1 mark. (He had been 1–1 in the West before making the
jump.)

The 19-year-old Gibson had taken over the catcher's job full-time. Having caught perhaps the best black pitcher of all time—Williams—as a rookie, he now caught perhaps the best black lefty ever, Foster.

Josh found himself playing with a powerhouse. The top hitter, Scales, batted .393; a later Grays standout, Buck Leonard, would call him the best right-handed hitter, and the best curveball hitter, he had ever seen, and that, presumably, included Gibson. Charleston hit .380 with four homers in 34 games, second highest total in the league. The new third baseman, burly Jud Wilson, hit .373, and Ted Page .308.

They didn't awe young Josh, who batted .367 with six home runs to lead the league. He came to bat 128 times. That's about 26 homers for 550 at bats.

Eric "Ric" Roberts, who covered the Grays for the *Courier,* reported that Josh hit 75 homers while batting .608. It is not clear where the numbers came from, but if authentic, they have to include the many contests the Grays played against white semipro clubs in the Tri-State area of Ohio, Kentucky, and western Pennsylvania. In all, the Grays claimed, they won 186 and lost only 17 that year.

The Grays played their home games in Forbes Field, home of the National league Pirates, when the Pirates were on the road. (They used the field, that is, not the locker room.) It was the worst park in the National league to hit one out of. Left field was 365 feet from home, and center field a distant 457.

The Gibson swing had been perfected. "He had a fluid swing, a classic swing, like Ted Williams," said Monte Irvin, who later starred with the New York Giants. "He attacked the ball. He was as strong as two men."

"He didn't have Babe Ruth's eight-foot cut," said Ric Roberts. "His bat blurred through the strike zone like a swarm of bees, on a short, six-foot cut. Josh always said the ball came up there as big as a balloon, no matter how fast it was coming."

Those who saw him say Gibson stood flat-footed, like Joe DiMaggio, taking hardly any stride. He was one of the first of the modern wrist-hitters. When Ruth or Jimmie Foxx swung and missed, they often ended up sitting on the ground, their legs twisted like corkscrews from the force of their swings. Not Josh. He always kept his balance.

Newark pitcher Max Manning remembers:

> I never saw Josh take a leaving-the-ground swing. It was always a smooth, quick stroke. A lot of guys would swing, the ground would

shake, the air would move, and their hats would fly off. But he'd just take that short, quick stroke, and that ball would leave any ballpark.

Gibson took a very short stride, Cool Papa Bell said. He hit mostly line drives like Gehrig, not flies like Ruth.

Bob Burnes, sports editor of the St. Louis *Globe Democrat,* said Gibson reminded him of Cardinal catcher Walker Cooper at bat:

> A real short stroke. A lot of line drives. Stood straight up, legs spread fairly wide apart. A huge upper torso, which gave him his power. He didn't wag his bat too much, just kept it cradled in his arms, then let go with a really short stroke.*

Gibson didn't take a back swing, said Judy Johnson. Like Williams, Josh could swing late and hit it out of the catcher's mitt.

Roy Campanella would later write that Josh "was the only power hitter I ever heard of who hit the ball where it was pitched." Most young sluggers are taught to pull, but Josh's power was to all fields:

> Nobody has a smoother, more rhythmic swing than Josh. That was the thing that used to impress people more than anything else, the distance he would get with the easiest sort of a swing. I used to take a real hefty cut myself, and he'd always tell me, "Roy, you don't have to swing that hard to give the ball a ride. If you hit it right, it'll go."

Senators owner Clark Griffith reportedly said Gibson "hits for more distance with less effort than any player I ever saw," and Clark had seen Ruth, Gehrig, and Foxx.

Gibson was a great curveball hitter. "That was his main pitch!" marveled Leonard, who would later join Josh on the Homestead Grays, forming the black equivalent of a Ruth–Gehrig home run duo. "You stay in this league, you got to hit a curveball," Josh advised Buck. "He'd look at three fastballs, then hit that curveball! He figured sooner or later that pitcher was going to throw him that curveball, and he was waiting for it."

Gibson hit with power to all fields, as Willie Powell of the American Giants later learned:

---

*Burnes said his uncle usually took him to see the Cardinals or Browns, but sometimes he'd say, "Let's go see some *real* ball players," and took him to a Stars game.

Josh hit a bad pitch through that tin fence at Pittsburgh's Greenlee Field. And it was a bad pitch. I knew what I was doing—or thought I knew. I wanted him to hit it to right field. I didn't believe anyone could reach out that far and hit it that far. Boy, he talked about that ball all the time we got together. He said he had that ball till he died. And I was having a good year too. That's the year I beat the Crawfords a doubleheader. They had a team, boy.

Pitchers were in a quandary. As Powell muttered, if you threw a curve outside, Josh would kill the ball; if you threw a fastball inside, "he'd kill the third baseman."

Catcher Quincy Trouppe told young pitchers to keep the ball at Gibson's knees. If you pitch high outside, he warned, Josh will hit it over the right field fence. If you pitch high inside, he'll hit it over the left field fence.

Chet Brewer's strategy was even more effective: "Keep the ball low and behind him."

"Don't let him stretch his arms out," moaned Newark pitcher Leon Day.

Memphis lefty Verdell Mathis threw Josh screwballs low and away, and "he never hit a homer off me." But,

You couldn't fool him—don't think you're gonna fool him. Josh will hit you with one hand as quick as he will with two. I've seen him reach out on a sharp-breaking curveball on the outside from a right-hand pitcher, almost fooled him—almost. The ball almost got by him, and he reached out with one hand and hit it over the right field fence. And he ran the bases hollering, "Ha, you like to fooled me that time, but don't try that no more."

Philadelphia center fielder Gene Benson remembered:

Josh Gibson in Washington did something I can't believe. Henry McHenry had been getting Josh out all day. He got two strikes on Josh in the ninth and threw him a curveball—and he had a good curveball—and fooled Josh. Josh stepped back—you know how you step in the bucket when the ball fools you? He swung with one hand, and it went over my head. All I did was look at it, didn't even turn around. McHenry broke up the water cooler! He had a fit. He was high strung, you know.

Pitcher Dave "Impo" Barnhill also learned not to throw Gibson a curve.

His hand slipped off the bat, and he just followed through just like that with this right hand and hit the ball in the cemetery beyond the fence. I've never seen a ball hit that hard before in my life!

Every time I left a town, some young kid would say, "Heh, see over there? Josh done hit one right there." And that was about four blocks from the ballpark where he was pointing. He was the greatest, as far as I was concerned.

Some hurlers, like Bill Harvey, *wanted* Josh to hit to right. Harvey watched him line one back through the box and hit the pitcher on the top of his cap as the ball bounded into center field. "If it had hit him in the face, it would have killed him." Thereafter, Harvey was careful to keep the ball outside—and let the first baseman worry about it.

Ted Page thought Josh's worst weakness was right down the middle. Leonard had pretty much the same theory. Before he and Josh became teammates, Buck said, the opposition would pull the infield and outfield toward the center of the diamond

and put the center fielder out of the ballpark if we could. And then throw the ball straight down the middle of the plate. He could hit the ball 500 feet to center field, and we would catch it—I say 500 feet, but I mean extreme center. No, he couldn't pull it, not a fastball. You'd hear the crack of the bat—bam!—400 feet to centerfield. Or if it was on the ground, it would handcuff somebody in the infield.

Bill Foster said Gibson's only blind spot was a six-inch area right at his belt buckle. "But you get it at his knees and it would be gone a mile. When Gibson turned that cap bill around and got in that crouch at the plate, you had your problems. Anywhere he caught it, he could hit it."

Along with Suttles, John Beckwith was another right-handed slugger often compared to Gibson for sheer distance. But the hurlers agreed they'd much rather pitch to John than to Josh, even though Beckwith posted several .400-plus seasons. Beckwith was strictly a pull hitter, and pitchers kept the ball outside to him. Said Streeter: "A pitcher that knew Beckwith could get him in the pinches and kind of work with him, but Josh, you couldn't fool him any time."

Added Kansas City second baseman Newt Allen: "Beckwith never learned how to step into [an outside] ball. That's the reason he was a much easier out than Josh was." The infield could shift on Beckwith. "He'd hit a couple fouls, a smart pitcher would throw one on the outside, he can't reach it, and it's an easy bounce out."

New York shortstop Bill Yancy admitted that Beck could hit the ball a long way, "but he'd strike out a lot. Josh didn't strike out as much."

As for Suttles, Bankhead said, the Mule "hit them way up high, and they'd drift over the fence. Josh hit 'em on a line, and they'd still go over. I don't want to be segregationist, but Josh was the greatest slugger who ever lived."

Josh's drives whistled to center on a low line, said Monte Irvin, then backspin seemed to take over, and the ball appeared to jump forward anew.

Streeter's strategy was to make Josh hit it on the ground for a single or double "and maybe have a chance to get the next man out." The strategy backfired one day in Forbes Field when Josh hit a ground ball home run. It bounced over the center fielder's head. Josh was fast, Sam said. "When the ball came back in there, he was already back sitting on the bench."

Gibson's long-time buddy, shortstop Sammy Bankhead (older brother of Dodger pitcher Dan Bankhead and model for the character Troy Maxon in August Wilson's prize-winning play, *Fences*) said Josh hit a grounder to him in Mexico. Bankhead sidestepped it like a matador "and just let that bullet go."

And remember, Johnson pointed out, the Negro leagues used the cheaper Wilson ball, which didn't have as much spring to it. And some wily teams froze the balls in the refrigerator before the game when the Crawfords came to town.

And, of course, Gibson was hitting against all kinds of illegal pitches—emery balls, spit balls, grease balls. As Cool Papa Bell said:

> In our league they threw the spitter, the emery ball, shine ball—that means Vaseline ball; there was so much Vaseline on it, it made you blink your eyes on a sunny day. Then they threw the mud ball—the mud on its seams made it sink. The emery ball would break either up or down, but if a sidearmer threw it and didn't know what he was doing, it could sail right into the hitter. Ray Chapman [of the Cleveland Indians] got killed with an emery ball, that's why they don't throw it any more. It was a dangerous pitch.

From Gene Benson:

> What we had to hit at was much worse in our league than in the major leagues. In the majors you didn't have to worry about being

thrown at, you didn't have to worry about anybody cuttin' the ball or sailin' the ball, or throwin' spit balls. I've had balls come in on the heart of the plate; when I'd swing, it would be over my head! Now *no* ball jumps that much unless it's cut.

And you couldn't get a toehold at the plate. You see those batters today dig a hole with their toe. The pitchers would tell us, "Let's see how you hit it layin' down."

In personality, Josh was "the biggest kid you ever saw in your life," Judy Johnson said. "Like he was just 12 or 13 years old. Oh, he was jolly *all* the time. You had to love him."

Baltimore outfielder Crush Holloway related:

We called him "Big Boy," because he wasn't nothing but a boy. He liked to play, liked to have fun. Easy to handle. All those home runs and everything never did go to his head. Some stars, you know, it goes to their head, they think they're greater than anybody else. But Josh was always the same.

Leonard recalled:

He wasn't loud or rowdy. He always wanted to have some fun, and he was always saying funny things. Everybody liked him, nobody disliked him. He never did molest anybody, never did ride the umpire.

From Ted Page:

Josh was just a big overgrown kid. After a game we'd go to an ice cream parlor. The older fellows would go out drinking or looking for women, but we'd find a field where the kids were playing. I remember after one doubleheader in Kansas City, it was 110 degrees. We went back to the hotel, and there was a ball game in session behind the hotel, and he and I went right out there and got in the game, and he played just as hard with those kids as he had in the two games that afternoon.

As for women, Josh was shy, remembered first baseman George Giles. "He didn't know what to do with them." The life of an itinerant ballplayer—a game, a quick snack, and a long overnight bus ride—didn't encourage romance anyway. The traveling salesman's life is not nearly so glamorous as popular myth indicates.

On August 18, Satch and Josh faced each other for the first time that we can confirm. The Grays had just knocked the Craws' Harry Kincannon out of the box with a five-run fourth inning, and Paige was rushed in to put out the fire. "The feature of the game," wrote the *Courier,* "was the masterful and sensational pitching of Paige." Satchel held the Grays scoreless the rest of the way, striking out six, as the Crawfords rallied to win. Josh went hitless for the day.

Josh's owner, Posey, had seen enough of both Gibson and Paige to name them to his authoritative black all-star squad for 1931.

That October for the first time, Josh faced a white major league pitcher, right-hander George Uhle (11–12 with the seventh-place Tigers). Gibson drove two homers and two singles in six trips. The blacks, with Streeter pitching, walloped Uhle and his relief, Frank "Dutch" Henry, formerly of the White Sox, 18–0.

They also challenged 40-year-old lefty Wilbur Cooper, who had won 216 National league games before retiring five years earlier. Josh got one hit, as his club won 10–7.

Radcliffe remembered a third game that fall against another former National leaguer, Cardinal right-hander Bill Doak, who, incidentally, invented the modern webbed glove. No corroborating box score has been found, but Duty said Josh hit the ball over the fence and onto a front porch, sending the startled family scattering for cover.

Meanwhile, Satchel traveled to California that winter to play the white stars such as Babe Herman, who had hit .313 for the Dodgers that season and .393 the year before that. In one night game in Los Angeles on October 23, Paige struck Herman out four straight times and beat the San Francisco Seals 8–1. Satch whiffed eight men in all that night.

On that trip one of Paige's most enduring legends was born, possibly as a result of a racial slur. As Satch's chirpy little catcher, Larry Brown, told the story:

> We were playing a game out in Los Angeles, and were only leading 2–1 against Joe Pirrone's All-Stars—Babe Herman, Walter Berger [.323 with the Boston Braves], Fred Haney [formerly of the Tigers]—big men. The guys kept hollering, "Come on, he ain't got nothing but a fastball." But it was so fast, they couldn't hit it. The speed was so rapid, it would take off. Anyway, Satchel called the outfield in on the grass and struck out the next two men coming up, Frank Demaree [who would go to the Cubs in '32] and Walter Berger. And we only leading 2–1. He did it

against the major leaguers—I know, 'cause I was catching! I said, "Satch, you're the biggest fool ever I've seen in my life." I said, "Long as I been playing ball, I never saw anybody do that but you with a one-run lead."

Next Satchel and Larry went down to San Diego. Again Brown recalled:

A guy had come up and got me and Satchel for a battery. Now we were going to play on a high school team against one of the top white teams down there. He said, "I want you fellows to give us a good exhibition."

I said, "Well, goddam, that's all Satchel *got* is a good exhibition!" The ball game gets under way. Satchel struck out so many men until he started handing them the ball so they could hit it, to give 'em some kind of play, you know. So one guy hits the ball way past the outfielders. Satchel lobbed in another one like that, the second guy hit it way out yonder out there. Then he got on the rubber and struck out the rest of them.

1932

One out of four workers was unemployed ("Brother, can you spare a dime?"). MacArthur routed the Washington bonus marchers. The Lindbergh baby was kidnapped. Japan attacked Shanghai. Hitler and Roosevelt were elected ("Happy Days Are Here Again").

"Night and Day," "April in Paris," "I'm Getting Sentimental Over You," "Shuffle Off to Buffalo," "I've Told Every Little Star," "How Deep Is the Ocean?," Duke Ellington's "It Don't Mean a Thing If It Ain't Got that Swing," "Tiger Rag" by Louis Armstrong,

Grand Hotel, I Am a Fugitive From a Chain Gang, Tarzan with Johnny Weissmuller, *Farewell to Arms, Freaks.*

Radio: Burns and Allen, "One Man's Family," Jack Benny, Fred Allen, Walter Winchell ("Good evening, Mr. and Mrs. America").

Books: *Studs Lonigan, Tobacco Road, Brave New World, Death in the Afternoon.*

Radio City Music Hall. The jitterbug.

Jimmie Foxx hit 58 homers. Ruth called his shot as the Yanks beat the Cubs 4–0. Sonja Henie and the Lake Placid winter Olympics. Babe Didrikson, Eddie Tolan, Buster Crabbe won the gold at Los Angeles. Jack Sharkey beat Schmeling.

The two men who were to become living legends finally met on the same team, the Pittsburgh Crawfords, in 1932.

Posey, like many another black owner, had found his gate receipts going down, down, down. It grew harder and harder to meet the payrolls, until, over the winter, Greenlee dangled some of his numbers money in front of Posey's stars and captured almost all of them—Charleston, Wilson, Stephens, Ted Page, and Gibson. Josh apparently was tempted by a $100 a month raise. Virtually the only Grays to remain loyal to Cum were Joe Williams and manager Vic Harris.

Josh was on his way to spring training on the team bus when he was seized with appendicitis and was rushed to a hospital. But he made a lightning recovery from the surgery and was back in the lineup within two weeks. He was moved to left field to make room for Perkins behind the plate.

Later, Gus also picked up Cool Papa Bell and second baseman Pistol Johnny Russell from Posey's Detroit Wolves, and Judy Johnson from the Philadelphia Hilldales.

The Crawfords stayed out of the league, which was a wise move—it folded in June—but they were surely the best black club in America. Paige would call the Craws the best team he ever saw, including the world champion Cleveland Indians of 1948, who featured four future Hall of Famers—Bob Feller, Bob Lemon, Lou Boudreau, and Satch himself.

Gradually Josh won the catcher's job back. By mid-May Perkins was hitting only .207, and Greenlee let him go to the Grays (where, ironically, he slugged .462 to end with .407 for the season). Frank Duncan, another excellent defensive catcher, came from the Monarchs to replace him, but by mid-June he too was gone, and Josh was finally called in from the outfield.

Most of the newcomers—Charleston, Page, Stephens, and Gibson—were northern blacks. There was friction, as a subtle caste system developed between the northerners and the less polished fellows from the South. Stephens, a native of York, Pennsylvania, put it this way:

> You take Satchel and those, they were all southern boys. They lived a different life than we lived. We didn't even much associate with them off the ball field, because they were what you'd call clowns. They didn't dress the way we dressed, they didn't have the same mannerisms, the same speech. Paige was a big mouth, didn't have any education, saying, "You all" and stuff like that.
>
> And you have this other problem with southern boys. They've never been used to making money. Give them $150 a month, first thing you know they go all haywire, living on top of the world, walking around with their jackets on: "Pittsburgh Crawfords." The older fellows, we had neckties on when we went to dinner, I mean because that's how you were supposed to do. You're a gentleman, you're a big-timer.

Jake, who had been around since 1923, considered both Satchel and Josh upstarts.

> They were wearing didies (diapers) when I was playing. Satchel Paige is the most overrated ballplayer ever God put breath into. . . . Satchel was a good pitcher, don't let anyone tell you anything different about that, but as far as him being so great, hell, you take Bill Holland, Rats Henderson, Joe Williams, Cannonball Dick Redding, Nip Winters. Let me tell you: Those men were *pitchers*, they weren't just throwers.

Stephens was right about Satchel spending money. "Money," Paige admitted, "was just something I passed along." He was always broke. He bought five suits and fancy ties—red, green, yellow, and bright blue—and even wore flowers on his underpants. He bought a bright green Packard convertible that had belonged to movie actress Bette Davis. He had another car that was so long he had to walk three blocks to check the tires. At the Crawford Grille, he harmonized with the Mills Brothers, who played there. When he walked down the street in Pittsburgh, people noticed him. He felt like a kid, he said—he had never really been a kid before. Impetuously, he got into the ring to spar with John Henry Lewis, Greenlee's light-heavyweight contender, and was knocked cold, almost giving Greenlee a heart attack.

Paige was given the honor of opening Greenlee Field, the country's only black-owned baseball stadium, on April 29. His opponent was the New York Black Yankees, owned by dancer Bill "Bojangles" Robinson, Shirley Temple's dancing partner. The Black Yanks had second baseman George Scales, first baseman Showboat Thomas, and center fielder Clint Thomas, whom Monte Irvin called "the black Joe DiMaggio." The pitcher that day was sandpaper specialist Jesse "Mountain" Hubbard. It was 0–0 going into the ninth, Hubbard recalled at the age of 78 in his home in Los Angeles. Paige had given four hits, Hubbard three.

> The ninth inning Ted Page [who had moved from the Craws to New York] came up, said, "I'm gonna get you a run." He walked up to bat and he laid one down and beat it out.
>
> I told Clint Thomas [the next batter], "Don't move your bat until Page gets to second." Bill Perkins was catching; now Perkins threw harder than Satchel! So the first pitch Ted was taking off for second. The ball beat him there, but Page knocked it out of [shortstop] Chester Williams' hand, and the ball went to center field. Ted got up and went to third. Oscar Charleston got the ball and throwed it to the third baseman, and Ted was coming into third. The third baseman moved away from third, let him come on in, so he wouldn't get cut, see?
>
> Thomas just topped the ball, just did get it over Satchel's head, and Williams came in, and he couldn't throw Clint Thomas out going to first. That's how soft it was hit. So Ted Page scored. Then Satchel struck them out. When he was going off the mound, I said, "Satchel."
>
> He said, "What?"
>
> I said, "Kiss this one good-bye."

In the last of the ninth, Hubbard struck out Rap Dixon and Charleston popped up. That brought up Gibson. "The damn stands went crazy," Thomas remembered. Josh's mother was sitting in a box seat. She called him over, planted a kiss on him, and told him to smack one out of there and win the game for Satchel.

Meanwhile, the Yankees were imploring Hubbard, "Keep that damn ball outside low, don't give him nothing inside, or it will be long bye-bye."

"Two strikes and no balls," Hubbard said, "and I threw one right over the heart of the plate," but the umpire called it a ball. The next pitch Josh drove a screamer to deepest center field.

Thomas said the fence was 459 feet at that point. Right fielder Page estimated it as 480 to 500 feet. "There were some flagpoles sitting right back in that corner. There were maybe four-five-six feet between the flagpoles and the fence. Clint turned his back on that ball and charged for that corner."

Thomas remembered Page and left fielder Fats Jenkins screaming at him as he ran, "Can you get it, Hawk? Can you get it, Hawk?"

Page said Clint "went right back into that pit, and just as he turned around, there was the ball."

"I put my right hand against the fence and put my left hand up, and the ball struck in the center of my glove," Clint said.

"He was so graceful," Paige said. "He came out with that ball, shaking it."

The New Yorkers had won it 1–0.

On July 16, Satchel gained his revenge by throwing a no-hitter against New York in the same park. The papers printed only a sparse box score with no details (I have added the batting average as a matter of interest):

BLACK YANKEES		R	H	A*	CRAWFORDS		R	H	A*
lf Jenkins	.288	0	0	0	ss Stephens	.202	0	0	3
3b H Williams	.364	0	0	1	cf Dixon	.310	0	0	0
rf Holloway	.438	0	0	0	rf Page	.315	2	2	0
cf C Thomas	.293	0	0	0	lf Gibson	.286	2	2	0
2b Scales	.218	0	0	2	3b Johnson	.270	1	2	2
1b D Thomas	.233	0	0	0	1b Charleston	.286	1	3	0
ss Yancey	.188	0	0	4	2b Russell	.275	0	0	2
c Burnett	.176	0	0	1	c Radcliffe	.234	0	1	0
p Stanley		0	0	2	p Paige		0	2	0
		0	0	10			6	12	7

---

*The box score says E, but presumably it means assists. If so, seven of Paige's outs came on ground balls. We are not told how many he struck out or walked.

Paige enjoyed a fine year on the mound, with a record of 14–8 against black opponents. He led the leagues in wins and just about everything else. Radcliffe, who caught Satch's no-hitter, was second in wins with a 13–5 mark.

For a home run slugger like Gibson, Greenlee Field was some improvement over Forbes Field, but not much. The left field wall was about 350 feet from home, Buck Leonard estimated. Cool Papa Bell called it "way over 300 feet." The wall was not high, but a hill in left field added to the height a ball needed to clear it.

Still, Josh smacked seven homers in 46 games, a pace of about 26 for a white major league season, and again enough to lead the league. He was also tops in triples, five. His average dropped, however, to .286.

Two semipro players from Martin's Ferry, Ohio, recall one game Josh played against the Martin's Ferry Westlakers at the local football field. The left field fence was more than the length of the field, Bill Brown said, "more like 150 yards." He told historian Lee Douglas that Gibson, playing third base, smashed five home runs in the contest. "We near run out of balls."

On their rare days off, the Crawfords were encouraged to go to see the white big leaguers play. "Josh just loved Yankee Stadium," Judy Johnson told Bankes. "He loved to see Ruth and Gehrig hit." Unfortunately, Gibson never got a chance to play against them.

That fall, the Crawfords hooked up for a seven-game series against Casey Stengel's All-Stars, including Hack Wilson (.297, 23 homers) and Johnny Frederick (.299, 16). The Craws won, five games to two. Unfortunately, few box scores have been found in the Depression papers, but against lefty Larry French (18–16) and right-hander Bill Swift (14–10), both with the second-place Pirates, Josh drove out three hits in an 11–2 victory. Then he and Satchel teamed up to defeat right-hander Roy "Tarzan" Parmelee (0–3) with the third-place Dodgers. Gibson slashed four hits as Paige won by a score of 10–2 with 15 strikeouts.

Another of Stengel's pitchers, Fred Frankhouse, remembered Josh throwing out runners without getting up from his crouch. In a wild car ride through the Allegheny mountains with Charleston, Frankhouse said he thought the day would come when blacks would get into the white majors.

1933

Hitler became dictator. FDR was sworn in ("The only thing we have to fear is fear itself"). Fifteen million unemployed. Six million pigs were killed to raise prices. Bank holiday. TVA. Prohibition was repealed. Frances Perkins became the first woman in the Cabinet. The United States recognized Russia. Japan and Germany walked out of the League of Nations.

"Stormy Weather," "It Was Only a Paper Moon," "Smoke Gets in Your Eyes," "Lazy Bones," "Easter Parade," "Let's Fall in Love," "Who's Afraid of the Big Bad Wolf?", "Sophisticated Lady," "I Cover the Waterfront."

Dinner at Eight, King Kong, Gold Diggers of 1933, The Three Little Pigs.

Radio: "Romance of Helen Trent;" "Jack Armstrong, the All-American Boy;" "Ma Perkins."

Broadway: *Ah, Wilderness.*

Books: *God's Little Acre, My Life and Hard Times* by James Thurber, *Life Begins at 40.*

Esquire magazine.

Chicago World's Fair; fan dancer Sally Rand.

Ruth homered in the first All-Star game. The Giants beat the Senators 4–1. Primo Carnera KO'd Sharkey. Helen Wills Moody won her sixth Wimbledon. The Rens beat the Celtics seven out of eight.

As the 1933 season opened, Gus Greenlee warned that it was "a crucial time for the game. One thing is certain: There will be no big salaries for any of the players this year."

Gamely he took the lead in re-forming the old Negro national league.

His Crawfords lost the pennant by one game to Chicago. One of the reasons was Paige, who suffered the first losing season of his life, with a 5–7 record. However, Satchel's TRA, 3.68, was actually slightly less than his league-leading 3.79 of the year before.

Fortunately, Josh made up for him. He brought his batting average back up to .362, second only to the 36-year-old Charleston's .372.

Cool Papa Bell, who had joined the club in '32, had played with Suttles in St. Louis. "They said Josh was better than Mule," Bell says, "and I wanted to see." Cool says he kept count of Gibson's home runs in '33 and counted 72 of them—Suttles' best (unofficial) mark was 69 in 1927. (Both totals, if accurate, would of course include semipro games.)

However, only 34 league games have been found, and they show Gibson hitting only six homers in 116 at bats (28 for 550 at bats). Though a far cry from 72, they were enough to edge out Suttles, Charleston, and Stearnes for the league lead by one.

Among Gibson's homers may have been one of the longest he ever hit. It came in the grimy coal-mining town of Monessen, Pennsylvania, against the Chicago American Giants.

There is disagreement about the date. Leonard said he saw Josh hit one in Monessen for the Grays about 1939 or '40 against a white semipro team. He said the ball cleared the fence and a school behind the fence. Double Duty Radcliffe said Josh hit one in the same park against Duty's Memphis Red Sox, which would have been 1938–41; he said the ball bounded into a passing freight train for a 500-mile home run. Perhaps there was more than one long shot at Monessen. But the actual date must have come sometime in the 1932–35 period, because those are the years that Larry Brown, an eyewitness, was catching for Chicago.

Old-timers still talk of the blow with an incredulous shake of the head. Monessen clings to a winding valley southwest of Pittsburgh, just off the present-day Pennsylvania Turnpike and not far from Stan Musial's hometown, Donora, or Joe Namath's Beaver Falls. The Crawfords often played there, and townspeople still proudly point out to visitors where the ballpark used to be where Josh Gibson hit his famous home run.

The site is a coal field now, but a watchman's old shack still stands beside the railroad tracks beyond what had been the center field fence. Right field was the short field. The left field foul pole was a long poke away, and a merchant had enticed Depression-day hitters with a sign offering a suit of clothes to anyone who could clear the wall there. Center field was even longer, with an apple tree just beyond it.

Brown said Gibson hit his blast against one of Sug Cornelius' curveballs. It cleared the fence and tree and landed with a splat on the concrete sidewalk outside the shack and bounded onto the tracks, where the watchman ran out and snatched it.

The mayor of the town was so amazed that he ordered a tape measure brought immediately and announced that the drive had traveled 512 feet, or about seven feet longer than the 1930 Yankee Stadium blow.

The blow (or blows) is still the biggest thing that ever happened in Monessen, and folks there still point out the exact spot where the ball came down before the startled watchman.

Gibson himself would call it his longest home run.

Brown, who had called the pitch that Josh hit in Yankee Stadium in 1930, was behind the plate this time too—and Larry was rated one of black ball's top receivers. He stomped back into the dugout and slammed his mask against the wall. "What'd you call for, L.A. (a Brown nickname)?" the players asked.

"A fastball," Larry snapped.

"Why didn't you call for a curve?"

"God damn!" Larry exploded. "If I'da knowed he was gonna hit the fastball, I *woulda* called for the curve!"

Meantime, a cocky 20-year-old rookie from Virginia, Ray Dandridge of the Detroit Stars, got his first look at the Great Paige, whom he remembered as "the best pitcher in all baseball":

> And he was the coolest man out there on the mound I ever saw. I tried to get his goat one day. I was a youngster then—you know, wild— and we were in Pittsburgh to play the Crawfords.

Ray, now a Hall of Famer like Satchel, hit only .211 that year, but between games of a doubleheader, Ray stood on tiptoes to peer over the partition into the Craws' dressing room. "All right, you're next," he called to Satch. "You just come out here, talkin' 'bout how you can throw hard. We'll see how hard you throw. We're gonna rack you back."

On Ray's first at bat, he later admitted, he did feel a little nervous. A moment later a fastball exploded under his chin. When he stepped back in, he remembers with a grin, he was a lot looser. The next pitch was another fastball, but in the strike zone, and Ray said he lined it out for a hit. "That's one thing I'll say: I don't believe any man alive could throw that fastball by me."

Quincy Trouppe remembered swatting Satch for a single, triple and homer in one game in Pittsburgh. Paige threw an occasional curve to right-handers, Trouppe wrote, but since Quincy was a switch-hitter, he knew Paige would work him with fastballs. His third hit "bounced off the wall of the hospital next to the playing field," Trouppe said.

At the Crawford Grille that night, Paige asked Trouppe amiably what his name was, told him he had a great future, then imparted some fatherly advice: "Don't be a know-it-all, take it easy with the girls, and lay off the liquor." Trouppe thanked him warmly and from that day on, looked on Satch as "a great man."

The two met later that summer out in Bismarck, North Dakota, where a chubby auto dealer, Neil Churchill, was laying out big money for top Negro leaguers to fill out his team of local whites. Paige won 12 out of 13 games, Trouppe said.

Tickled with his new star, Churchill put a '29 Buick at Satch's disposal. But he did ask Trouppe to talk to Paige about one thing: "I understand a man has to go out with a woman, but there is a way to do it in any walk of life. Just tell him to be careful about riding white girls around in broad daylight."

That autumn Paige headed for southern California to play winter ball. But when it started getting chilly, "I jumped for Venezuela. That was because I didn't have a topcoat."

In his first game in South America, Satchel was playing outfield, where he chased after a long drive, reached down for the ball in the grass, and found himself staring eyeball to eyeball with a boa constrictor. At least, he said it was a boa, although they are generally found in trees. At any rate, Satch picked up a stick and "beat the devil out of that snake," while the batter sprinted around the bases with the winning run. "The crowd chased me right out of the park, and the manager of the club wouldn't pay me for that game."

Gibson spent the winter in Puerto Rico. No statistics were compiled, but Bankes says Josh hit so many balls into the palm trees behind the fence, about 500 feet away, that they began hanging placards up to mark where the different blows landed.

1934

The Dust Bowl. Bonnie and Clyde, Baby Face Nelson, Pretty Boy Floyd, and John Dillinger were all gunned down. The Townsend Plan. The Dionne quintuplets.

"Blue Moon," "I Only Have Eyes for You," "What a Difference a Day Makes," "On the Good Ship Lollypop," "You and the Night and the Music," "Isle of Capri," "The Very Thought of You," "Moonglow," "Stars Fell on Alabama," "Let's Fall in Love," "The Darktown Strutters' Ball."

It Happened One Night, The Thin Man, Treasure Island, Donald Duck. The Hays office.

Radio: "The Bob Hope Show," "Major Bowes' Amateur Hour," Father Coughlin, Joe Penner ("Wanna buy a duck?").

Books: *Tender Is the Night; Tropic of Cancer; I, Claudius; Goodbye, Mr. Chips; The Ways of White Folks* by Langston Hughes.

Li'l Abner, Terry and the Pirates, Flash Gordon, Jungle Jim.

Carl Hubbell struck out seven straight in the All-Star game. Dizzy Dean said, "Me 'n Paul" will beat the Tigers, and they did 4–3. Max Baer KO'd Carnera.

The Craws fielded one of the strongest teams in blackball annals. It may have been the greatest black team of all time—Monte Irvin said it was—and, who knows, perhaps the best *team* of all time, period. Yet they didn't win the pennant.

The 28-year-old Satch came back strong with a 13–3 record and a splendid 1.99 TRA—that's *all* runs, not earned runs—the best season of his life.

Josh, who was 22, hit .295 and slugged 12 home runs, almost twice as many as the next highest man. Gibson's 12 homers in 190 at bats equaled about 35 in 550 at bats. Charleston hit seven, and Josh's two rivals, Stearnes and Suttles of Chicago, six apiece.

If, as legend has it, Gus Greenlee did indeed advertise Paige to strike out the first three men in a game and Gibson to hit at least one home run (against semipro opponents, presumably), this was the year they were most likely to keep his promise for him.

But some of the star-studded Crawfords resented the attention being poured on Josh and Satch. The self-effacing Bell, as sweet a human being as was ever elected to the Hall of Fame, found himself in the shadows, both in fame and finances, of the two glamorous stars. Cool Papa said that in 1933 he stole 175 bases, but that wasn't good enough to star on the Crawfords:

> When I went to the Crawfords, they had Charleston, Gibson, Paige. They weren't going to build anyone over them. They never did advertise you over those guys. The Crawfords advertised Satchel. They just kept dramatizing and dramatizing him, but we had guys who would win more games than him. His ball was faster, but we had some guys you couldn't hardly beat them because they were smart, they knew how to pitch.
>
> Now when we played in California, they would bill Satchel, and he would get 15% [of the gate].
>
> When they billed me, they had those wagons all going around saying, "Bell's going to be here tonight." But I didn't ask for anything. I only got a cut like the rest of the ballplayers got. I'm not the guy wants to be praised too much. I never wanted to be a big shot. I don't have enough money to go around to places where an outstanding guy should go. They'd "go off" (tour), they'd come back with a new suit of clothes. I said, "I want to go off too."

As for Gibson, "Of course he deserved all the attention," Ted Page said. "He was a terrific ballplayer, terrific hitter."

Paige had only one complaint about Greenlee's publicity campaign. "Even though he advertised both Josh and me," Satch wrote, "Gus knew I was pulling in the big crowds. . . . Those other players ate that lean meat because I pulled like that. If it wasn't for me, they'd have been eating side meat, that's what."

Unfortunately, Satch's fine year was topped by a super one. A skinny rookie left-hander named Stuart "Slim" Jones—a left-handed version of Satchel himself—posted one of the greatest seasons in blackball history.

Paige started off with a three-hit shutout May 13. A week later he lost a ragged 10–5 decision to the new kid, Jones, but he bounced back with an 8–2 victory.

From June 4 to July 4, Satch reeled off four straight shutouts, including a one-hitter. The last one came on the Fourth of July, a no-hitter, the second of his career, over the Grays with 17 strikeouts.

It's true that the Grays were still rebuilding after Greenlee's raid of two years earlier. Officially, they weren't even in the league, and

GRAYS		R	H	PO	A		CRAWFORDS		H	R	PO	A
2b	Lyles	0	0	2	2		cf	Bell	1	1	1	0
ph	Strong	0	0	0	0		rf	Crutchfield	0	0	1	0
3b	Binder	0	0	2	2		1b	Charleston	0	2	2	0
1b	Leonard	0	0	12	1		1b	C Harris	0	0	3	0
rf	J Williams	0	0	0	0		c	Gibson	0	0	17	0
cf	Brown	0	0	0	0		3b	Johnson	0	0	0	1
ss	H Williams	0	0	0	5		lf	V Harris	1	1	1	0
lf	Robinson	0	0	1	0		2b	C Williams	0	1	3	0
c	Burnett	0	0	2	0		ss	Morney	2	2	0	1
c	Palm	0	0	5	0		p	Paige	0	1	0	2
p	Dula	0	0	0	2				4	8	28	4
p	Stewart	0	0	0	0							
ph	Jarnegan	0	0	0	0							
		0	0	24	12							

e: Leonard, J Williams, Morney
3b: Bell, Charleston
bb: Paige 1, Dula 3
so: Paige 17, Dula 2, Stewart 2

except for rookie Buck Leonard, who hit .438 in eight other games against league clubs, the Grays presented no big names. But they were probably as good as some of the weaker teams that were in the league.

Satch fanned the side in the first. He whiffed two more in the second, and struck out the side again in the third—eight of the first nine men to face him had gone down swinging, and the ninth had grounded out.

"He threw *fire,* that's what he threw," Leonard whistled.

I'd say Satchel was the toughest pitcher I ever faced. Satchel had an exceptional fastball. That was his main pitch. We knew he was going to throw a fastball, and yet we could not hit it. It would get up to the plate and just rise a little, just enough for you to miss it. If you finally did get a piece of it, it wasn't much.

("Buck was a number-one hitter," Paige said, "but he was trying to pull me all the time." Satch pitched him on the outside corner.) Writer Ric Roberts said:

Leonard kept calling for the ball, wanted to know if there wasn't something wrong with it. The umpire saw nothing wrong with it, threw it back into play. When the next two men protested, the umpire threw the ball out. Paige said, "You may as well throw all of them out, because they're all gonna jump like that."

In all, Satch threw three ground balls, two pop flies and two outfield flies. He walked one man, and another reached on an error.

Paige recalled that "someone kept shooting off firecrackers every time I got another batter out."

Satch got the only run he needed in the first, when Bell's fly was misplayed into a triple, and Cool Papa scored on Gibson's sacrifice.

Paige went into the ninth with 15 strikeouts, two short of Dizzy Dean's white big league record of 17, which Diz had set just the year before. Satch got one more to make 16 before Posey sent up a pinch-hitter to try to break up the no-hitter. Satch mowed him down on strikes too, to equal Diz' mark.

Satch wrote that the firecrackers were still popping when he ran out of the park, hopped into his car, and drove all night to Chicago, arriving just in time to beat Ted Trent and the American Giants 1–0 in 12 innings. A great story. Unfortunately, no newspaper, not even the Chicago *Defender,* reported any such game.

Actually, the afternoon ended anticlimactically. In a twilight nightcap between the same two clubs, Satch was called in in the eighth inning to relieve Leroy Matlock with two men on base and the Craws leading 2–1. Paige whiffed the first hitter, his 18th victim of the afternoon. But the next man, the pitcher, lined a double to score both runners, and the Grays went on to win 4–3. The final run would have been charged to Satch, breaking his string of scoreless innings.

Paige did go to Chicago next—his recollection is correct in that respect—but he faced, not Ted Trent, but Bill "Sug" (for Sugar) Cornelius, who, if anything, pitched an even finer no-hitter than Satch's. The American Giants were winners of the first-half flag, and Cornelius, who was 4–3 on the year, hurled 9.2 hitless innings at the powerful Crawfords. He walked only one man, Bell, then picked him off first. The outfielders were lolling in the field, when Judy Johnson came up in the tenth with two out and lifted a routine fly to right-center. Cornelius recalled:

I rolled up my glove and started back in the dugout. But when I looked up, Stearnes was just standing there with his legs crossed. The ball could have been an easy out, but he wasn't expecting it. Jack Marshall at second base went out for it, but it fell between them.

I walked back to the mound. My arm was tightening, and I said, "If I get by this inning I'm going to tell Dave Malarcher, our manager, to get someone else ready." The next man up, Josh Gibson, hit me for a single. The pitch was that far outside—three feet—and he threw his bat at it and was lucky enough to make contact and get a single out of it. The next man came up and hit a little pop fly to left-center field, and that fell in and they beat me. After two outs.

Six days later, against red-hot Philadelphia, winner of the second-half flag, Satch was losing 1–0 after six innings, when he came to bat and hit a ground ball to the infield. The Phils' defense kicked it around, but Satch never saw it. He had already trotted back to the dugout without running it out. Charleston was so mad, he pulled Paige from the lineup. The Craws went on to tie the game, then lost it in the ninth, sparing Paige a loss.

A day later, two conflicting box scores illustrate the problems of researching Negro league records. Newspapers came out weekly and often didn't tell the exact date of the game they were reporting. In addition, different papers reported presumably the same games differently. The Baltimore *Afro-American* reported that Satch pitched five innings against the Phils, losing 1–0 on three hits. The Philadelphia *Tribune* said he pitched six innings, gave four hits, and ended up in a 1–1 tie. Were they two different games? or the same game reported erroneously by at least one paper? Arbitrarily, I have decided to accept both games as reported. It would have been Satch's second loss against seven wins.

Satch followed with a relief win and a 12–3 victory over Chicago to give him a 9–2 record for the season thus far.

The Crawfords might have had a shot at beating Philadelphia for the second-half pennant, but Paige jumped the team in early August to head for Denver and pick up some money at the Denver *Post* semipro tournament. He played for the bearded House of David, managed by ex-major league star Grover Cleveland Alexander. Satch didn't grow a beard but compromised on a mustache. They mowed the semipro players down. Paige struck out 14 men his first game and 18 more two days later.

Then, with only one more day's rest, he faced the great Kansas City Monarchs—Rogan, Brewer, and Allen, plus Stearnes and Foster borrowed from the American Giants. It was a battle between the only two undefeated teams left in the tourney, and a record crowd of

11,000 fought for seats, with several thousand more turned away. Satch whiffed 12 more men, making a total of 43 in five days, and beat Brewer 2–1.

Paige returned to the Craws a week before the East–West game, beating Philadelphia 6–4 and giving him a won–lost record of 11–2 for the season (counting the Monarch game).

But his formidable new rival, the 20-year-old Jones, was having an even better year; in fact, possibly one of the greatest in the history of black ball.

Jones stood about 6'5", and his arm hung down to his knee. "He was just like a dishrag," said Craws outfielder Jimmie Crutchfield.

Slim had been discovered by the Baltimore Black Sox a year earlier playing softball on the Baltimore sandlots. He didn't stick with the Sox, and ex-Detroit Tiger Johnny Nuen tipped off the Stars.

That winter, Slim went to Puerto Rico with Leonard and others to gain confidence, and struck out 210 men in the short season there. "He developed a pretty good curve down there," Buck said, "and he could get it over the plate."

By the spring of 1934, Slim was ready for a great year, pitching to the nonpareil catcher, Biz Mackey, perhaps the greatest handler of pitchers of any color ever. Slim arrived in Philadelphia without even a pair of baseball shoes, recalled infielder Dick Seay. "We had to buy him a pair." But could Slim pitch! "Oh yeah, he was better than [Sandy] Koufax. He had better control."

Monte Irvin agreed: "He was faster than Koufax."

"Of course, he didn't have the curveball Koufax has got," Leonard conceded. Slim developed a curve later, but "at the beginning, he was just like Satchel, he had a fastball."

"*Did* he have a fastball!" exclaimed Stars owner Eddie Gottlieb (who discovered basketball star Wilt Chamberlain). "Every time Vida Blue pitches—they talk about his speed—he reminds me of Slim Jones."

"Blue wasn't as fast as Jones," said Baltimore fireballer Laymon Yokely. "And his curve—you've seen how a snake moves? That's how Jones' curveball was. He threw it sidearm, and it would break and then break back the other way"—aerodynamically questionable, but the hitters apparently didn't know that.

Paige himself described Jones:

> Best pitchers I ever saw was Slim Jones, Bob Feller, Dizzy Dean. Slim Jones could throw harder than everybody put together, if you want me to

tell you the truth. I never did see Walter Johnson, but I don't believe there was a man on earth could throw as hard as Slim Jones. Just like I told them at Cooperstown, we had a lot of Satchels back in those days.

Yeah, we had some battles. We had some tough battles out there. Jones used to beat me out there. 'Cause he was on his left side, he could throw hard, had number-one control, and we had a lot of left-hand men on my team. To tell you the truth, of the four years I was out there with him, I know he came out ahead.

Jones was also an excellent hitter. Satch, who liked to brag about his own (feeble) hitting, would bet Slim who would get more hits when they faced each other. Holding court at his own inauguration in Cooperstown in 1971, Satchel lamented that it seemed that every time he pitched, the opposing pitcher was Slim.

Crutchfield shuddered as he recalled:

I'd get sick the days we had to face Slim. He believed he could beat any team Satchel could beat. That was the kind of guy he was. He loved to win. I'd have to put Satchel in a class by himself, but if you had a doubleheader to pitch, I'd just as soon have Slim Jones and Satchel pitch it for me. Wally Moses of the Athletics played with Lefty Grove, and he said Slim Jones was the toughest lefty he'd seen.

Jones started the year with a 3-hit, 12-strikeout shutout, then lost 4–3 to the Grays in relief, and beat Satchel 10–5. Slim gave up 15 hits, one of them a homer by Gibson.

Starting with that game, Jones reeled off 18 straight victories. Four of them were shutouts, including a one-hitter against the weak Bacharach team that won only three games in the second half. He also saved a game. He beat the Crawfords twice more, 4–3 and 9–4, although Gibson tattooed him for two more homers.

Jones' string was broken in August, when the Craws battered him 8–2, mauling him for 14 hits. Josh smashed five hits—a single, double, triple, and two homers. Of his 12 homers that year, five came against Jones! His batting average against the skinny one was .529.

Still, on the eve of the East–West game in August, Jones was 19–2 and threatening to become only the sixth man, at that time, to win 20 games in one Negro league season. The other four all had done it in the 1920s, when the league season was more than twice as long as in 1934. They were:

Bill "Plunk" Drake	20–10	in 1921
Nip Winters	21–10	in 1925
Bill Foster	21–3	in 1927
Ted Trent	21–2	in 1928.
Connie Rector	20–2	in 1929

Yet, amazingly, Jones didn't win the fans' vote to start the Classic. For one thing, nobody was keeping count of his amazing won–lost record. For another, the papers promoting the game, the Pittsburgh *Courier* and Chicago *Defender,* gave the Chicago and Pittsburgh players a big edge in the voting. Third, Satchel had established a reputation, while Jones was just a rookie. When the votes were all counted, Satch out-polled Slim 7,000 votes to 5,000.

(Gibson beat Newark's Johnny Hayes for the starting catcher's spot by a narrow 5,500 to 5,300. One can only wonder why it had been even close.)

Nevertheless, for some reason Jones started the Classic for the East before 25,000 fans—about 4,000 of them white—while Paige went to the bull pen.

Slim began shakily. The first four hitters were all from Chicago, due to meet Jones' Phillies in the coming play-off. Jones started by walking Willie Wells (.240), then balked him to second. But he bore down and struck out Alec Radcliff (.309) and Turkey Stearnes (.374), and Gibson rifled a throw to third to nip Wells stealing.

In the second, Mule Suttles (.279) lined a single to left off Jones. Charleston's error put men on first and second, and they each moved up a base on Jones' wild pitch. With no out, Slim bore down again. He whiffed Sam Bankhead (.338), his fourth strikeout of the game. Larry Brown (.431) hit a grounder to third, and Suttles was thrown out at the plate, Wilson to Gibson. Sammy T. Hughes (.229), perhaps the best black second baseman before Joe Morgan, rolled out to end the inning, and Slim left the game with the score still 0–0.

Josh was having a good day. He hit a double and a single against Chicago's Ted Trent (4–4) and the Monarchs' Chet Brewer (5–1). Defensively, he dropped a ball as Sammy Bankhead broke for second on a steal, but recovered and snapped a beautiful throw to catch Sam at the bag.

But Gibson's rival, Suttles, was having an even bigger day for the West. The hero of the first East–West game a year earlier, Mule got three hits, one of them a triple when center fielder Chester Williams somersaulted trying for a shoe-top catch. But when Mule tried to score on a sacrifice fly, Crutchfield uncorked a great throw to Josh, who caught it on the fly and tagged out the big runner, as the crowd rose and roared.

After five innings, the teams were still tied 0–0, when Pittsburgh's Harry Kincannon gave up a lead-off double to Wells. As the Chicago fans cheered noisily, Satchel was hurriedly waved in to the mound. Josh moved to left field, and Bill Perkins came in to catch Satch.

A hush fell on the stands as Satch ambled in from the outfield to face Radcliff, followed by the dangerous Stearnes and Suttles, the hometown home run heroes. Satch described the moment:

> I headed for the mound, and when I passed first base I ducked over toward the bench to toss my jacket in there. That's when I heard this guy in the stands.
> "It's Paige. Goodbye ball game."
> He didn't know how right he was.

Using his famous double windup, Satch burned five balls in to Alec and fanned him for one out. The left-hander Stearnes swung late and flied to left. Mule also flied out and the threat was over.

In the eighth, Brewer turned the shutout over to Bill Foster, who walked the first man, Bell. Cool Papa stole second, and with two outs, Jud Wilson hit a broken bat single to shortstop Wells, while Bell raced all the way home to score.

Satch then nailed down the victory with two more shutout innings. In his four-inning stint, he whiffed five, walked none, and gave just two hits. As Pop Lloyd observed after the game, "You can't beat unbeatable pitching."

Later Paige added a 7–6 victory to his regular season total, making it 13–3.

Jones went on to win his 20th game 2–1 to lead the Stars into the play-off against Chicago. Since there was only one league, this was tantamount to the black World Series.

He was beaten in his first Series game 3–0, as Chicago took a two-nothing lead in the Series.

Then, in a scenario that could happen only in the Negro leagues, the World Series was interrupted, while promoters hyped a big Yankee Stadium showdown between the two greatest matadors of the day—Paige and Jones—*mano à mano*. Those who saw the game called it the greatest contest they ever witnessed.

"Get me two runs," Jones muttered, "and I'll win this game." They got him one.

The Stars scored in the first, and for six innings Jones had a no-hitter going, until Charleston finally broke it up with a single in the seventh. The Stars got six hits off Paige, but some sensational plays by second baseman Chester Williams got Satch out of trouble. Williams "dived on his eyebrows," one reporter wrote, to steal a base hit from Biz Mackey and get a force-out at second.

Monte Irvin said Jones would have won the game 2–1 but for a controversial catch by Ted Page of the Crawfords. The circumstances are not clear, but Ted either caught or trapped a low liner at a crucial moment. One ump called it a hit, but plate umpire Frank Forbes overruled him and declared it an out, nullifying the run.

The "Colored Baseball and Sports Monthly," supplied by historian Larry Lester, described the drama of the last two innings: In the eighth Pittsburgh's Judy Johnson doubled, Leroy Morney walked, and Johnson scored the tying run on an error. Jones set the Craws down one-two-three in the ninth, getting Gibson on a hard grounder for the final out. He had finally stopped his nemesis cold in four at bats.

In the last of the ninth, the Craws' Williams raced behind first to make another great play, spearing a drive by Chaney White (.194) and throwing the runner out at first. Dangerous Jud Wilson (.342) beat out a slow roller to Williams, who threw wildly to first, as Jud chugged all the way into third base. Mackey walked. Manager Webster Mac-Donald, a good hitter for a pitcher, put himself in to pinch-hit with only one out. A squeeze or a long fly would win the game. It was getting dark, and both pitchers were almost invisible. Satch fanned Mac on a called third strike. "Mac never got the bat off his shoulder," Page said. Another pinch-hitter, Brooks, also fanned—Satch's 18th of the game—as the stands erupted in hysterical screams. The umpires called it after that, leaving a 1–1 tie in the record book.

Then the Philadelphians went back to their World Series, which they were losing, one game to three. Rocky Ellis pitched a 1–0 win, and Paul Carter won 4–1 to tie the Series. At this dramatic moment, there was another long layoff, while Slim returned to Yankee Stadium for the more important business of two exhibitions. The first was against the Black Yankees, a weak non-league team. Slim won it 4–1, for his record-tying 21st victory.

The second was a rematch against Satch and the Crawfords. Before the game Judy Johnson stopped by one Harlem barbershop where Satchel liked to play some pinochle, get his shoes shined, and

CRAWFORDS		AB	R	H	C*	E	STARS		AB	R	H	C*	E
cf	Bell	.317	4	0	0	0	0	ss	Stephens	.255	2	1	0	2	0
lf	Perkins	.174	4	0	0	0	0	3b	Creacy	.223	4	0	1	1	0
1b	Charleston	.298	4	0	1	8	0	lf	White	.194	4	0	1	1	0
c	Gibson	.295	4	0	0	14	0	1b	Wilson	.342	4	0	2	10	0
3b	Johnson	.255	3	1	1	2	0	c	Mackey	.281	3	0	1	11	0
2b	Williams	—	2	0	0	5	0	pr	Holmes	—	0	0	0	0	0
rf	T Page	.109	2	0	0	4	1	rf	Dunn	—	2	0	0	2	0
ss	Morney	.151	3	0	1	4	0	ph	Casey	—	0	0	0	0	0
p	Paige	—	2	0	0	2	0	cf	Washington	—	2	0	0	2	0
ph	Palm	—	0	0	0	0	0	ph	McDonald	—	1	0	0	0	0
pr	Crutchfield		0	0	0	0	0	2b	Seay	.137	3	0	0	5	0
			28	1	3	39	1	ph	Brooks	—	1	0	0	0	0
								p	Jones		3	0	1	4	0
											29	1	6	38	0

2b: Johnson
sh: C Williams
sb: Creacy
Pitching:

	IP	H	R	SO	W
Paige	9	6	1	12	3
Jones	9	3	1	9	0

*total chances: putouts plus assists

"shoot off his mouth." The crowd would get so big that cars outside blocked traffic while people crowded to listen. This time Satchel wasn't there, and the boys were whooping about what Jones was going to do to him.

At the game the Phils had the bases loaded with nobody out, and Johnson called time.

> I said, "Satch, the gang at the barber shop said they want to close your big mouth."
> Did they say that?"
> I tossed him the ball, and he struck out the side. Then he walked all the way over to the other dugout, stuck his head down there, said, "Go over to the barbershop and tell them that!"

Paige pitched a six-hitter. A first inning Philly error let in two runs, and Satchel won the game 3–1.

The victory gave Paige a final total of 13–3, plus the East–West win, compared to 22–3 for Jones.

The comparative totals:

	W–L	IP	H	R	SO	BB	TRA	SO/G	PA*
Paige	13–3	156	74	31	101	22	1.92	9.2	.176
Jones	22–3	192	108	38	92	18	2.11	7.7	.189

*Pitching Average (opposition batting average). The white major league record is .169 by Luis Tiant in 1968.

The numbers are not complete, that is, some box scores did not give data on SO, BB, and even hits. TRA, SO/G and PA (pitching average, i.e., opposition batting average) are calculated on innings for which runs, strikeouts or hits are also known.

Which man was better? Cum Posey had no access to the numbers we have today. But he did see both men in action, and the man he picked first on his annual all-star team was Satchel. He may have been influenced by Paige's greater reputation, as well as by the no-hitter Satch had hurled against Posey's team.

At last, the Stars could resume their twice postponed World Series. On October 11, just one month after the first game had been played, the Stars and Giants battled to a 4–4 tie, setting up the final showdown the next day. "Pitch Slim," Mackey begged, "pitch Slim." Jones did pitch and won 2–0 to give the Stars the pennant.

Jones had one more victory in his arm that year, against another World Series hero, Dizzy Dean (29–7),* the conqueror of the Detroit Tigers. Both Diz and Slim were sharp. Dean fanned three men in the first two innings. Jones whiffed four. At the end Slim had beaten the Great One 4–3.

Satch and Josh also faced Dizzy. Dean told me Josh hit the longest ball ever hit off him, in Washington that autumn. Unfortunately, the two do not appear to have faced each other there. They did face off, however, in Cleveland in a game Paige won 4–1 with 13 strikeouts and no hits in six innings pitched.

In Philadelphia, Gibson drilled three hits, including a triple, against the Dizzy One.

*The record books say 30–7; however, author G. L. Fleming (*The Dizziest Season*) says one of Dean's wins was actually a save.

Their next meeting was at York, Pennsylvania against Dizzy and his brother Paul. According to Bell, Josh slammed a two-run homer in the first and another in the third. "The people started booing," Bell said, "and Diz went into the outfield for a while; he hated to just take himself out of the game." At game's end (the Craws won it 11–1), Diz trotted past the black's dugout, mopped his face, and puffed, "Josh, I wish you and Satchel played with me 'n Paul on the Cardinals. Hell, we'd win the pennant by July 4th and go fishin' the rest of the season."

Shortstop Bill Yancey told Jackie Robinson that in one exhibition Dean asked Josh to strike out to get the game over with faster. "OK with me," Josh smiled, then hit the next pitch over the fence. "That's more fun than striking out," he laughed.

The series moved to Pittsburgh, where a riot broke out on the field. George Susce, who caught for five different big league clubs, was behind the plate for Diz that day. A Pittsburgher himself, Susce said his son and Josh's went to school together. When I interviewed him, Susce recalled the game but not the riot:

> Old Satchel come in, loaded the bases, struck the next three guys out. Struck me out on three fastballs. Dick Goldberg, playing minor league ball, told me, "George, you missed those three balls by a foot!" That's how alive that fastball was. You play the games at twilight, look out! Somebody says, "What was that went by?"

The Craws' Vic Harris ("I was a little fiery") was called out on a close play, grabbed the ump's mask, pulled, and let it snap back on his face. That did it. In an instant, both teams were swinging their fists in a general melee. Temperamental Oscar Charleston was punching away with the greatest enthusiasm.

Ted Page ran all the way in from the outfield to get into it and recalled:

> Josh and George Susce were the main attraction, because they were rolling around, and Gibson and Susce down in the corner between the fence and the dugout. Dizzy Dean and I were trying to pull Josh out of there, because he was strong, and there was no telling what he would do to any man, it didn't matter who, when he got him in a crack like that. We tried to pull him off, but, heck, he threw Dean from here to there, just shook him like this and shoved him out of the way and never let go of Susce with the other hand.
>
> I can see Josh today, right now, when that was over. He was kind of scratched up and had lost his cap in the scuffle, but he had a big grin on

his face, you know, one of those satisfied grins, like, "Well, that was a good one."

Josh would never pass up a fight, but he was not the kind of guy would pick a fight with anybody, because life was just a beautiful thing with him. He enjoyed it. Big and strong, able to take part in any kind of ruckus that came along, or play baseball. He was happy with life.

It took Gus Greenlee's friend, Pittsburgh Steelers owner Art Rooney, to intercede with the judge and keep everybody out of jail.

Even Charleston was afraid of Gibson. Once, Cool Papa Bell says, Oscar was threatening to punch Bell, when Josh stepped in and grabbed the manager in a headlock. From then on, Bell told Jim Bankes, "Charleston stayed clear of him."

Beneath his boyish demeanor, Josh was tough. All the pitchers threw at him to try to scare him, said Bell, "but it didn't work." According to Bankes, Bell recalled a game in the South when the crowd grew noisy over a play. One fan hurled a chair onto the field, narrowly missing Cool in the on-deck circle. Josh charged into the stands, "which wasn't very smart. But he looked so powerful that nobody tried to do anything to him." The miscreant meanwhile disappeared.

On October 26, Greenlee threw a big party at his grill to celebrate the marriage of his star pitcher, Satchel Paige, to Janet Howard. Bojangles Robinson was best man. "We had to lock the door to keep the fans out," Paige wrote. "There was a bunch of fine-looking girls out there with the fans," he sighed. He wished he had a tranquilizer to get through the ceremony, "but they hadn't been invented yet."

The newlyweds honeymooned in sunny California, where Paige beat Lee Stine of the White Sox with 12 strikeouts.

Bill Veeck said he saw Paige and Dean duel for 13 innings in Hollywood Park. The legendary game has not yet been verified in newspaper files, but one story says Dizzy tripled off Paige and hollered triumphantly, "I gotcha!"

"No you ain't," Satch replied, "you're not goin' no further."

The Boston Braves' Wally Berger (.298, 34 homers) joined Dean's All-Stars for one game. As reported by Richard Beverage, editor of Berger's autobiography, still in manuscript, the game took place in Los Angeles' Wrigley Field before 18,000 people. Berger wrote:

Paige could fire the ball. He and Dean were about the same size, and they both pitched the very same way with about the same speed—about

95 mph. I saved the clipping on the game, because I got the only hits off Satchel, a double and a triple. I was real proud; I'd hit a famous pitcher, teed off on his fastball. . . .

I thought he might have a curveball, so I looked for the curve. I wasn't going to try to kill the ball. I cut down on my swing and waited to see how he was pitching 'em.

First he pitched me high, then he raised it, then he brought it down. No curves. He finally got one down a little too low, and I hit it off the center field fence. . . . He followed me around to second and said, "How'd you hit that one?" I got a kick out of that.

Satchel went back to the mound and struck out the next three batters in order—Dolph Camilli, [.267 with the Phils]; Frank Demaree, [.325 in '35 with the Cubs], and Gene Lillard [with Los Angeles].

In the fourth inning I got a triple, and he did the same thing, followed me with his eyes to third.

He struck out seven in four innings. . . . Dean struck out seven in seven innings. . . .

That season was both the beginning and virtually the end of Slim Jones' career. The next year he slumped to a 4–10 record and never had a good season again. Had he ruined his arm with his magnificent 1934 season? Jones wasn't too robust anyway. Many of those who knew him blamed his fall on too much running around to bars.

In the winter of 1938–39, a bitterly cold winter, Monte Irvin said Jones asked owner Ed Bolden for an advance so he could buy a coat. Bolden apparently wasn't able to give it to him. "The way I understand it," said Leonard, "he was drinking one night, and he got wet and cold and contracted pneumonia."

"The boy was sick only a day or two," McDonald said, "when his parents sent me a telegram that he had passed. We all went down for the funeral, all the team were pallbearers, and it was a big funeral, because he had been so popular."

"He was a big kid," said Stars infielder Dick Seay sadly. "He just came up too fast."

"Nice boy," added Jake Stephens. "Wasn't nothing but a kid. Booze and women killed him. It was a shame. He was the greatest left-hander in baseball."

Slim Jones 1934

Date	Score	W–L	IP	H	R	SO	BB	
5/12	12–0	W	9	3	0	12	—	
5/17	3–4	L	1	—	1	—	—	
5/20	10–5	W	8	—	5	5	3	vs Paige
5/27	4–3	W	2	—	0	6	0	
6/4	6–2	W	9	3	2	—	—	
6/5	6–2	W	9	3	2	0	4	
6/9	5–1	W	9	4	0	10	1	
6/11	0–1	—	—	—	—	—	—	
6/17	7–2	W	9	4	2	—	—	
6/23	1–0	W	9	4	0	9	0	
6/28	1–0	W	9	4	0	—	—	
7/1	10–9	W	—	—	—	—	—	relief
7/8	9–2	W	9	6	2	—	—	
7/10	4–3	W	9	9	3	—	—	
7/14	9–4	W	9	9	4	7	2	
7/22	3–2	W	9	4	2	—	—	
7/29	7–0	W	9	1	0	9	—	1-hitter
8/1	3–2	W	—	—	—	—	—	Chicago
8/5	4–2	W	9	11	2	—	—	
8/12	8–0	W	9	6	0	—	—	
8/18	6–3	W	—	—	—	—	—	relief vs Craws
8/20	2–8	L	8	14	8	9	—	Craws
9/1	2–1	W						
9/9	1–1	—	9	3	1	9	0	vs Paige
9/23	4–1	W	9	2	1	9	4	2-hitter
9/30	1–3	L	8	7	3	6	2	vs Paige
10/7	1–6	—	2.2	5	—	2	0	vs Matlock
Total:		20–4						

East-West

8/21	1–0	—	3	1	0	4	1	

Playoff

9/15	0–3	L	8	7	3	7	—	
10/1	2–0	W	9	5	0	6	1	

Satchel Paige 1934

Date	Score	W–L	IP	H	R	SO	BB	
5/13	7–0	W	9	3	0	9		2	Chicago
5/20	5–10	L	9	15	10	11		4	vs Jones, Phila
5/27	8–2	W	9	—	2	—	—	
6/4	5–0	—	9	4	0	—	—	
6/17	6–0	W	9	1	0	7		1	1-hitter
6/30	6–0	W	7	5	0	—	—	Nashville
7/4	4–0	W	9	0	0	17		1	no-hitter
7/4	3–4	—						
7/7	3–0	W	10	5	0	—	—	Chi (Cornelius lost no-hit in 10th)
7/14	1–2	—	6	6	1	3		1	Philadelphia
7/15	0–1	L	5	3	1	—	—	Philadelphia
7/15	1–1	—	6	4	1	—	—	Philadelphia
7/22	9–7	W	4	—	0		—	—	relief
7/25	12–3	W	9	5	3	4		2	Chicago
8/ ?	2–1	W	9	—	1	—	—	Kansas City
8/19	6–4	W	9	6	4	10		3	Phila
9/3	7–6	W	9	8	6	9		3	
9/15	1–1	—	9	6	1	18 @		3	vs Jones, Phila
9/ ?	2–11	L	—	—	—	—	—	
9/30	3–1	W	9	5	1	7		0	vs Jones, Phila
Total		13–3						

East-West

8/26	1–0	W	4	2	0	5		0

Dates are approximate.

1935

Social Security, CCC (Civilian Conservation Corps), WPA. Eight million persons unemployed. Roosevelt's National Recovery Act died in the Supreme Court. Lawrence of Arabia, and Will Rogers died in accidents. Huey Long was assassinated. Italy invaded Ethiopia.

"I Got Plenty O' Nothing," "Begin the Beguine," "The Music Goes 'Round and 'Round," "It Ain't Necessarily So," "I'm in the Mood for Love," "Red Sails in the Sunset," "These Foolish Things Remind Me of You," "You Are My Lucky Star," "Stairway to the Stars," "When I Grow Too Old to Dream," "Zing! Went the Strings of My Heart," "Lullaby of Broadway." Ella Fitzgerald, Count Bassie.

Mutiny on the Bounty, Captain Blood (Errol Flynn), *The Informer, A Night at the Opera, The 39 Steps.*

Radio: "Your Hit Parade," "Fibber McGee and Molly."

Broadway: *Three Men on a Horse, Dead End, Porgy and Bess, Waiting for Lefty.*

Books: *Tortilla Flat, Lost Horizon, Black Reconstruction* by W. E. B. Du Bois, *Ferdinand the Bull.*

Life magazine. Knock, knock jokes, rumba, bingo, chain letters, vitamins, roller derby, Gallup poll.

The first big league night game. Babe Ruth hit three homers in a game and retired. The Tigers beat the Cubs 4–2.

Josh Gibson wintered in Puerto Rico, where Harry Salmon and Ted Page witnessed another of his mammoth blows. Gasped Salmon:

> Left field was 500-some feet. And the wind blew in hard from the ocean. Josh hit the ball over the left field fence. God, it went over 500 feet, over the fence!

Page was playing outfield. He disagreed on details but confirmed the main thrust:

> He hit an awful long ball, over the center field fence and right there on the beach. There was a lot of wind, and the fence was 475 feet, and he

73

hit it another 50 feet beyond that. The ball had to travel at least 500 to 525 feet.

The St. Louis Cardinals' Hall of Famer, Johnny Mize, also saw the drive and agreed that the wind was blowing in. "He was at second base when the ball cleared the fence. He jumped straight up in the air, figured no one was going to hit one out of there."

At spring training in Florida, former Senators pitching great Walter Johnson watched Gibson catch. "That boy is worth $200,000 of anybody's money," he whistled.

> He can do everything. He hits the ball a mile. And he catches so easy he might as well be in a rocking chair. Throws like a rifle. Bill Dickey [of the Yankees] isn't as good a catcher. Too bad this Gibson is a colored fellow.

Johnson wasn't the first man to notice that Josh had developed into a good defensive player, as well as a slugger. Dean had already remarked on it:

> Josh was the greatest catcher back in those days. He could sit on his haunches and throw you out at second base. A good receiver, a strong arm. And watch him work that pitcher; he was tops at that. He was terrific all the way around.

"Josh didn't really learn to catch until he played winter ball," Buck Leonard believed.

> Down there in those winter leagues you can work out all morning on your weakness, whatever it is, hitting, running, pop flies, anything. Josh would work out by the hour perfecting his catching. After two or three winters of that, he could catch anything.

In his autobiography, Campanella also remarked on Josh's defense:

> Now after all I've said about his hitting, I'm going to say something that might sound a little crazy. I always looked to his catching more than his hitting. Nobody but a catcher would say that, I know, but I was a catcher. . . .
>
> He had a huge chest, tremendous shoulders, and the biggest arms

I've ever seen. With all that weight, he moved around behind the plate with such effortless grace that everything he did looked easy. There never was a better receiver. His arm was strong and always accurate.

Josh and Judy Johnson had a play they put on. With a man on third, if Judy wanted a snap throw to catch the runner, he "gave a little whistle," and Josh would fire a strike to the bag. "Josh threw a light ball," Cool Papa Bell said. "You could almost catch it bare-handed. Campanella and Perkins threw a brick."

Gibson and Bell also had a little play, Cool Papa said. With a man on second, the infielders crept in toward home, and while the unsuspecting runner lengthened his lead, Bell dashed in from center field to take Josh's throw for the putout.

It was an era of cutthroat sign-stealing. When Gibson signaled the pitcher, Willie Wells kept his eyes glued to Josh's muscular right forearm. The muscle twitch told Wells if it was two fingers or one. When Josh caught on, he began giving decoys with his fingers. The real signal was the glove—if he held it horizontally, it meant a curve, vertically was a fastball.

Bell said Gibson also had his own system for signaling pitches to the outfielders. If he stood up with his glove across his chest, it meant a fastball was coming; if he held the glove down at this side, it meant a curve.

Meanwhile, Satchel was learning that married life is expensive. "After the honeymoon," he wrote, "I started noticing a powerful lightness in my hip pocket." When his bills exceeded his income, he went to Greenlee for a raise. Gus turned him down.

So Paige stomped out and drove all the way to North Dakota, to the little town of Bismarck, where the mayor, auto dealer Neil Churchill, was recruiting a black battery to go with his blond Nordic local semipro team.

One of Satchel's first problems was finding a place to live. Mysteriously, when he and Janet knocked on doors with "For Rent" signs out, they learned the house or room had just been taken. Finally Churchill found a place—a railroad freight car that had served as a bunkhouse for work gangs.

Radcliffe came along to catch. He recalled Churchill as a fine man, but Duty lost his patience with Paige.

The first of the season he couldn't throw across the street. He caught gonorrhea. I said, "Just roll it up there. They're ascared of your name, they ain't gonna hit it."

Then I said, "Why don't you send him to the Mayo Clinic [in Minnesota] and get him some shots?" He was back pitching within two days.

But every game, I caught four innings and pitched the last five. I remember one time we were playing out in Nebraska against all those Western league teams. I had to pitch five days in a row, while he went fishing with some rich man and didn't show up till the next Sunday. You couldn't fine him 'cause he'd quit. That's a bitch, ain't it? I used to say, "He's bigger than the game. You can't find him and you can't fine him." I could give him hell, 'cause he and I were buddies. I don't care if he could throw the ball so hard you couldn't see it. If he couldn't take orders, I wouldn't want him, would you?

Satchel once described the itinerant life that might have applied to that summer:

Mostly the crowd would come to our games in their cars and ring them around the outfield for a fence, because there was no fence. Then they'd pass the hat and drop in a few silver dollars. We'd use the money for gas—and to get out of town.

Paige wrote that "a bunch of Indians up there . . . took a real liking to me." One, Dorothy Running Deer, had a father who raised rattlesnakes in a pit behind his house. To cure rattlesnake bites, he gave Satchel some snake oil, which, he warned, was too hot for anything but snake bites. Paige, who hated cold weather, tried some on his pitching arm, liked it, decided to use it after every game, and credited it with keeping his arm young. He bottled it but promised the Indians to keep the formula secret until he died, when he would reveal it in his will. Unhappily, no such magic formula was ever found, and the secret went to the grave with Satch.

Satchel was already formulating the training regimen that helped him pitch until the age of 65. He took a bath "hot as I can stand" every morning, and one hotter than that after every game—near boiling. "It's kept my arm alive." He also claimed that he rested his muscles by using three sets in every game—one for overhand, one for sidearm, and one for underhand.

Then too, "I kept my belly down and my legs in shape and avoided hurry-ups, which is what kills a lot of pitchers." He lived on boiled chicken and greens, broccoli, spinach, or beans. Once in a while he broiled a steak or baked a fish.

Psychologically, he advised:

Never let your head hang down. Never give up and sit down and grieve. Find another way. And don't pray when it rains if you don't pray when the sun shines.

At some time in his career, the rules got distilled into the famous set of aphorisms which he said "some sports guy on the East Coast" actually composed:

Avoid fried meats, which angry up the blood.
If your stomach disputes you, lie down and pacify it with cool thoughts.
Keep the juices flowing by jangling around gently as you move.
Go very lightly on the vices—the social ramble ain't restful.
Avoid running at all times.
And never look back: Something might be gaining on you.

Duty, who caught Paige's first no-hitter, in 1932, said he caught two more that summer. One was in Burlington, Iowa. The second was in Toronto against the Canadian Club whiskey team, featuring 43-year-old Happy Felsch of the infamous 1919 Chicago Black Sox. (Unfortunately, confirmation has not been found in the Toronto press files).

Bismarck's big rival, Jamestown, also hired Negro leaguers, such as Perkins and pitcher Barney Brown. They even hired Bill Foster of the American Giants to come up and pitch one game against Paige. Trouppe said Satch knocked in all three runs to win it 3–2. (Foster claimed that he and Satch matched up 13 or 14 times over the years and that he ended with a one-game edge.)

With Janet nagging him, Satchel said, he began riding his teammates. One day his outfield just walked off the field behind him. The fans, thinking it was a stunt, cheered, so Satch buckled down and struck out the side, muttering, "That'll show them who needs who." But he knew he couldn't do it indefinitely, so he apologized to the players, and "from then on, I decided I'd be the quiet guy, like I'd always been before"(!)

Satch called his fielders in deliberately to strike out the side. The signal was to turn to them and wipe his forehead. One hot day he took off his cap and absentmindedly wiped the sweat, then turned to face the batter, who hit a soft fly to short right field. Paige turned to see his fielders all sitting down laughing uproariously while the batter legged it around the bases for a homer.

While Paige was bumping around out in the wheat fields, what of the Crawfords without him? They had the greatest season they would ever enjoy, winning the only pennant of their history. Bell led the club with .341, far below the league leader, Stearnes, who hit .450. Perkins hit .337, new second baseman Sam Bankhead .336, Charleston .309, and Johnson .288.

Josh, .304, slugged 13 home runs, again comfortably ahead of runners-up Stearnes, Suttles, and Cubans manager Martin Dihigo, with seven each. (Stearnes and Suttles played in the wide open Chicago park; Dihigo played in a much smaller bandbox, Dyckman Oval in the Bronx.)

Biggest surprise of all was Gibson's speed on the bases—he stole eight bases to lead the league—twice as many as Cool Papa Bell! Only three other men have ever led a major league in both homers and steals—Ty Cobb in 1909, Chuck Klein in 1932, and Jose Canseco in 1988. Even Willie Mays never did it.

"Josh was fast for a big man," his teammates Judy Johnson and Buck Leonard maintained.

"He was one of the fastest big men I ever saw," agreed Carl Hubbell, the New York Giants' pitching ace.

"He came in with spikes high," Gene Benson said. Usually catchers and infielders were circumspect about how they slid, because they themselves were targets for retaliation (Cobb and Charleston, two of the most notorious slashing base runners, were outfielders.) But Gibson ran bases in the Negro league tradition. "Runners would jump at your chest," Benson said. "I've seen ballplayers get their suits cut off. Josh was good at that. He'd jump at you."

Oddly however, Josh had stolen only three bases before in his life, and it would be another three years before he stole another.

But he was known to bunt for a base hit occasionally, especially when he caught the third baseman playing left field.

He was even known to get a home run on a ground ball! Sam Streeter shuddered at one Gibson homer. "It hit the ground and bounced over the center fielder's head. When that ball came back in there, he was sitting on the bench."

The Craws did indeed boast a powerful offensive team. But how could they have survived the loss of their ace pitcher and gone on to rule at the summit of black baseball? One reason, of course, was the fall of Jones, whose 4–10 mark dragged the Stars down to 28–27.

The Craws' veteran pitcher, Roosevelt Davis, helped mightily with a 12–4 record.

The biggest reason, however, was another left-hander, who, if possible, had an even more sensational year than Jones had had in '34. The savior's name was Leroy Matlock.

"To me," said Ted Page, who had moved to the Stars, "Leroy Matlock was the best left-hander that ever toed the rubber. I couldn't hit him with a paddle."

"Matlock gave me a fit," Leonard nodded grimly. "I had more trouble with Matlock than any other left-hander. There wasn't anything about pitching he didn't know."

Radcliffe, Crutchfield, and others recalled Matlock as a control pitcher, who could spot the ball wherever he wanted to, a man who had made himself into a pitcher through sheer determination.

Matlock had been born 29 years earlier in Moberly, Missouri, on the same prairie that produced John J. Pershing, Omar Bradley, Walt Disney—and Big Bill Gatewood, Satchel Paige's old mentor. Leroy grew up shining shoes in the Moberly barbershop and playing ball, along with his fellow townsman, Crutchfield, for the Gatewood Browns.

In 1929, Gatewood sent Leroy to the St. Louis Stars. He lost his first game and recalled that he took quite a razzing from the fans. His wife urged him to go home, but he said no, he was going to stay and make good. He did. He ended 1929 with a 5–2 record, then helped pitch the Stars to the pennant in 1930 with an 11–3 mark. "No, they didn't razz me then," he grinned. "It was my turn then, and I could cuss them out on anything."

In '31 Matlock lost the only game we've found for him that year. But that fall he faced Bill Walker, who was 17–9 for the New York Giants and led the National league in ERA. Walker was supported by Bill Terry (.349), Babe Herman (.314), and the Waner brothers, Lloyd (.313) and Paul (.298)—three Hall of Famers in all. Matlock beat them 18–1. He even hit a homer. He also defeated Vern Kennedy (11–11 with the fifth-place White Sox) 3–2 in 11 innings.

As the Depression deepened, Matlock bounced around to Detroit, Washington, the Grays, and finally, the Crawfords, where he was 7–3 in '33, and a modest 5–3 in '34.

Then came 1935.

Matlock wasn't overpowering: He averaged only two strikeouts per nine innings. But he had good control, under three walks per game. He won all five of his starts in April, all six in May, and all four in June. Every one was a complete game, except for one 15–3 laughter, when he came out after six innings.

The Craws ran away with the first-half pennant.

Then they traveled to Denver for the big semipro tourney there, while the Cubans, led by Dihigo, came from next-to-last to win the second-half pennant.

By the East–West break Matlock was 15–0, but, surprisingly, he did not lead the vote of the fans for the East–West game. Nor did he start the game. Raymond Brown, 11–4 with the Grays, won both honors.

This time the Crawfords were assigned to the West team, which meant that the two foremost black sluggers of the day, Gibson and Suttles, were teammates for the first time ever. Josh hit cleanup and Mule fifth.

Josh had a splendid afternoon with two doubles and two singles in five at bats. In the sixth, center fielder Dihigo crashed into the wall trying to catch Gibson's long double, a line drive into deepest center field in Comiskey Park, 436 feet away. That drove in one run. In the seventh, Gibson's fly fell safely to knock in another. And his tenth-inning single ignited a four-run rally that tied the score.

Meanwhile, Mule was frustrated by three walks and after ten innings had only one official at bat, a strikeout.

In the eleventh, Dihigo, now pitching for the East, walked Cool Papa Bell, and after two outs had the choice of pitching to Gibson or Suttles. As Josh stepped into the batters' box, Mule sent pitcher Sug Cornelius up to "pinch-kneel" for him in the on-deck circle. Thinking Suttles was out of the game, Dihigo walked Gibson then cursed as Suttles, not Cornelius, stepped up to bat. Mule lashed one of the most famous home runs of black ball history into Chicago's upper deck to win the game and steal the glory.

Matlock pitched two more games at the end of August, winning both, one of them a three-hit 1–0 shutout of the Grays. He added another easy triumph in September to end with a season's record of 18–0. Actually, Matlock had won his final game in 1934, so he had now won 19 in a row, tying the white big league record of Rube Marquard in 1912. And if Matlock had not missed most of August out in Denver, there's no telling how many he might have won.

Every game but one was a complete game. His TRA was a solid 2.47, and he held enemy hitters to an estimated .208 batting average. One senses that he bore down only when he had to, winning by scores of 1–0, 5–4, 8–6, etc. If necessary, he probably could have brought that TRA down even lower.

Meanwhile, Satchel and Bismarck traveled to the big national semipro tournament in Wichita, Kansas. Duty recalled:

Churchill wired for reservations for 30 people. The guy wired back OK. When we got there, me and Satchel walked in with the rest of them white boys. "Oh, I didn't know you had those colored boys. We can't take them all."

Churchill said, "I got your telegram, goddam it. I'll sue you."

I spoke up. "Well, the man didn't know. Mrs. Jones got a nice rooming house up here, we'll go up there and stay." (I had some girl friends there I knew years before—'course I knew they weren't gonna let me bring them in the hotel.) Mrs. Jones even cooked for us. We stayed there for three dollars a day, two meals a day. Churchill would come out every day and give us some money, thought we were mad. Heck, we weren't mad.

On the field, Radcliffe said, "We were playing against the nine ball players and the two umpires." Nevertheless, Satchel whiffed 13 men in the first game, 17 in the second, and 16 in the third.

In the fourth game we started a young white pitcher. They had us 3–2. Satchel was playing pepper with two little white kids. I told him to go down there and warm up. "Are you ready?"

"I am that."

I said, "Come on, then." He threw nine balls and three strikeouts.

In the finale, Satch said, "that skinny arm of mine was flapping just as good as ever." He whiffed 14 more, setting a tournament record that may still stand. Duty added:

We won the pennant in seven straight. I caught two and pitched two. In those days we got $1,000 a game, so that gave us $7,000 for the tournament.

Those teams from Texas and Oklahoma and Georgia said they weren't going to come back and play any more, 'cause they didn't have a chance with me and Satchel. They said, "Those are big league players. They're niggers, but they're big league players."

That night they went to Kansas City to play the Monarchs* and made $177 apiece.

That was big money for those days. Satchel struck out 16 of them, and we beat 'em 9–0.

Satchel had bought one of those cars from Churchill. He owed him

*One of the Monarchs was outfielder Eddie Dwight, whose son would go on to become a U.S. astronaut.

$970, I think, on it. Churchill gave Satchel the car. And gave Satchel $500 to go out to California to play winter ball.

Meanwhile, the Crawfords were in the play-offs, battling the Cubans, who had charged from next to last in the first half to the pennant in the second half. The Craws lost the first two games, including a 4–0 defeat of Davis.

Matlock was sent in to stop the slide against the Cubans' rookie, Schoolboy Johnny Taylor, who was 7–3 on the year. Gibson's long triple off the center field wall on a 3–2 pitch drove in the first run, and Leroy went on to win 3–0, his 19th straight victory of the year and 20th overall.

Dihigo (6–4) won the fourth game to take a three-to-one lead, but Davis won the must-win fifth game to keep the Craws alive.

Matlock started the sixth game, also a do-or-die contest, against young Taylor. Leroy was losing 5–2 in the eighth, and Cubans business manager Frank Forbes was already counting out the winners' share under the stands, when Dihigo suddenly yanked Taylor and put himself in to pitch. Charleston quickly slugged a three-run homer to tie it, third baseman Pat Patterson doubled, Matlock was safe on an error, and slumping Judy Johnson drilled a 3–2 pitch through the infield to win the game, as Forbes threw the pile of bills disgustedly across the room. The Craws had tied the Series, and Matlock had won his 21st in a row.

In the seventh game, the Craws came from behind again. With the score 7–5 against them, Gibson homered over the center field fence against Luis Tiant Sr (7–4). Charleston also homered to tie the game, and Bell singled and scored on an error to win it.

There was no one left to beat but the whites.

In October, Josh and Dizzy Dean (28–12) met again, in Yankee Stadium. Paige was supposed to be there too, but, as Greenlee explained to 15,000 angry fans, Satchel had "stopped off" in Chicago to pitch for the Monarchs for $500. "This caused him to forget all about his agreement to appear in New York."

In the game, Bell was on second with Gibson up, and Diz turned his back to the plate to wave Cincinnati's center fielder Jimmy Ripple back. Ripple retreated a step or two. Dean waved him further back. Ripple took two more steps to the rear. Still Dean shooed him back. Apparently satisfied, Diz stepped onto the mound and fired to Gibson, who drilled one deep to the monuments, about 460 feet away, where Ripple was waiting. Bell tagged up, raced around third and slid home under the throw. But the umpire called him out. "You don't *do* that against big leaguers," he scolded.

Josh and Judy Johnson also went to Cincinnati to play Leo Durocher and another all-star team. The Lip reached third base and began dancing off—"Lippy was a show-off," Judy smiled. Judy called time and went over to Matlock, the pitcher. "You dumb son of a bitch," he said—loud, so Leo could hear it. "He's gonna steal the cover right off you."

Then he gave Josh "the whistle." Durocher started toward home, Judy moving up with him. Then Judy backed up to about three feet from the bag, and Josh snapped a throw, as Durocher scampered back with a perfect hook slide into Johnson's leg. "You're out!" the umpire bawled.

"What! Me out?" Durocher screamed.

"Heh, Lip," Johnson chuckled, "get off my foot." Leo was still three feet from the bag.

Durocher never forgot. Twenty years later he bumped into Johnson at the Braves–Yankees World Series (Judy's son-in-law, Bill Bruton, was playing outfield for Milwaukee), and still sputtered about that play.

Dizzy and Paul, meanwhile, headed west, where Paige intercepted them in Springfield, Missouri. Satch said he heard Diz tell a radio audience that Satch had a great fastball but no curve. That afternoon "I fired my fastball right by his boys." When Dean came up, Paige showed him a curve. "Tell me what *this* is," he yelled. Satch said he threw two more curves, and Dizzy missed them all.

A week later, Dean got revenge with a 1–0 victory in Kansas City, but he gave Paige a hug and admitted, "You're a better pitcher than I ever hope to be, Satch." Dean told one Chicago newspaper:

> A bunch of the fellows get in a barber session the other day, and they start to arguefy about the best pitcher they ever see. Some says Lefty Grove and Lefty Gomez and Walter Johnson and old Pete Alexander and Dazzy Vance. And they mention Lonnie Warneke and Van Mungo and Carl Hubbell, and Johnny Corriden tells us about Matty, and he sure must of been great, and some of the boys even say Old Diz is the best they ever see.
>
> But I see all them fellows but Matty and Johnson, and I know who's the best pitcher I ever see, and it's old Satchel Paige, that big lanky colored boy. Say, Old Diz is pretty fast back in 1933 and 1934, and you know my fastball looks like a change of pace alongside that little pistol bullet old Satchel shoots up to the plate. . .

It's too bad those colored boys don't play in the big leagues, because they sure got some great ballplayers. Anyway, that skinny old Satchel Paige with those long arms is my idea of the pitcher with the greatest stuff I ever saw.

That was enough to convince Paige: Dizzy Dean was just about the smartest fellow he ever met.

Satch continued to the coast, where he and Janet spent the winter with "baseball and dancing and dancing and baseball." They even did a little "quarteting."

Paige visited San Diego, where a skinny 17-year-old high school kid took away a vivid memory of him. Ted Williams said:

Even then he had built up a reputation as the fastest pitcher that baseball had known at that time. So I made it a point to go to the stadium. He was pitching against the local sandlot players, and I waited for him to come out of the dressing room. I looked him over real good. He was real skinny. He had trouble keeping his pants up, because the bands weren't tight enough. ["If I stood sideways," Paige once said, "you couldn't see me."]

I remember how loose he was and how fast he was. He just made the ball pop! The only hit he gave that day was to a young kid catcher, and he was far from the best one on the club. I'm convinced that he just let him hit it. The other guys, he just breezed by them and made it look real, real easy.

In Oakland, Paige faced a big league all-star team—Ernie Lombardi (.343), Augie Galan (.314), Gus Suhr (.272), "Rowdy Dick" Bartell (.262), and a minor leaguer who had hit .398 with San Francisco—Joe DiMaggio. Satchel threw sidearm fastballs "that would rise and sink and sail," Bartell said. His delivery was as hard to hit as his pitches. "He'd look like he was looking at third base, but he'd throw to home plate." Paige had a four-hitter 1–1 with two out in the tenth. Then Bartell singled, stole, and took third on a passed ball.

DiMag was up. So far he had been hit with a pitch, bounced to short, bounced to second, and flied to center. On the 0–2 pitch Joe hit a bounder to Paige's left and just beat the throw from second, as Bartell scored to win it.

"I just got a hit off Satchel Paige," DiMaggio beamed. "I know I can make the Yankees now."

1936

The Dust Bowl. The Spanish civil war. The Moscow purges. New King Edward abdicated to marry an American. Mussolini defeated Ethiopia. Roosevelt swamped Landon ("a rendezvous with destiny"). Boulder Dam. Rudyard Kipling died.

"I'm an Old Cowhand," "Is It True What They Say About Dixie?," "I've Got You Under My Skin," "The Night Is Young and You're So Beautiful," "There's a Small Hotel," "The Whiffenpoof Song," "Let's Face the Music and Dance," "The Way You Look Tonight," "Pennies From Heaven."

Mr. Deeds Goes to Town, Modern Times.

Radio: "The Kate Smith Show," "The Shadow" ("Who knows what evil lurks in the hearts of men?"), "Gangbusters," Charlie McCarthy, "Pepper Young's Family."

Books: *Gone With the Wind* sold one million copies in six months.

Joe DiMaggio and Bobby Feller made their debuts. Cobb, Wagner, Ruth, Mathewson, and Johnson were elected to Cooperstown. The New York Rens were voted into basketball's Hall of Fame. The Yanks beat the Giants 4–2. Slingin' Sammy Baugh was All-American. Max Schmeling beat Joe Louis in 12 rounds. Jesse Owens won four golds in Berlin.

In May, Greenlee meekly took Satch back. With the money he made, Paige wrote, he went to Mobile to see his mother. "You been playin' any on Sundays?" she demanded. He assured her he hadn't and bought her a new house.

Meanwhile, Satchel buckled down to pitching and showing Matlock who the ace of the Crawfords was. Matlock won his first two games, making a total of 23 straight victories, before Philadelphia finally snapped his streak 7–6. Leroy pitched only two more league games all year, both in June, and split them for a 3–2 record. Whether his arm had given out or he simply jumped the team, we don't know. But historian Bob Hoie reports that Matlock went on to enjoy two excellent seasons in Mexico 1940–41.

With Matlock gone, Satchel was king of the hill again, with a 10–3 record. No one on the Craws was even close; the next best man, Streeter, was 3–1. Paige topped the league in wins but was out-pitched by Webster McDonald, the soft-spoken skipper of the Stars, who was 9–1.

Gibson also had a stellar year. He led the league in homers again, with 11—Suttles and Dihigo each hit ten. Josh slugged his 11 in only 23 games; it works out to 81 in a 550 at-bat season. One report, unverified, says he hit 84 homers in 170 total games, or one every other game, which is consistent with his league pace. If true, of course, that would include semipro games. His .360 league BA ranked third behind Jim West, .403, and Lazaro Salazar, .367.

The Crawfords were virtually a two-man team—Satch and Josh. No one else on the team won more than three games and no one else hit .300—the aging Charleston was .285, Bell .256, Johnson .239, Perkins .232. But thanks to Satch and Josh, the Craws finished third in the first half, behind the Washington Elite Giants. They copped the second half, although this time there was no play-off between the two champions.

Instead, the two clubs joined forces in Denver at the *Post* semipro tourney and swept through all seven games without a defeat. Paige won his three 7–2, 12–1, and 7–0, the last one with 18 strikeouts. Bell hit .469 and Josh .433.

After the tourney they barnstormed home against a white big league all-star club led by Johnny Mize (.329), Gus Suhr (.312), Harlond Clift (.302), and Ival Goodman (.284). For some reason Gibson didn't play in the series. Rogers Hornsby, 40 years old, put himself in the lineup, though he'd played in only two big league games that year. "I want you to tell me when Hornsby comes to bat," Paige told Bell.

"Here's Hornsby," Cool Papa yelled obediently, as the fans gave Rajah a hand. "When the ball hit the catcher's glove, Hornsby would swing," Bell said. Satchel fanned him on three pitches. "Hornsby never touched the ball," Clift said. Rogers also went down on called strikes in his next try, then popped to shortstop and finally reached on an error.

Mize was held to a double. In all, Satchel gave six hits in nine innings, whiffed nine, and beat Jim Winford (11–10 with the third-place Cardinals) 6–3.

In the second game, Bob Griffith of the Elites beat Big Jim Weaver, formerly of the Cubs, 6–4 in seven innings. Matlock got Hornsby on a fly for the final out with two men on base.

The two teams met again in Davenport, Iowa, where Paige and Andrew "Pullman" Porter threw a two-hitter—both hits by Mize—but lost to Winford 2–1. It was a rainy, foggy night, Bell said, the game was tied 1–1 when Mize hit a pop fly behind second. The outfielder lost the ball in the fog, then threw wildly to first, as big Jawn streaked all the way home.

The next day in Des Moines, Matlock beat Weaver 5–2. Charleston, who was as old as Hornsby, knocked in three key runs and got into a brief but lively fight with the umpire. Five hundred fans swarmed onto the field to help out before police stopped it.

The teams were back in Des Moines the following day to face the 17-year-old Iowa phenom, Bobby Feller, who had whiffed 17 Cards in one exhibition and was 5–3 for third-place Cleveland. Bobby gave only one scratch hit in three innings and struck out eight. Paige also gave one hit and whiffed seven. After Bobby left, the blacks scored two. The whites tied it and had the bases loaded with one out against Porter, but both Hornsby and Mize left them stranded. Perkins' triple to the wall broke the tie, and Wild Bill Wright saved the win with a great throw to catch Goodman trying to score on a double.

Repoıted Bell drily: "They just canceled the rest of the games."

That winter, Greenlee took his club to Mexico. For some reason, Paige didn't go. Bell recalled:

> The first thing the Mexicans said was, "Come out and play the big leaguers tomorrow."
>
> We said, "Big leaguers? We didn't know *they* were here!" They had Jimmie Foxx [.338, 41 homers] and Rogers Hornsby in the infield, Heinie Manush [.291] and Doc Cramer [.292] in the outfield, and Earl Whitehill [14–11 for fourth-place Washington] pitching. It takes about a week to get used to the altitude, and they'd been down there about two weeks, while we'd just arrived.
>
> We had them beat 6–4 with two out in the ninth, when Manush was safe on first. Foxx took a 3–2 count, then he got a ball up around his letters and hit it into the bleachers for a home run.

The game ended 6–6 in the eleventh with the bases loaded, as the Craws' Roosevelt Davis got both Foxx and Hornsby on ground balls. Gibson was held to one single in six at bats against Whitehill and Vern Kennedy (21–9 with the third-place White Sox).

"That night," Bell said, "we all had dinner at an American restaurant, and Foxx told us that that was a strike, the third ball the umpire called, but he said he wasn't going to argue." Jimmie picked up the dinner check. "I owe you guys one," he said.

Next, Ted Lyons (10–13 with the White Sox) whipped them 11–0—Josh went 0 for 4—as Hornsby smashed a long home run into the French cemetery outside the park.

Finally Jack Knott (9–17), who had pitched a no-hitter for the seventh-place Browns that summer, beat the Crawfords 7–2. Hornsby hit a three-run homer. Gibson went 2 for 4.

Manager Earl Mack, Connie's son, sidled up to Bell after the game. "If the door was open, you'd be the first guy I'd hire," Earl said. "I'd pay you $75,000 a year. You'd be worth it in drawing power alone."

It was the last hurrah for the great Crawford team, that may have been the best black team of all time. They would never play together again.

1937

The blimp Hindenburg exploded and burned. Amelia Earhart vanished. Roosevelt tried to pack the Supreme Court. George Gershwin, movie queen Jean Harlow, and John D. Rockefeller died.

"I've Got My Love to Keep Me Warm," "September in the Rain," "In the Still of the Night," "Where or When," "Let's Call the Whole Thing Off." Toscanini and the NBC Symphony Orchestra. Teen fans mobbed Benny Goodman, "the King of Swing."

Captains Courageous, Dead End, In Old Chicago, Lost Horizons, a Star Is Born,

Radio: "Stella Dallas," "The Guiding Light," "Our Gal Sunday," "Dr. Christian."

Books: *Of Mice and Men.*

Carl Hubbell's two-year 24-game win streak ended. Yanks beat Giants 4–1. Joe Louis, 23, beat Jim Braddock for the heavyweight title. Byron "Whizzer" White made All-American prior to going to law school.

This was the year all the Crawfords stars deserted Greenlee for the Dominican Republic. Gus was suddenly having big troubles. He was used to having the cops raid him, but only after he'd banked all the day's take from the numbers racket. But the Pittsburgh municipal elections brought a reform ticket into power, and Gus found that the cops were arriving *before* he had gotten his loot out of sight. His business shriveled, and with it, his freewheeling spending on ballplayers. The first sign of trouble was the announcement that the players would have to pay their own expenses at spring training.

Meanwhile, dictator Rafael Trujillo of the Dominican Republic was sending his agents up north with suitcases full of greenbacks. Greenlee swore out a warrant to have them jailed. He even went to the State Department to try to have them deported. Nothing worked.

Naturally Satchel was the number-one target of the raiders. One team, *Estrellas Orientales,* had offered pitcher Spoon Carter $725 to jump the Craws. But that was just "jingling stuff," Paige sneered. The Trujillo team, the *Dragones,* pursued him to spring training in New

Orleans, cornered him on the street with a big, black limousine, pulled a pistol, according to one account, opened up a suitcase with $30,000 in bills, and told him to pick eight other players at $3,000 each and keep the change.

That sounded good to Paige. The newspapers attacked him for ingratitude after all Gus had done for him, but, Paige retorted, "I wasn't the only one heading down to the islands like that." He brought Bell, Bankhead, Perkins, Matlock, and a few others. The Aguilas club picked up Chet Brewer, Martin Dihigo, Pat Patterson, Bertram Hunter, Showboat Thomas, and Luis Tiant Sr. While a sputtering Greenlee announced they would all be blackballed from the league, Satchel and his friends got a hero's welcome when their flying boat landed on the island.

Gibson, playing winter ball in Puerto Rico, was not among them. Cum Posey and the Grays were negotiating to buy Josh and Judy Johnson ("the punch and Judy show") for $2,500. Meanwhile, Paige wired Josh an even better offer, and he too hopped a plane to Santo Domingo.

The Trujillos were not doing too well, and, according to Bankhead, Josh also got off to a slow start, coming to bat ten or 12 times without a hit.

In one game, nobody got a hit, as Brewer beat Satchel on a no-hitter, though the Dragones got two runs on an error. But Brewer said Santos Amaro and Spoony Palm each hit a homer, "and we beat them 4–2."

Trujillo didn't like that. Elections were coming up, and he was counting on his team to give him a boost at the polls. "El Presidente doesn't lose!" the militia shouted, firing rifles into the air for emphasis. ("They don't kill people over baseball?" Bell asked. "Down here they do," he was told.)

A voodoo priest from neighboring Haiti slipped over the border and gave Paige a *wanga,* or magic charm, to help him win. He later discovered that a *wanga* actually was an evil charm to make him lose.

Josh meanwhile buckled down at bat, and the hits began flying. Paige also went into the final game with a 7–2 record.

Just before the big game, Brewer strolled over to visit his buddies on the *Dragones* and found their hotel room deserted. "Where is everyone?" he asked a kid. "In the *carcel,*" he replied, jerking his thumb toward the jail.

The whole team had been locked up to be sure they were in good shape for the game. "You'd have thought we had the secret combination to Fort Knox," Satchel said.

Before the game supporters of each team lined up in military uniform along the foul lines. "They looked like firing squads," Satch said. "You never saw old Satch throw harder." He was losing 3–2 in the seventh, when he singled and Sam Bankhead homered. Then Paige went out and got the next six men out, five on strikeouts.

Baseball, his manager told him, is a spiritual experience. Satch was glad he didn't end up a spirit himself.*

Paige's record for the season was 8–2, easily the best of anyone. Dihigo was next with 6–4.

Gibson ended up batting .453, 100 points above his nearest rivals, Clyde Spearman and Dihigo, though he hit only two home runs. He did, however, lead the league in triples with five.

It was the last time Josh and Satch ever played together. When the truants got home, Josh was sold to the Grays for $2,500 plus two players, a trade hailed as "the biggest player deal in the history of Negro baseball." (One of the two players Greenlee got was catcher Lloyd "Pepper" Bassett, whom he made famous as a "rocking chair catcher." The trick was to be rocking forward when the pitch comes, Pepper said, or it would knock you over backwards.)

Josh "put new life into everybody. He was the whole team," said Grays first baseman Buck Leonard, who had been carrying the team at bat almost single-handedly. For almost a decade, Gibson and Leonard would become the black Ruth and Gehrig. With those two at the heart of the batting order, the Grays built the greatest dynasty in baseball history, winning nine straight pennants, 1937–45, a feat unmatched by any American professional team in any sport at any time. (Actually, Josh missed two of those years in Mexico.) In the same period, the Yankees won six flags. The Grays' only rivals are the Tokyo Giants of Sadaharu Oh, 1965–73, who also won nine straight.

The trade put new life into Josh as well. With Leonard (.333) hitting behind him, pitchers had to give Gibson strikes to hit. As "Half a Pint" Israel of Newark put it: "If you walk him, you're going to have to pitch to Buck, so what's the difference?"

Said little Dave "Impo" Barnhill of the Cubans:

---

*Dragones hurler Rudolfo Fernandez said the stories about minatory police are exaggerated—he never even saw Trujillo attend a game. Fernandez was a top reliever in his native Cuba, and his manager, Dolph Luque, former Cincinnati Reds pitcher, often called him into the game with the desperate plea, "!Fernandez, ven por Dios!" (Come on, for God's sake!") until "Ven Por Dios" became Fernandez' permanent nickname.

You could strike Josh out; you might throw a fastball by him. But Buck Leonard, you could put a fastball in a 30-30 rifle, and you couldn't shoot it across the plate by him. That's right!

In the same way, Ruth was helped by Gehrig, Hank Aaron by Ed Mathews, Roger Maris by Mickey Mantle, and Oh by Shigeo Nagashima. With Leonard behind him, Josh ran up some of the highest batting averages compiled by any man in black ball annals.

But Gibson had one big factor going against him on his new team—the park. His lifetime record for bad timing continued. For in 1937, the same year Josh joined them, the Grays decided to play half the games in Washington's Griffith Stadium, the most notorious hitters' graveyard in baseball, with a left field foul line 407 feet away. The power alley was a more reachable 383 feet, but in the "coffin corner," center field, 427 feet away, loomed a formidable 30-foot wall. So now Josh would play half his home games in the worst home run park in the National league, and the other half in the worst park in *any* league.

Like Forbes Field, Griffith Stadium was a wide-open park that had stopped the finest home run sluggers in the white majors. Babe Ruth hit only 34 of his 714 homers there. If Babe had played all his home games there instead of in Yankee Stadium, he'd have hit more like 400 homers instead of 714 and would have come nowhere close to 60 homers in one year. Though Josh's new park didn't entirely stop him, it must have hurt him considerably.

Meanwhile, Suttles moved to Newark's bandbox Ruppert Stadium with a left field foul pole only 305 feet away. Mule could hit the ball as far as Gibson without help from the park, but the short fence offered an inviting target, and if he didn't hit the ball squarely, there was still a good chance that a long fly would go out. On the other hand, Gibson may have seen more hittable pitches in Washington than Suttles saw in Newark, as the pitchers figured they might get away with a loud out in Washington but couldn't run that risk in Newark.

After returning from the Dominican Republic, Gibson got into 12 league games with the Grays, hit .500 with seven homers and four triples in only 42 at bats. Mule won the home run crown with 12 in 27 games, equal to about 73 in a 550 at-bat season. Josh's equaled 92!

In one semipro contest, Gibson slugged what he would call one of the two longest homers of his life—the other was the famous 1930 Yankee Stadium drive. This one came at East Orange, NJ, at the home field of the Farmers. "I hit the ball over the left field fence and over a two-story station outside the park," he said.

Gibson hit another mammoth blast into the Yankee Stadium bull pen, almost as far as the 1930 shot. Chicago second baseman Jack Marshall told author Bob Peterson *(Only the Ball Was White)* he saw Josh hit it against Slim Jones of the Philadelphia Stars, and that the ball went over the roof. Marshall is mistaken on the details, but not on the main thrust.

The ball was hit against the New York Black Yankees, who were not in the league that year but did include some top black players, such as Bill Holland, Jake Stephens, Bill Yancey, Clint "Hawk" Thomas, and Fats Jenkins.

Both Stephens and Thomas swore to me they saw the blow, which I at first confused with the famous 1930 homer, since both men had played in that game too, Stephens as Josh's teammate and Thomas with the opposition Lincolns. The key to the mystery was Stephens' statement that he watched the ball land from his vantage point at shortstop, a tipoff that it had to have come after Jake had left the Craws and moved to New York.

"It went over the roof and fell in the bull pen and bounced into the bleachers," Jake said.

Cool Papa Bell disagreed that it went over the roof. But he said there is a telephone in the bull pen for messages from the dugout. "He hit it way over that."

Yancey called it one of the "quickest" home runs he'd ever seen. "It was out of the park before the outfielders could turn their heads to watch it." He said it landed "behind" the bull pen, some 500 feet away. (Yancey also told William Brashler that Josh hit three homers that day, which is incorrect.)

"Jesus Christ!" Thomas whistled to left fielder Jenkins, as they both stared in awe from the bull pen gate, "I ain't *never* seen a ball hit like that before!"

"Neither did I, roomie," Fats replied.

The ball bounded into the bleachers 13 rows back, where a white fan caught it. "You want it?" he called to Hawk.

"Yes, if you don't mind," Thomas called back, and the fan tossed it down.

"Bill," Clint told his owner, Bill Robinson, "I'm gonna make you a present of this ball." "Bojangles jumped five feet in the air," Thomas chuckled.

That night, Thomas and Robinson hailed a cab downtown to appear on Ed Sullivan's radio program. Sullivan, later a famous TV variety show host, gave them $50 for the appearance, and, Clint said, Robinson gave Sullivan the ball.

The Grays had already won the first half of the season without Josh and repeated as champs in the second half. Part of their success, of course, was due to the breakup of the once great Crawfords. Charleston, an overweight 41 years old, had to carry a new club on his own shoulders. He hit only .154, and the Crawfords sank to fifth, a bare half-game out of the cellar.

In a postseason contest against the western champion Kansas City Monarchs, the Grays and Eagles won a six-homer 14–12 free-for-all. Josh got a triple and a homer. Stearnes and Willard Brown homered for the Monarchs.

Technically, Gibson had gotten permission before he flew to Santo Domingo. Paige, Bell, and the others had not, and the unforgiving Greenlee blacklisted them from all league teams when they returned. So they formed their own team, the Trujillo All-Stars, and toured in competition with the league.

In August they went to Denver for the tournament. Brewer, Matlock, and Bob Griffith won two games apiece, each yielding just one run. Paige pitched the clincher in order to collect the bonus offered for doing it. But the other players thought that wasn't fair and, whether by design or not, lost the game 6–4. The next day, with Matlock on the mound, they clinched the title 11–1 and picked up the winners' check of $5,000, while Matlock presumably took home the one-grand bonus.

On September 20, the All-Stars played a Negro National league all-star team in the Polo Grounds in a game that Paige would call "the worst time" of his life. (In his autobiography, he places the game in Hartford in 1941, but this is a case of faulty memory.) Actually, Paige pitched an excellent game that day. But 21-year-old Schoolboy Johnny Taylor of the New York Cubans pitched an even better one.

"You don't want to cancel out, do you?" Satch said he asked Taylor's manager, Dihigo. "We're liable to kill that boy." Dihigo just smiled and said that maybe Satch was the one who should cancel.

Actually, Taylor had been pitching for three years in the league and had faced the Craws in the 1935 World Series and would have beaten them for the clincher if Dihigo had not lifted him for no apparent reason.

Johnny took the mound before 20,000 fans, including his mother and the diminutive, mustachioed, ambitious district attorney of New York, Tom Dewey, who would later run for President. Dewey was at the game presumably as part of his investigation of racketeer Alex Pompez, who owned the Cubans. Taylor said he wasn't nervous—"the crowd was usually with me in New York. They'd give you lots of applause." His overhand curve was sharp that day, and he was pitching to the best catcher in black baseball, perhaps in all baseball, Biz Mackey, who was even then giving tips to his young protege, Roy Campanella.

For eight innings Taylor and Paige pitched to a scoreless tie. Satch had pitched out of one jam by purposely walking Wild Bill Wright (a league-leading .410) to fill the bases, then striking out pinch-hitter Henry Kimbro (.276). "I gave up only eight hits and struck out eight," Paige wrote, "but it was nowhere near as good as that kid did."

Taylor gave up a walk to lead-off man Bell, another walk in the second, and his third walk to Bell in the sixth. Three spectacular fieldings plays, two by shortstop Chester Williams and one by first baseman Shifty Jim West, got him through the seventh and eighth, and he still hadn't given up a hit.

In the bottom of the ninth, West (.374) swung late on a two-strike fastball from Satch and hit it into the upper deck in right to give Taylor a 2–0 lead.

In the ninth, Taylor retired George Scales and Spoony Palm, pinch-hitting for Satch. The last man, Bell, grounded out on an overhand curve, and Johnny had his no-hitter, as his mother leaped over the box seat railing to hug him, and Dewey stood and cheered with the rest of the crowd.

Satchel, ignored by the crowd,

> ran to the hotel and locked myself in my room. You've never seen an old man if you didn't see me after that game.
>
> "Maybe I'm over the hill," I kept asking myself. It's a mighty bad feeling when a young punk comes along and does better than you, and you know it. And you know you ain't young like you used to be. . . .
>
> For a couple of days I just moped around.

Paige was hardly old; he was only 31. And what he forgot to mention, probably because it didn't make nearly so great an impression on him, is that he met Taylor again a week later and beat him 9–4.

Gibson, meanwhile, went barnstorming against a Cincinnati Reds squad that included pitchers Bucky Walters (14–15), Jim Weaver (6–5), and Wild Bill Hallahan (3–9), plus Ernie Lombardi, Frank McCormick, and Leo Durocher. Josh reportedly hit three home runs in eight games, as his club won five out of the eight, although the box scores have yet to be found. Durocher gulped. He later told a reporter:

I played against Josh Gibson in Cincinnati, and I found out everything they said about him was true, and then some. He hit one of the longest balls I've ever seen. He caught hold of one of Weaver's fast ones, and I'll bet you it's still sailing.

1938

G ermany invaded Austria. Chamberlain met Hitler, ceded part of Czechoslovakia, and came home with his umbrella proclaiming "peace for our time." The Nazis looted Jewish shops on Kristalnacht.

"You Must Have Been a Beautiful Baby," "September Song," "My Heart Belongs to Daddy," "Thanks for the Memories," "You Go to My Head," "One O'Clock Jump," "Beer Barrel Polka," "A-Tisket, A-Tasket," Kate Smith's "God Bless America."

You Can't Take It With You, The Adventures of Robin Hood with Erroll Flynn; Spencer Tracy and Mickey Rooney in *Boys' Town, Love Finds Andy Hardy, Bringing Up Baby* with Cary Grant, *Snow White and the Seven Dwarfs*.

Radio: "Information Please," "Young Widder Brown," "The Green Hornet," "Kay Kyser's Kollege of Musical Knowledge." Orson Welles' "The War of the Worlds" terrified millions on Hallowe'en.

Broadway: *Our Town, Hellzapoppin'*.

Books: *How to Win Friends and Influence People*.

Johnny VanderMeer pitched double no-hitters. Hank Greenberg hit 58 homers. The Yanks beat the Cubs 4–0. Joe Louis KO'd Max Schmeling in round one. Helen Wills Moody won her eighth Wimbledon.

In May, Greenlee swallowed his pride and agreed to take Satchel back.

OUTLAWS WON'T BE FIRED
National Loop
Goes Soft on
Bad Boys

the headline read. Gus even offered his star a $450 a month salary.

Satchel was insulted. "I wouldn't throw ice cubes for that kind of money," he sneered. He was learning to dance the boogie woogie and was weighing an offer from Argentina—Satch's business acumen was as sharp as ever, though his geography was weak. Besides, he said, Joe DiMaggio had advised him to hold out.

Abe Manley, a Newark numbers king and owner of the Newark Eagles, wanted Satch and paid Greenlee $5,000 for him. But, Satchel scoffed, Gus "was only selling a piece of paper and not the real stuff."

Abe's young white wife, Effa, the glamour girl of Negro baseball, and some say the brains and energy behind the team, opened a lengthy parley with the pitcher. Thirty-five years later at the age of 73, she disclosed the nature of the negotiations. Paige agreed to join the Eagles, she said coyly, "if I would be his girl friend."

Apparently she said no, because Paige decided to jump the Newark contract to play in Mexico instead.

SATCHEL PAIGE
BANNED FOREVER
FROM BASEBALL

the Baltimore *Afro-American* reported.

Mexico almost ended Satchel's career. Something snapped in the golden arm. Pain shot through him. "All I could see was white," as the ball dribbled a few feet away. With pain cutting "clear through my head," Satch tried again—another shot put. "The ball'd bloop up a little and then drop."

In the past, boiling hot showers had always kept his arm loose, and "I ain't gonna miss none of those pay checks just 'cause (my arm's) complaining a little now." But now he couldn't even get his arm up to his shoulder, and he later admitted ruefully that "being greedy like that just about ended my career."

In all, Paige got into only three games that year, couldn't complete any of them, won one, lost one, and gave up a disastrous 5.21 ERA.

His final game, against Martin Dihigo, the Cuban *inmortel,* is considered a classic in Mexican annals. Still throbbing with pain and relying on underhand and trick pitches, Satch dueled Dihigo 0–0 for six innings. In the seventh, he loaded the bases with a hit and two walks, then wild-pitched the game's first run home. He was lifted for a pinch-hitter in the eighth, but his club tied the score. Dihigo won it in the ninth with a homer.

The Mexicans sent Satch to a specialist, who told him grimly: "Satchel, I don't think you'll ever pitch again."

Meanwhile, Josh had returned from wintering in Cuba, where he had hit .344, second to Bankhead's .366. He hit only three homers in

61 at bats, which is only 27 per 550 at bats. But Cuban parks were wide open; the co-leaders, Willie Wells and pitcher Ray Brown, hit only four. Old-time fan Pedro Cardona said Tropical Park in Havana had no left field fence at all; many of Josh's longest drives were caught for outs.

Some reports claim that Josh opened the Negro league season in Washington and pumped the first two balls he saw into the distant bleachers and blasted the next two against the fence for triples. If so, the Washington newspapers remained unaware of the feat.

Gibson reportedly hit 65 homers that year, four in one game. Like many numbers that are passed along in Negro league history books, these are hard to track down. Scientifically, one cannot prove a negative, so one cannot prove that Josh didn't do all the things he's credited with doing—some day scholars may uncover proofs that he did. Meantime, until some hefty research is done, some hefty skepticism is in order.

Josh's known league homers totaled a modest four, compared to Mule Suttles' league-leading nine. Though Gibson's power output was down, he batted .350.

And he has never received credit for another skill, perhaps the most important for any catcher, more important even than hitting home runs, and that is handling his pitchers. As an 18-year-old rookie back in 1930 he had caught Joe Williams' 27-strikeout masterpiece. Two years later, he caught Paige's first no-hitter. In 1935, he caught Leroy Matlock's 20–0 perfect season. Thirty years later, Johnny Bench was called a top defensive catcher, but Bench never handled a great pitching staff or even a great individual pitcher (except for Tom Seaver, who had been a star before he joined Bench's Reds).

In 1938, Gibson showed once again that he was a master handler of his pitching staff, especially the temperamental but talented Ray Brown. If Gibson and Paige had been the best battery of all time, the combination of Gibson and Brown was almost as good.

George Scales called Brown the greatest pitcher he ever saw, better even than Joe Williams or Paige. Sam Bankhead conceded that Paige was the best—for one game—but he would take Brown for one season, because he knew Brown would be there, while Satch might or might not show up.

The light-skinned Brown came to the Grays from Wilberforce College and married the boss's daughter at a home plate ceremony on July 4, 1935. He threw a fastball and a curve, to which he added a knuckler. Brown had a rubber arm, Johnny Taylor said, and he was a threat at bat as well: He could pitch the first game of a doubleheader, play right field in the second, and come in in relief again if needed.

Leonard had this thumbnail appraisal:

> Ray Brown is my iron man, because he could play outfield, pitch, play a little infield too. Could pitch doubleheaders. Whenever you called on him to pitch, he was ready, and he always pitched a good game. The score was going to be low. He learned to throw a knuckleball that really danced. And he could always get the ball over the plate. With 3 and 2 a lot of ballplayers, you can't depend on them throwing that curveball over the plate, but he would get three balls on a good hitter and then throw three curveballs over the plate.

In 1936–37, Brown (called "Brinquitos" in Spanish) set a Cuban record with a 21–4 mark in the short, 69-game season. One of his losses was 1–0 in 11 innings to Luis Tiant Sr. One of his wins was a no-hitter.

But Brown had a temper. And being Posey's son-in-law didn't make him any easier to handle, as manager Vic Harris continually discovered.

But Josh handled Brown skillfully, and Ray posted a perfect 12–0 record in '38.

Harris was pleased with his new catcher:

> Gibson would ask a lot of times during the game—I was in left field—he'd holler out: "How 'bout walking him?"
> I'd say, "Suit yourself."
> "What you want me to do?"
> I'd say, "Just get him out." I let Gibson use his own judgment. There was no one easier to handle than Josh Gibson.

"Josh was very playful, just like a big kid," Monte Irvin said. One day in Newark's Grand Hotel, Josh strode in, calling, "Monte, where are all the girls?" Then he spied Newark first baseman Lenny Pearson, one of the league's leading ladies' men, sitting with some girls. "What do you say, lover boy? Come on, lover boy, you can give me one of them (girls). Just one. We're playing a doubleheader tomorrow. You want me to be tired out, don't you? What about this one right here?" and he nudged Lenny's date.

"Well," Pearson said sourly, "if she wants to go with you, it's up to her." The girl quickly weighed her options, got up, and took Josh's arm.

The next day, "Brown was popping that ball" when Pearson came to bat. Josh ignored him but called to Irvin in the on-deck circle: "Heh, Monte!"

"Yeah, Josh, what is it?" Irvin called back.

"Tell Lenny something for me."

Strike one.

"What you want to tell him?"

Strike two.

"Tell him I took his girl out last night."

Strike three.

The next time Pearson appeared, Josh repeated the routine: "Tell him I screwed her."

Another strikeout.

On the third at bat, the punch-line was: "Tell him we're gonna do it again tonight!"

"Pearson went 0 for 9 that day," Irvin said. "Calm down," Monte told him, "don't you see what Josh is trying to do?"

Another time Josh was behind the plate while Philadelphia's Webster McDonald was serving up his submarine "junk" stuff. Gibson casually picked each pitch off with his bare hand. "Don't you ever do that to me again," McDonald fussed, "insult me in front of all those people."

Mac got his revenge in another game, Irvin recalled;

> Bases loaded. McDonald threw three curveballs in a row, Josh fouled them off, taking a good cut. Count was 3–2. A fastball down the middle. Josh was so surprised he took the ball. Mac did the boogie from the pitching mound to home plate. The people just died.

Amid the chuckles, the everyday life of a black ballplayer in Depression America meant nights of boring shuttling by bus between Pittsburgh and Washington, 265 miles each way on the new Pennsylvania Turnpike. Buck Leonard described the grind in *Voices From the Great Black Baseball Leagues:*

> Sometimes we'd stay in hotels that had so many bedbugs you had to put a newspaper down between the mattress and the sheets. Other times we'd rent rooms in a YMCA, or we'd go to a hotel and rent three rooms;

that way you got to use the bath, by renting three rooms. All the players would change clothes in those three rooms.

After a Sunday doubleheader—nine innings the first game, seven innings the second—the players went back to their hotel for a quick shower, darted into a lunch counter for a bite, then piled into the bus. They tilted their seats back, sang some barbershop harmony, replayed the games, and finally drifted off to sleep to the drone of the motor.

We'd get back in Pittsburgh 7:30 in the morning, go to bed, get up around three o'clock, go up the river somewhere about 25 or 30 miles, play a night game.

They played semipro steel mill teams all around the metropolitan area, starting at 6:30 and ending when it was too dark to see the ball any more. The team might get $75–100 a game—"for the whole *team.*"

The next evening the same thing. We used to play a doubleheader at Bushwick in New York on a Sunday and go out to some place on Long Island and play Sunday night. Man, you're spent. You're trying to save a little from the day game for tonight's game. Then you go out there at night to play, you're stiff, tired, and you're just forcing yourself. We logged 30,000 miles one summer. Of course, you get tired around July or August. The people didn't know what we went through. They'd see us dragging around, they didn't know we'd ridden all night getting there.

Sundays at Forbes Field, Griffith Stadium, Yankee Stadium, etc. were the big pay days. Leonard called them the "getting-out-of-the-hole days." Wilmer Fields, who joined the team in 1940, remembered Posey sitting in the front seat as the bus raced dark rain clouds to the park. "He was going to get in four and a half innings of this game *some*how!"

Players filled up on junk food. Fields recalled playing a game on a hot dog, a Coke, and lemon meringue pie. They kept sandwich boxes under their seats—bread and sandwich spreads—for snacks on the road. Or they stopped at hamburger stands.

Fields, who was light enough to pass for white, usually got the assignment to go in and order for the team. Gibson called him Chinky, presumably meaning Chinese. Once at four in the morning, Josh got hungry and told the driver to stop at a roadside all-night diner. "Here, Chinky, wear my hat," he said. Wilmer pulled it down low and sauntered in. Suddenly pitcher R. T. Walker jumped up and followed him in to order an extra hamburger. The waiter shot a second look at Fields and ordered them both out. Fields returned to the bus empty-handed to find Gibson already licking his lips until he got the bad news. "He like to killed Walker for messin' up the eatin' deal," Fields said.

One of Josh's practical jokes was to wait until the bus entered a tunnel, then order the rookie Fields to holler at the top of his voice. The shout echoed in the narrow tunnel, as the startled players all jumped awake and Gibson guffawed at their expense.

The Griffith Stadium staff in Washington never was sure if the bus would arrive on time for the game. "If you're not here by 11:30, we're not going to open the gates." Once the bus broke down out near Hagerstown, Maryland, and Posey had to call Washington to send three taxicabs out to pick them up.

The Grays would also play a midweek night game, usually on Tuesday, at Griffith Stadium, using the Redskins' football lights. They were pretty dim compared to later lighting plants; fly balls went up out of sight of the lights, and neither outfielders nor infielders could get a good jump on a ball. Presumably, batters couldn't follow the pitched balls any better.

"And we didn't have a paid trainer," Leonard said. "We rubbed each other. If my back was hurting or my arm was sore, I'd get another player to rub it. And you'd tape yourself up the best you could."

Leonard remembered needing three stitches in his leg, but the team couldn't spare him, so he just played until the leg healed. "Had I been in the major leagues, I would have had proper attention."

That summer New York Yankee outfielder Jake Powell created a furor when he blurted out in a radio interview that he was a sheriff in the off-season and "enjoyed cracking niggers' heads." Commissioner Kenesaw Mountain Landis ordered him to apologize.

For some reason Josh didn't play in the East–West game in August, though he was first in the vote of the fans.

There was a flurry of excitement that summer that the white majors might at last open their doors to Gibson and the others.

During the white major league meetings that winter, Ches Washington of the Pittsburgh *Courier* had wired manager Pie Traynor of the third-place Pittsburgh Pirates with a revolutionary proposal:

KNOW YOUR CLUB NEEDS PLAYERS STOP HAVE ANSWERS TO YOUR PRAYERS RIGHT HERE IN PITTSBURGH STOP JOSH GIBSON CATCHER 1B B. LEONARD AND RAY BROWN PITCHER OF HOMESTEAD GRAYS AND S. PAIGE PITCHER COOL PAPA BELL OF PITTSBURGH CRAWFORDS ALL AVAILABLE AT REASONABLE FIGURES STOP WOULD MAKE PIRATES FORMIDABLE PENNANT CONTENDERS STOP WHAT IS YOUR ATTITUDE? WIRE ANSWER

Traynor's reply was eloquent: No reply at all.

By September, the Pirates were locked in a pennant race with the Giants and Cubs, and New York *Daily News* Columnist Jimmie Powers impatiently demanded to know why the Giants didn't pick up Gibson and six other black stars. With Josh, Leonard, Bankhead, and Ray Brown of the Grays, plus infielders Pat Patterson and Ray Dandridge, along with Giant stalwarts Mel Ott, Carl Hubbell, and Dick Bartell—Powers wrote—the Giants could wrap up the pennant for sure.

But, like the Pirates before them, the Giants ignored the idea as preposterous—as indeed it was at that time. So the Cubs won the pennant on Gabby Hartnett's famous "home run in the gloaming," while the Pirates faded to two games behind and the Giants to five. Either team might have used blacks as a nucleus for a dynasty. Instead, the Giants waited 13 years for a pennant and the Pirates 22.

National League president Ford Frick was asked why the doors were not open to blacks. He blamed it on the fans:

We cannot do anything we want to until public opinion is ready for it. The problem of traveling with Negro players in the South and other cities will cause embarrassment and dissatisfaction for all. . . . Baseball is biding its time and waiting for the social change, which is inevitable. I think that in the near future, people will be willing to accept a Negro ballplayer just as they have the Negro boxer and college athlete. Times are changing.

Satchel Paige and Josh Gibson. (Photos from author's collection unless otherwise credited)

Satchel Paige with
Miami Marlins.

Josh Gibson.

Josh Gibson (second from left) in a Veracruz uniform with (from left)
Barney Brown, Ray Dandridge, Leroy Matlock, Johnny Taylor and
Bill Wright.

Satchel Paige (far left) with Crawfords pitching staff. Others pictured (from left) are Leroy Matlock, W. Bell, Harry Kincannon, Streeter and Hunter.

As members of the Pittsburgh Crawfords, Satchel Paige and Josh Gibson (second to right and far right) with light heavyweight champ John Henry Lewis (center). Also shown is Oscar Charleston (second from left).

Satchel Paige and Josh Gibson (back, second and third from left) with the 1932 Pittsburgh Crawfords. Others include L. D. Livingston (back, far left) and, completing the back row, Ray Williams, Walt Cannady, Bill Perkins and Oscar Charleston. Front row, from left, Chester Williams, Harry Williams, Harry Kincannon, Henry Speaman, Jimmie Crutchfield, Bobby Williams and Ted Radcliffe. (Courtesy Craig Davidson)

Bill Foster.

Turkey Stearnes (left) and James "Cool Papa" Bell. (Courtesy Craig Davidson)

Josh Gibson (second to left) with (from left) Oscar Charleston, Ted Page and Judy Johnson.

Jackie Robinson.

Satchel Paige (center) with Tom Baird (left), owner of the Kansas City Monarchs, and Lefty Gomez.

Satchel Paige and Josh Gibson (far left and center) with Bill Perkins in the Dominican Republic in 1937.

Josh Gibson (seated) with Ray Brown.

Satchel Paige with Bill Veeck.

Roy Campanella.   Joe Williams.

Gus Greenlee. Courtesy Craig Davidson.

Satchel Paige (far right) with 1942 Kansas City Monarchs pitching staff. Others pictured, from left, Hilton Smith, Jack Matchett, Booker McDaniels, Jim LaMarque and Connie Johnson.

Josh Gibson running the bases at Griffith Stadium.

Bill Byrd.

Ted Page.

Satchel Paige with Cecil Travis and Dizzy Dean.

Josh Gibson with Mrs. Joe Louis.

Josh Gibson touching home plate in the East-West Game, Comiskey
Park, 1942. Catcher is Ted "Double Duty" Radcliffe.

Satchel Paige with Dizzy Dean.

Satchel Paige with his teammate, Jackie Robinson, on the Kansas City
Monarchs, 1945.

Satchel Paige.

Josh Gibson.

Buck Leonard.

Josh Gibson batting in his final year, 1946.

Josh Gibson.

Satchel Paige.

1939

Germany invaded Czechoslovakia, signed a nonaggression pact with Stalin, invaded Poland. England declared war on Germany. Russia invaded Finland. The New York and San Francisco World's Fairs. Fermi split the atom. Sigmund Freud died.

"I'll Never Smile Again," "All the Things You Are," "South of the Border," "Frenesi," "Oh, Johnny, Oh," "Body and Soul," "In the Mood," "Over the Rainbow." Harry James, Charlie Parker. Marian Anderson, barred from the DAR hall, sang at the Lincoln Memorial before a crowd of 75,000.

Gone With the Wind ("Frankly, my dear, I don't give a damn"); *Dark Victory* with Bette Davis, Humphrey Bogart, and Ronald Reagan; *Goodbye, Mr. Chips, Mr. Smith Goes to Washington, Ninotchka, Destry Rides Again, Stagecoach, The Wizard of Oz, Wuthering Heights, Gunga Din, Jesse James, Pinocchio.*

Radio: "Henry Aldrich" ("Coming, Mother"). Ed Murrow broadcast war news from London.

Broadway: *Life with Father.*

Books: *Finnegan's Wake, The Grapes of Wrath, The Yearling, Mein Kampf.*

Ted Williams debuted. A dying Lou Gehrig retired ("the luckiest man on the face of the earth"). The Yankees whipped Cincinnati 4–0.

A change had come over Gibson. Ted Page, who was retired and operating a bowling alley, recalled:

Josh loved life. He was one of the happiest persons in the world until about the 1940s. Then he began to realize that he was perhaps the greatest hitter in the world, and yet he was deprived of a chance to make $30–40–50,000, while Babe Ruth had pulled down $80,000. He realized that he was just as good as Ruth. . . .

He changed from the Josh I knew: a kid, just an overgrown kid who did nothing but play ball and eat ice cream or go to the movies. Strictly play, this was Josh. Well, that changed, all that.

He started to drink. I wasn't close enough to him to have found out why, but it seems to me that his wife had misused some money, like when you're playing down in the tropics and you send some money home. If this is true, I don't know. But I would like to say this: Something caused the man to change from what he was—a congenial, big, old, young boy— to a man who was kind of bitter with somebody, or mad with somebody, he wasn't really sure who. He realized as he started to get older that his good days were behind him as a baseball player, and I feel certain that in the inside of his mind, Josh realized that he was never going to make the big leagues, so who cares?

Meanwhile, his arm now useless, Satchel Paige tried to get a job managing or coaching. "You'd figure they'd want my name. But nobody needed coaches all of a sudden. . . . All of a sudden nobody knew me any more."

He was reduced to selling off his precious shotgun, fishing gear, suits, even his car. "Mr. Pawnshop must have thought I was a burglar the way I kept coming back to see him. . . . I was a broken bum just wandering around looking for a piece of bread. . . . When you been at the top and hit the bottom, it's a mighty long fall." He was only 32.

Then he got a phone call from Kansas City Monarchs owner J.L. Wilkinson. "I just got your contract from Newark," Wilkie said. "When can you report in Kansas City?"

"Tomorrow," Paige replied.

"I'd been dead. Now I was alive again."

But it was now sadly clear that Paige could no longer pitch as he once had—in fact, he couldn't pitch at all. "He couldn't even wipe the back of his neck," said Newt Allen. But Wilkie gave him a job playing first base on the Monarchs' "B" team that toured the prairies under former third baseman Newt Joseph.

"My name ain't gonna lure that many fans," Satchel said.

Satch and the other vets "have done a lot for the Negro leagues and made us some money," Wilkinson replied softly. "I'm just trying to pay you back a little."

So Paige got in the bus and headed for the little towns of Kansas, Oklahoma, and the Dakotas. He turned out to be a liability at first base and at bat, so Joseph patiently told him, "Maybe we can work that arm of yours out."

The Monarchs' masseur, Frank "Jewbaby" Floyd, arrived to help work on the arm, and Satch soaked it in boiling water every night until it got numb, then he threw an inning or two—"Alley Oops and bloopers and underhand and sidearm." But the arm still "ached like a tooth" and fans asked each other, "How'd he ever get anybody out?" That hurt worse than the arm did.

Then one day before a game, he wound up and threw. There wasn't any pain! He threw again. "I'm gonna try a fast one," he yelled.

"A *what?*" the catcher said.

Even Satchel hesitated. What if he threw it, and the pain returned? He gulped and fired. It wasn't the old "be ball," but it was fast enough. He threw another. And another.

The muscles tingled, the sweat appeared.

"I can throw it again, Newt!" he shouted. "I can throw it again!"

So Joseph taught Satchel how to pitch all over again and how to throw a curve.

Several players have taken credit for teaching Paige the curve, starting with Willie Powell back in 1927. Satch had thrown a few in his 1934 no-hitter as a waste pitch, and Jack Marshall said he was fooling around with the pitch in the 1936 Denver tournament.

Cool Papa Bell told him to develop the pitch seriously:

> Satchel was the fastest pitcher I ever saw. He was so fast you couldn't time him. But he was in the league four or five years before he learned how to pitch. I used to say, "Satchel, why don't you learn how to pitch? You don't throw the curve, you don't have control of it. And you have to have a change-up. As hard as you throw, you'd really fool the batter."
>
> In 1938, his arm got sore, and I told him, "See, Satchel, you've got to learn how to pitch." I showed him how to throw the knuckleball [Bell was originally a knuckleball pitcher], and he was throwing it better than I was. That's what I liked about him, he didn't want anybody to beat him doing anything.

Newt Allen recalled:

> When he came back [with Newt Joseph], the second team played us out in Kansas City, Kansas, and Satchel pitched and wore us out. And he went from there. He started pitching around three-four innings. Then he pitched every day, every ball game almost, and the people started coming back to see him.

"That hummer of mine just sang a sweet song going across the plate," Satch wrote. "It was the finest music I ever heard." At 33, most ballplayers were "curling up," he said, "but not Ol' Satch. When everybody's calling you ageless, you got time for those comebacks."

Still Wilkinson kept Paige on the "B" team. Even without him, the Monarchs were the powerhouse of the new Negro American league and breezed to their third straight pennant. Turkey Stearnes and

Willard "Home Run" Brown led the league in homers, and Hilton Smith topped the pitchers with an 8–2 record. Presumably Wilkie considered Paige more valuable as a drawing card in the small towns, where baseball-hungry townsfolk flocked to see him. "We played in some towns where they didn't want us in *town*, let alone the ballpark, unless I pitched," Satch said.

With Wilkinson's lights, the Monarchs could play up to three games a Sunday. Satch wrote that he once won a game in the morning, won in relief in the afternoon, and won a nine-inning contest under the lights that night. (Negro leaguers Johnny Taylor and Wilmer Fields claimed the same distinction.) "I know some ballplayers who don't win that many all season," he bragged.

Meanwhile, Josh had wintered in Cuba. The Grays lost four out of six to Cuban teams; then, in the regular winter season, Gibson set a home run record—11, compared to the old mark, seven, by Suttles a decade earlier. It works out to about 37 for a normal season, but as we have said, Cuban parks were huge. He also batted .356.

Back in the States, Gibson walloped homers at an unbelievable rate—16 in only 72 known at bats. That's one homer every four and a half times up or—take a deep breath—122 in 550 at bats! And this was in Griffith Stadium and Forbes Field.

The next highest man, Suttles, slugged ten.

Josh's 24 hits included 16 homers, two triples, two doubles, and only four singles. He batted .333, but his slugging average was an unheard of 1.083, which means that he averaged more than one single every time he stepped to the plate. To put that in perspective, Babe Ruth's best slugging average was 0.847 in 1920.

Leonard recalled one homer in Beckley, West Virginia. "Josh hit it up on the side of a mountain. There was a mountain in center field, and you could see little boys up there on the mountain looking for the ball."

A 17-year-old catcher with Baltimore, Roy Campanella, had a similar story about four homers in West Virginia. The first one just cleared the fence, the second reached the base of the hill, the third one was higher on the hill, and the fourth halfway up it. "I always figured that if he had come up one more time, he just might have hit the ball clear over the hill."

Newark pitcher Leon Day reported:

> I saw Gibson hit the top of the left field bleachers in Washington, missed by about that far of going out. I don't think there's ever been one hit out of there, but that was the closest one I've ever seen.

Actually, Mickey Mantle hit one out, his famous 565-foot tape measure blast, in 1953. Rick Roberts insisted that Gibson had already done it: "I saw the one that Mantle hit. Josh's was higher than Mantle's. Mantle's just got over; Gibson's went over with room to spare. [Senators owner] Clark Griffith almost ate his cigar!"

Said Judy Johnson:

> Mr. Griffith thought so much of Josh, he'd come in the dugout, sit alongside of him, say, "Josh, you gonna hit a home run for me today?"
> Josh said, "Well, I'll try, Mr. Griffith," and before the game was over, somebody was looking for it over the left field fence.

Gibson said his favorite park was the old Polo Grounds in New York, only 279-feet down the left field line (250 to the overhanging second deck) and an irresistible 257 feet in right—and Josh loved to reach out and smash curves to right. But center field was 505 feet, about two golf drives, away. Sammy Bankhead, who also had moved to the Grays, remembered one blow Josh hit there. The bull pen was in extreme left-center of the horseshoe-shaped park, the deepest corner, farther even than center field. Sam said Gibson's drive "went upstairs, above the bull pen, second tier, out of the park."

Leonard said he saw one that left the same park *between* the roof and the upper stands. No lobbing mortar round could have found that small opening; it must have sprung from his bat like a cannon shot. "A man came in from the el train: 'Who the hell hit that ball over here on the train track?'"

How many homers could Gibson have hit there in a 154-game schedule? He probably would have broken all records.

Of course, he would have faced the best black *and* white pitching in an integrated league. But then, so would Ruth, Jimmie Foxx, Mel Ott, and others. "I'd have taken a few points off those big fat batting averages," Paige said. So would Smokey Joe Williams, Rogan, Slim Jones, Matlock, etc.

According to Campanella, one impish young shortstop for the semipro Brooklyn Bushwicks finally figured out how to stop Gibson. The kid's name was Phil Rizzuto, and he froze the balls in a refrigerator overnight to be sure they'd be dead by game time. Another Bushwick, future Boston Brave Tommy Holmes, laughingly verified the tale. The frozen balls were marked with dots, Holmes grinned, and drives that should have flown over the fence, sank like lead balls in a pond.

For the rest of the Grays, Leonard hit .319 with four homers and Bankhead .333. But manager Vic Harris slumped to .216. On the pitching staff, Ray Brown had slipped to 4–1, and rookie Roy Partlow was only 2–2, though seven years later he would follow Jackie Robinson into the Dodgers' organization at Montreal. They won both halves of the split season, but it was clear that the Grays were a one-man team—if you stopped Gibson, you shut down the whole team.

That summer the Young Communist League in New York launched a citywide drive to collect 100,000 names on a petition to open the white major leagues to blacks. Kids of both races covered the beaches, parks, athletic fields, and even Yankee Stadium, and succeeded in collecting 20,000 signatures. One of them, reportedly, was Gibson's.

The Grays again won both the first- and second-half flags. A new play-off scheme, somewhat like pro basketball's, was tried. The Grays would play the fourth-place Philadelphia Stars, the runner-up Cubans would play third-place Baltimore, and the two winners would meet for the pennant. The Ruppert Cup, donated by New York Yankee owner Colonel Jacob Ruppert, would go to the winner.

The Grays lost their opener to the Stars 5–3, in spite of Josh's home run. In the second game, he drove out a single, double, and triple in a 15–9 rout. The Grays won the third game 6–4, though no box score has yet been found. They then wrapped the series up with a 3–0 victory in the fifth and final contest.

The Elites, meanwhile, upset the Cubans three games to two.

Baltimore had a good club. Little Tommy "Pee Wee" Butts hit no less than .485. In later years, Negro leaguers would compare him to the Yankees' Phil Rizzuto or the Dodgers' Pee Wee Reese.

Butts' DP partner, Sammy T. Hughes, hit .345. Campanella, Monte Irvin, and others who saw him, consider Hughes the best black second baseman until Joe Morgan came along 30 years later. At 6'3", Hughes stood half a foot taller than Butts, but they still could turn the double play together.

An ex-football running back, Wild Bill Wright, played outfield and hit .404. He weighed about 205, Paige recalled, "and he could go down to first base fast as anybody we had." Wright led the league in steals and triples that year.

Next to him, Henry "Jumbo" Kimbro patrolled center field and hit .310.

Young Campanella hit .287. He had moved up to the number-one catching job, as the great maestro, Biz Mackey, was traded to

Newark after teaching the kid everything he knew about the position. "You saw Campanella catch, you saw Mackey catch," old-timers said. But in his autobiography, Campanella also gave Gibson credit for giving him critical help and encouragement:

> I had a very erratic arm when I broke in. It was strong enough, all right; but I never was too sure where the ball was going. I'll always be grateful to [Gibson] for the help he gave me when I was a skinny little catcher away from home for the first time, and he was the great man of baseball. He tried to show me how to set myself to improve my speed and accuracy, and when I'd have a bad day against the Grays, he'd come over to me in the locker room and try to give me a little confidence. "It's just a matter of practice," he'd tell me. "You got the arm, that's the important thing. The rest of it is just practice, practice, practice."

In later years Campanella would say the Elites "had five pitchers who could pitch in any league. There was Robert Griffith, Andrew Porter, Bill Byrd, Jim Willis, and a left-hander, Tom Glover. I would take those five pitchers, put them right on the Dodgers, and all of those fellows would be starters."

Byrd led the staff that year with a 9–4 mark. Byrd had none of Paige's color and as a result pitched in obscurity. But he won 115 Negro league games overall, only eight less than Satchel:

	W	L	Pct
Paige	123	79	.609
Byrd	115	72	.615

And Paige pitched for much stronger teams than Byrd did. If Bill had said, "Never look back, someone may be gaining on you," it is possible that he would be in Cooperstown today along with the more quotable Satchel.

But Byrd didn't say funny things. He just threw funny pitches. He had a fastball, curve, knuckler, slider, and cut ball. And "he was a tremendous spitball pitcher," Campy said, "tremendous control." He would have been "a consistent 15–20-game winner" in the majors. Thanks to Byrd, Campy would have no trouble in Brooklyn handling spitters thrown by Preacher Roe.

The Elites beat the Cubans and would face the Grays in the playoff. The first team to win three games would take the cup.

In the opening game, Byrd shut down Josh and held the Grays to only two runs. But young Partlow did even better, holding the Elites to one run to win it 2–1.

The teams played a Sunday doubleheader the next day. In the first game, Gibson smashed a two-run homer "far over" the left field wall at Baltimore off right-hander Jonas Gaines in the opening inning. The nervous Campanella dropped a third strike, but it caused no damage.

In the fourth, with the Grays leading 3–1, Bill Wright drove a "ponderous" double to spark a three-run rally and go ahead 4–3.

The Grays tied it 4–4 in the fifth on a single by Bankhead, a walk to Josh, and a single by Buck.

The Elites went ahead again in the sixth on a single and an error, plus two misplays by Gibson. First he dropped Campanella's third strike, then threw wildly to second, as the lead runner scored.

In the sixth, Wright singled in a run with two out to make it 6–4 Baltimore.

The Grays got one run back in the eighth on two singles and a wild throw by Kimbro. The tying run almost scored on a long fly, but Wright's great throw held the runner on third, and the Elites won 6–5 to tie the series.

Gaines completely shut Gibson down after that first-inning blow. For the day, Josh was 1 for 6.

The second game, a seven-inning affair, saw Campanella make an error, followed by a passed ball, to let in one run. He got the run back in the third, however, when he reached on an error and scored on a sacrifice and an error.

In the fifth inning, with the clock edging toward the six o'clock curfew, Wright lashed a long drive to right field with Sammy Hughes on base, but a great relay, Harris to Bankhead to Gibson, nipped Hughes at the plate, and the two teams ended in a 1–1 tie.

The fourth game the following Saturday was a duel between the rival catchers.

Campanella doubled in two runs to give Baltimore a 2–0 lead.

Gibson's homer off Byrd got one run back, and Leonard's single tied it 2–2. Campy dropped a third strike, but it did no damage.

In the fourth, Josh singled in two more runs to take a 4–2 lead, but Campy's homer tied it again.

Baltimore rallied for six runs in the seventh, capped by Roy's two-run double, and won it 10–5. Gibson had gotten a homer and three singles; Campanella topped him with a homer, two doubles, and a single.

The Grays were now down two games to one and had to take the fifth game, in Yankee Stadium, to stay alive. Partlow and Gaines locked in a 0-0 tie after the pesky Wright galloped back to the 467-foot sign to snare Gibson's smash. In the sixth, Wild Bill doubled and Campanella singled to put Baltimore ahead 2–0.

The Grays almost came back in the eighth. With two out Harris, Josh, and Buck all walked to fill the bases, but reliever Bubber Hubert rushed in and got Splo Spearman on a weak tap to the infield to end the threat. The Elites won the game and the pennant 2–0. Gaines had stopped Josh again in two official at bats.

(Did this break the Grays' eventual string of nine straight pennants? It depends on the definition of "pennant." Neither before nor after were the first-place finishers subjected to the extra danger of a play-off upset.)

That autumn, Josh and the Grays went back to Cuba, and this time they swept all six games against the locals, such as Louis Tiant Sr. and Martin Dihigo.

Then he reported to Puerto Rico, where he was named to manage Santurce, which was entering the league for the first time. His battery mate would be his recent protagonist from Baltimore, Byrd. Flashy Dick Seay played second—"he could turn a double play with a frog," the players said.

Josh reported about three weeks late because of the Cuba trip, and he started off slow, both as a manager and a hitter. His club languished near the basement for several weeks, and the best he could manage for himself was one home run.

Satchel also sailed to the Island to pitch for the Guayama team. "You're doing *what?*" Janet demanded.

"They ain't letting us take wives," Satchel fibbed.

For some reason Satchel reported about five weeks late. He pitched for the princely sum of $50 a week, while others were making $15–20, according to Puerto Rican historian Luis Alvelo. Paige's teammates included such stalwart Latin stars as Perucho Cepeda, the defending batting champion, who had hit .365 the winter before; most Puerto Ricans consider Perucho better than his son Orlando. The speedy Dominican, Tetelo Vargas, roamed the outfield; Satch always mentioned Vargas as one of the fastest men he saw, and his name survives in Tetelo Stadium in his native country. Best of all, Satch was pitching to his favorite target, Perkins, again.

Guayama was in third place when Paige arrived, and his first game was against Josh's club, Santurce. He blew them away by a score of 23–0 on only four hits. Poor Gibson got only one single in four tries. As the disaster mounted, the desperate manager moved to third base, first base, and finally even put himself in to pitch to try to stem the hemorrhage.

Three weeks later Satch and Josh met again, and again Paige mastered them, with Byrd in the box, 6–1. Again Gibson was held to a single in four tries.

In February they paired off again, and Paige beat Byrd 3–1 in 12 innings, holding Josh to another single in four at bats.

Finally, in March, Satchel whipped Gibson and Byrd 4–2, and this time Gibson couldn't get anything in four attempts.

In their four face-offs, Satch had held Josh to a .188 average. Paige himself hit .286 in the four games.

In fact, Paige played first base and pinch-hit when he wasn't pitching, and by season's end boasted a .313 average. His teammates on the Monarchs would later laugh at Satchel's boasts of his batting prowess. But the Puerto Rico figures suggest that he might have been a pretty fair hitter after all. Certainly, more research ought to be done on his offensive stats in the States.

When Gibson wasn't facing Paige, he was beginning to feast on the other hurlers down there, including Leon Day and his own Grays teammates, Ray Brown and Roy Partlow. Josh's average started to climb, and a few of his drives started clearing the walls as well. The Puerto Ricans hailed him as "Trucutu," a muscular comic strip character who carried a big club.

Life in Puerto Rico was paradise for the Americans. Alvelo says:

> They played Saturday afternoon and a doubleheader Sunday, and the rest of the week they were off. The people were crazy about them. Every night they had a different party. The rich people would take them home and prepare supper for all of them. During the day they would hang around bars in the plazas. In other words, they had a good time. And they didn't pay for anything, because all of the people loved them.

Week by week Josh slowly brought his average up to .380, only three points behind Cepeda, the leader. His home runs grew slowly to six—one of them a 450-footer—putting Josh one ahead of Cepeda, though he had only half as many RBIs. Still, six was a low total for Josh—it averaged out to about 22 in a 550-AB season. And Puerto Rico parks were generally smaller than those in the States, Alvelo says. "But, remember," he adds, "we had good pitching that year. Besides

Paige, Brown, and Partlow, Leon Day of Newark did well—he had 19 strikeouts in one 11-inning game—and several Puerto Rican pitchers also were effective.

Josh's behavior became erratic. "He went haywire," Seay said. After a game the two would go back to Gibson's house for a "tub of beer" and something to eat, then they'd "hit the hot spots." Seay traced the change in behavior to "those high society girls" Josh met in Washington.

> He never did smoke. But in the bars he'd go into the men's room. Twenty or 30 minutes later he'd start talking simple like, you know? We'd say, "What's wrong with the fellow? I'd go in the men's room, look everywhere, but I never could find what he was doing. I don't think it was liquor, I think it was marijuana—we used to call them reefers at that time.
>
> He used to come to my house in the morning, six o'clock, say, "Come on, let's go to the *picarina*"—a little tavern.
>
> I'd say, "Heh, Josh, it isn't open this time of day." He'd lay on the bed and fall asleep by himself.
>
> One time after he had gone bad, he went down to the main plaza in Puerto Rico. He was taking off all his clothes. They called the police, and they came for him with a wagon. They all knew him. One thing, he was afraid of policemen. They put him in back, and all three policemen rode up front. He ripped the spare tire right off the back of the wagon. Just pulled it off. It sounds unbelievable, but he did it. He was a strong man. Just a big, big kid.

Alvelo heard similar reports of drugs from Puerto Rican old-timers, and nods: "It probably is true."

For the last few weeks of the season, Seay had to don the chest protector and handle the catching himself. Gibson was *hors de combat* for the rest of the campaign.

But Paige was pitching magnificently, according to details furnished by Alvelo. In spite of his late start, Satch surged to a 19–3 record, outdistancing his closest rival, Byrd, who was 15–10, and setting a record for victories that still has never been broken in Puerto Rico. His ERA was 1.93, fourth best in the league. He struck out 208 batters, a league record, though Slim Jones had been credited with 210, presumably in non-league play, there in 1933–34. Satch whiffed 17 in one game and, Alvelo says, pulled his old stunt of calling in his outfield and striking out the next three men. He finished with a flourish, his sixth shutout, putting him just one behind Partlow, the league leader, and pitched Guayama right into the play-offs.

In the championship series, Paige faced Partlow (11–4) of San Juan (managed by Hiram Bithorn, who later pitched for the Cubs) and beat Roy 2–1. The run he gave up was unearned.

A week later, San Juan had a rally going in the sixth. They knocked two pitchers out of the box, had men on first and third, with one out, and Paige leading by only two runs. Satch gave up two hits and a fielder's choice to let three runs score. But then he settled down to pitch shutout ball the rest of the way to win it.

With Cepeda and Perkins both hitting over .500, Guayama went on to win the series four games to nothing.

Naturally they named Paige MVP.

The golden arm was back.

1940

Churchill became prime minister ("All I can offer is blood, toil, tears, and sweat"). The Nazis invaded Denmark, Norway, Holland, Belgium, Luxembourg, France. The British evacuated Dunkirk. The Germans entered Paris. The Battle of Britain ("Never have so many owed so much to so few"). FDR sent 50 lend-lease destroyers to Britain. The draft was passed. The NAACP protested segregated army units. Roosevelt won a third term, over Wendell Willkie. F. Scott Fitzgerald died.

"The Last Time I Saw Paris," "When You Wish Upon a Star," "All or Nothing at All," "You Are My Sunshine," "Beat Me Daddy, Eight to the Bar," "How High the Moon." The Andrews Sisters. Artie Shaw. Frank Sinatra joined Harry James' band.

The Grapes of Wrath, The Great Dictator, Fantasia, The Bank Dick, My Little Chickadee, The Road to Singapore with Hope, Crosby and Lamour. Bugs Bunny.

Radio: "The Quiz Kids," "Truth or Consequences," "Captain Midnight," Gene Autrey's Melody Ranch, "Portia Faces Life."

Broadway: *Cabin in the Sky* with Ethel Waters, Gene Kelly in *Pal Joey.*

Books: *For Whom the Bell Tolls, Darkness at Noon, My Name Is Aram, The Heart Is a Lonely Hunter, Native Son.*

The Reds defeated the Tigers 4–3. Tommy Harmon of Michigan won the Heisman.

This was the year Satch was finally discovered by the white world and was turned into a folk celebrity. Paige was still toiling for the Monarchs "B" team, the Travelers, where two national magazines found him and spread his story before white America.

Time was first. It devoted one whole page to Paige, hailing him as "one of the greatest pitchers of any hue in baseball history." Its story was made up of equal parts of error and dialect quotes.

It claimed that in 1939 his record had been 54–5, though where it got that number from is a mystery.

It said Satch got his nickname from his size 12½ shoes—that's not Paige's version—and had developed his pitching arm as a youth by carrying 200-pound blocks of ice on an ice wagon, a story Satch later left out of his autobiography. "That boy et mo' than the hosses," *Time* quoted his old boss as saying.

Time also pointed out that Westbrook Pegler and Heywood Broun (pronounced Broon), two of the country's most popular columnists, had led a chorus of journalists in protesting the discrimination that kept all the Satchels out of the white majors.

Six weeks later, *The Saturday Evening Post,* one of the nation's three leading weeklies, along with *Time* and *Life,* jumped on the bandwagon with a four-page feature called "The Chocolate Rube Waddell," after George "Rube" Waddell, another eccentric speedball hurler, who, 40 years earlier had, like Satchel, called in his outfield and struck out the side.

The piece, by Ted Shane, was filled with even more misinformation and stereotyped dialogue, neither of which would get past a self-respecting editor today.

It quoted one Negro fan as saying Satchel played in a league by himself: "He do jes' like he please, and nobody can do nuffin'." One "licorice-colored" opponent complained of Paige's pitching style: "You cain't see nothin' but dat foot."·

Satchel himself was quoted in his "Stepinfetchit accent" as saying, "Ah hit a dawg" with his car.

It said Oscar Charleston "tore his kinky hair" while explaining his strategy: "We plays for home run bunts."

Shane reported that Paige was still under contract to Newark— which came as a great surprise to both Wilkinson and Abe Manley in Newark. He said Satch played his first Negro league game for New Orleans in 1929 and was paid a fish fry supper for every victory.

He added that Josh (Rupert) Gibson (sic) had hit a ball over Yankee Stadium's center field bleachers.

In Mexico, Shane said, the players were paid in "Mex dollars unless the player is wary, which Negroes usually are not."

Prose like that would get Al Campanis and Jimmy the Greek kicked off their jobs in the 1980s. But in 1940—which is when Al's and Jimmy's youthful attitudes were formed—such language reflected the white view of the black world. No one thought of it as racist, a word that hadn't even been invented yet.

No matter how the article may look to us from the vantage point of a half century later, it was received as a positive development at the time. It elevated Paige onto the pedestal beside heavyweight champ Joe Louis and Olympic star Jesse Owens. Ric Roberts said:

> For the first time, a white magazine had burned incense at the foot of a black man outside the prize ring.
> It changed Paige into a celebrity. He immediately developed into a matinee idol among Negroes in this country. *The Saturday Evening Post* made him ten times more famous than the black press had. He cashed in on it by becoming a one-man barnstormer. He brought people back to the ball game. He got blacks in the habit of going to ball games and spending their money. It caught the eyes of Branch Rickey, who was a money changer from way back.

Satch claimed that he won "about 40 games" for the B team, though it is more likely that he meant he played in 40 winning games, going three innings to draw a crowd and then coming out.

Seventeen-year-old Connie Johnson, who would later pitch for the Monarchs, White Sox, and Orioles, watched Paige pitch a night game against the Ethiopian Clowns. The Clowns usually played "shadow ball" about the fourth or fifth inning, making beautiful leaping catches and throws without any ball at all.

In the first inning, Connie couldn't see Satch's pitch at all. He rubbed his eyes. "They're not supposed to play shadow ball until the fourth inning," he said to himself. The catcher threw the ball back, but Johnson assumed it was one he had hidden in his glove. He moved to the grandstand railing to get a closer look. Sure enough, Satchel was throwing a real ball, but it had been almost invisible from the stands.

In September, Paige played at least two games with the parent club against semipro teams. He beat Chicago's Palmer House 2–1 and the Detroit Atles Lagers, billed as the world amateur champs, on a no-hitter. It would have been a perfect game except for an error.

But, as far as is known, Paige pitched only two games for the parent team, winning one shutout and getting bombed for nine runs in the other. But he struck out 15 in the two contests and didn't walk a man.

The Monarch aces that year were Jack Matchett (6–0), Frank Bradley (6–1), and Hilton Smith (6–3). The threesome led the Monarchs to the pennant for the third straight year.

Meanwhile, Gibson was down in Mexico and missed the bright

spotlight that had been turned on Paige, though he was making good money. He had wintered in Puerto Rico with Hattie, an older woman he had been living with for several years. Then they went down to Venezuela for the spring season at $700 a month, plus a $1,000 bonus and per diem, much more than he could have made in the States. Reportedly he batted .419.

Mexican millionaire Jorge Pasquel offered Gibson $6,000 for the summer, and he snapped that up too. A number of other Negro stars—Bell, Byrd, Bill Wright, Dandridge, Wells, Brewer, Day, etc.— also followed the lure of pesos.

It wasn't only money, one of the jumpers, Johnny Taylor, said. "Playing in the Negro leagues, you were going in the back door. But in Mexico they treated you royally. No segregation." The American blacks were national heroes in Mexico, besieged by autograph hounds, their photos on the front pages of the papers. "It did a lot for the black ballplayers."

The crowds were big and the fans red-hot, Taylor wrote home. They played only three or four games a week. Sunday games were in the morning so as not to compete with the bullfights. Tampico boasted air-conditioned box seats, and travel was by train, not bus.

Gibson's club played in Vera Cruz on the east coast. But in higher elevations, such as Mexico City, pitchers couldn't get a break on their curve or a hop on their fastball, and batted balls flew farther in the thin air. Josh made some of those balls disappear like golf balls. Bell relates with a smile:

> We played in some parks that had no fences at all. Gibson hit them so far that if he had just kept running, there's no telling how many homers he'd have gotten before they found the ball.

In all, he hit 11 homers in 22 games (equal to 66 in 550 at bats), knocked in 38 runs, and batted .467. Yet he didn't lead the league in homers. The leader was, of all people, Bell, who was tops in just about everything—except stolen bases!

Meanwhile, in the East the Grays didn't seem to miss Josh. Leonard hit .383 to lead the league at bat. Josh's replacement, Rab Roy Gaston, hit .320, though he hit no home runs.

However, Gaston did handle a remarkable pitching performance by Ray Brown—24 wins and only four losses, breaking all records for victories in a single season. And, like Slim Jones, Brown did it in the shortened 50-game schedule, compared to the 1920s seasons which were almost twice as long, when most other 20-game winners had played. Historian Jim Riley says one of Brown's defeats was in an "exhibition" game against another league team that didn't count in the league standings. (I, however, count these the same as league games.) He was shellacked for 19 hits, as manager Vic Harris left him in.

The Grays finished first again, for the fourth time in a row.

The Monarchs declined a World Series challenge.

1941

Germany invaded Russia, advanced in Africa, Yugoslavia, and Greece. Roosevelt and Churchill issued the Atlantic Charter ("the Four Freedoms"). Pearl Harbor was bombed ("a day that will live in infamy"). The Philippines were invaded. Singapore, Hong Kong, Wake Island, and Guam fell. The Manhattan Project began work on an atomic bomb. James Joyce died.

"I'll Remember April," "Deep in the Heart of Texas," "The Jersey Bounce," "Waltzing Matilda," "The Anniversary Waltz," "Green Eyes," "You Made Me Love You," "Racing With the Moon," "By the Light of the Silvery Moon," "Dancing in the Dark," "This Love of Mine," "Chattanooga Choo Choo."

Citizen Kane, The Maltese Falcon, Sergeant York, Alfred Hitchcock's *Suspicion, Dumbo, Meet John Doe.*

Broadway: *Blithe Spirit, Arsenic and Old Lace.*

Books: *What Makes Sammy Run?, Berlin Diary.*

Kilroy, Sad Sack.

Williams hit .406 and won the All-Star game with a homer. DiMaggio was credited with hitting in 56 straight games. MVP Hank Greenberg traded a $40,000 salary for $52 a month as an Army buck private. Stan Musial debuted. The Yanks beat the Dodgers 4–1, as Mickey Owen dropped a third strike. Billy Conn almost upset Joe Louis. Sugar Ray Robinson. Whirlaway won the Triple Crown.

Paige finally got promoted to the parent Monarchs and really became a celebrity, as *Life,* the nation's number-one magazine, ran a three-page picture spread on him. Pitching on loan for the New York Black Yankees, Satch mugged with Mayor LaGuardia at Yankee Stadium, beamed at his new "wife," Lucy Figueroa of Puerto Rico ("just good friends," Satch insisted later), got trimmed, manicured and shined at a barbershop, shot some pool, played a riff on the piano, enjoyed the adulation of a mob of kids in Harlem, posed with a cigarette and a bright red auto in a suit, fedora, and narrow, two-toned shoes, and showed off his pitching form with his foot held high for the photographer.

It wasn't just Paige's pitching that attracted attention, of course. He was one of the great clowns of his time.

Satch protested that it was the photographers who made him look like a clown. "They figured I ought to look funny in pictures, and they did everything to make me look that way." But it wasn't entirely the photographer's fault.

"He was the most comical man you ever saw in your life," said his catcher, Othello Renfroe.

> When we were warming up, he'd take infield practice at third. Just *throw* it over the diamond, man, *flip* it to second. Oh, what an attraction, what a colorful man!

Paige liked to work out at third to loosen up instead of running. He wanted the fungo hitter to top rollers to him so he could run in and fire to first on the run. "He had more fun than the fans did," Monarch first baseman Buck O'Neil said. "The people would come to see us take infield practice. We'd go months without anyone juggling the ball. We'd put on a show."

"All the ballplayers were crazy about him," Newt Allen said:

> Remember the comedian Stepinfetchit? Satchel sounded and talked just like him. And he could sing and dance. Oh, he had a wonderful voice for singing. He was a solid comedian, another Bob Hope. He could think of more funny things to say and keep you laughing all the time. He was really a showman. He was a kidder, he could really rib a fellow. He used to make some of those ballplayers so mad that they'd want to shoot him. And if he knew he was getting under your skin, he'd really have your skin rolling up.

Buck Leonard remembered an exhibition game in Monessen with Satchel playing right field:

> Just messing around. Somebody hit a high fly in right field, and we rushed around and looked in the outfield for Satchel to be standing under it. Satchel was standing on the sideline getting a light on a cigarette from a fellow—getting a smoke! Wasn't even in right field!

The fans loved it. Ric Roberts grabbed pen and ink and reproduced the *Life* pitching pose with a list of attendance figures for Satchel's games: St. Louis 22,000, Washington 28,000, New York 29,000, Cleveland 29,000, Detroit 35,000.

Satchel reportedly began getting 15 percent, or even more, of the gate. His annual pay may have reached $40,000 at a time when DiMaggio and Feller were getting $35,000, Williams half that, and the average Negro leaguer about $1,000 a year.

Satch, of course, basked in the fame.

The folks in Kansas City treated me like a king, and you never saw a king of the walk if you didn't see Ol' Satch around 18th and Vine in those days, rubbernecking all the girls walking by.

Not all the Monarchs were happy about Paige's celebrity. The veteran pitcher, Chet Brewer, was one who wasn't.

They always starred Satchel, he had all the billing. Several nights when Satchel would pitch, I'd follow him, or Connie Johnson. All of us were tall and black, and the fans would say, "Which one of those niggers was Satchel? They were all throwing hard." They didn't know Satchel from the rest of us.

It was awful the way the white people talked about us. We'd ignore their insults and just beat the pants off them.

But the other players weren't jealous—after all, the more money Satch made, the more they made. Newt Allen said all the Monarchs got generous tips, up to $100 a game if the crowds were big.

"Satchel was the franchise," said Buck O'Neil—"Satchel was a *lot* of franchises."

"He kept our league going," said Renfroe. "Any time a team got in trouble, it sent for Satchel to pitch. So you're talking about your bread and butter when you talk about Satchel."

"He was a baseball player's man," O'Neil said:

When we played exhibition games, Satchel was supposed to get 25 percent off the top himself. But he never would take it. He'd only take a regular player's share. In regular games, of course, he had a separate contract, it wasn't like our contracts. He wouldn't let up on that. But in exhibitions after the season, he would do it.

From Double Duty Radcliffe:

Satchel wasn't hard to get along with. We never had trouble with him about money. Once he signed a contract, he didn't care how much money you made, what you did, just so he got his. He would do some ornery things, like go off and go fishing, wouldn't show up, you couldn't find him when you needed him. But when he came in there, you could count the game, 'cause he was going to win it.

Ted Page told us:

Now if we got in our bus, go some place to play ball, Satchel was the same as any of the rest of the boys, as us, his teammates. But he was always a little bit distant, or maybe arrogant, with a reporter, photographer, or something like that. Satchel wasn't the same kind of guy as Josh was. Josh would talk—Charleston would talk with writers or sign autographs. Satchel would be a little bit hesitant about this.

Ironically, Satchel's success might have slowed down integration. The Yankees made money renting four stadiums to black teams—in New York, Newark, Kansas City, and Norfolk. The Giants rented out the Polo Grounds. The Senators reportedly made $100,000 a year in rent from the Grays.

Paige had lost one-third of his former speed, Bell said, "but he could still pitch as fast as those other guys."

Satchel also enjoyed unveiling his new secret weapon, a slow curve. It tickled him to throw it on the 3–2. He wrote: "I got about 17 strikeouts on men waiting in that 3–2 spot for the fast one and then getting a slow curve."

Pee Wee Butts got his first look at Satch that year, took a called third strike, and trudged back to the bench muttering. "I thought you said Paige didn't have no curveball," he told the fellows on the bench.

"He don't," they answered.

"Well," Butts said, "if I'm not mistaken, he threw one to me on that last strike."

After the game Paige sidled up to the youngster. "They told you I didn't have a curveball, didn't they? Yeah, I was just saving it up for all you young ones who come up there and think I don't have a curve."

Newark utility man Clarence "Pint" Israel had a similar tale:

My coach told me, "You can't hit his fastball, because you can't see it, so take the first two fastballs, then he'll throw a curve, and he doesn't have a good one."

First pitch was a fastball, and I saw it good. But he gave me the same signal: Take. Next one, and I saw it good, was another strike. I got set for another fastball—I knew he didn't have a curveball. It was coming straight for my shoulders, so naturally I bailed out [ducked]. Looked up and heard the umpire say, "Strike!" In Yankee Stadium you had to walk a long way to the bench. I wanted to run!

Bell, who originally came up as a knuckleball pitcher, undertook to teach Satch that pitch as well. Pretty soon Paige was throwing it better than Bell, and, Cool Papa said, "The people all said, 'See how Satchel's teaching Bell the knuckleball!'"

Satch kept his teammates loose off the field as well as on it. O'Neil, one of his closest pals, was nicknamed Nancy. He earned it one night in a small town on the prairie when Satchel succeeded in smuggling two women, one black and one Indian, into adjoining rooms at the hotel. Tiptoeing out of one room, he rapped softly on the second door, whispering, "Nancy? Nancy?"

Just then the first door flew open, and an angry female demanded to know who Nancy was.

Hearing the ruckus, O'Neil opened a third door, sized the situation up, and said, "Yeah, Satch, what you want?"

From then on he was known as Nancy.

Like Babe Ruth (and Wade Boggs), Paige's off-field exploits were Rabelaisian. At the hotel after a game, Ric Roberts said, "the girls were lined up waiting their turn."

"I ain't married," Paige once grinned, "but I'm in great demand." "You're going to dig your grave with that tool," Senators owner Clark Griffith warned Paige. Roberts feels Satch might have done even better than he did in the American league if he had acted "less sophomoric."

Satchel was always late getting to games, or he wouldn't show up at all. So Wilkinson assigned Chet Brewer to ride with him.

Once, Chet remembered, they were in Three Rivers, Michigan, 200 miles from Chicago, with a game scheduled to start there in two hours. Satchel was pitching pennies with some girls, while Brewer tugged at him. "Oh, Dooflackem, you worry too much," Satch shushed him. They finally climbed into Satchel's Chrysler. He said, "If the red lights are going to make us late, I won't stop at any more." They covered the 200 miles with Paige leaning on the horn and Brewer covering his eyes. Satch finally skidded to a halt two blocks past the park, and they pushed past angry patrons on their way out demanding their money back.

In Philadelphia, Satchel turned his white Lincoln into a one-way street, dodging back and forth among oncoming cars, while Brewer screamed at him to stop. A cop finally did stop him. "But officer," Satch said innocently, "I was only going one way."

Another cop once stopped Paige and demanded, "Were you speeding?"

"No," Satchel replied honestly. "But I was fixin' to."

When a judge fined him $50, he peeled off ten ten-dollar bills and said, "Here, I'm coming back tomorrow."

In California, Brewer said, Satchel made U-turns through pedestrian safety islands and once led the cops a chase from Bakersfield to San Francisco. They finally caught up with him in Oakland. "I just wanted to see how fast I could go before you caught me," he told them cheerfully. Unamused, the judge lifted his California license.

The Kansas City cops considered giving him wholesale rates on tickets, Paige wrote.

At last Brewer begged Wilkinson, "Now instead of one pitcher being late, you got two late. I don't want to ride with Satchel any more. He's going to get *both* of us killed."

Renfroe, later an Atlanta sportscaster, recalled another night, in Washington. The stadium was packed to see Satchel—but no Satchel. He had been stopped for speeding, explained who he was and that he was late for a game. The obliging policeman turned his motorcycle around, turned on the siren, and escorted Satch to the park, where Wilkinson was nervously biting his nails at the prospect of refunding all those tickets.

There was one other Monarch who wasn't happy with Paige's success. That was Hilton Smith, who had been the ace of the staff until Paige came along. After that, Smith and Paige would become perhaps the best nine-inning hurler in baseball, a hyphenated entity known as Paige-Smith. Satchel started the game to draw a crowd, and Hilton trudged in to finish it.

Which was better? "Migod, you couldn't tell the difference!" exclaimed Roy Campanella.

"You better get your runs early," warned Gene Benson of the Philly Stars, " 'cause you ain't gonna get any runs after Smith came in." Paige still relied on his fastball, but Smith had both a hopping fastball and a crackling curve. Hitters could wait on Satch's fastball, but they couldn't guess with Hilton on the mound.

Quincy Trouppe compared Smith to Sal Maglie, but with a better fastball. Smitty had four pitches—a sinking fastfall, curve, slider, and change—and two motions—sidearm and overhand. "Hilton, in my estimation, had the most ability of any pitcher of my time."

Unfortunately, Smith had none of Paige's droll humor and quotable color. He never said, "Don't look back; someone may be gaining on you." If he had, it's just possible that he would be in Cooperstown today. Smith lamented:

I played 12 years with the Monarchs, 1937–48, but most people never heard of me. They've only heard of Satchel Paige. He'd go two or three innings. If there was a big crowd, and we had to win it, I'd go in there and save it. Then the next day I'd look in the paper, and the headline would say:

SATCH AND MONARCHS WIN AGAIN.

I just took my baseball serious, I just went out there to do a job. But Satchel was an attraction. He could produce, and he'd clown a lot. I guess it really hurt me. I tried to get away, but there wasn't anything I could do about it.

Now Satchel never did pitch much here in Kansas City. Oh no, he never did a lot of pitching here. But ooh, when he left here, my goodness, they'd eat him up all those other places, because he was an attraction.

Satchel was a great pitcher, I don't take anything away from him. I'd like to have seen him in his early age, back in '29 and the early '30s. Good God, he could throw that ball! And perfect control.

In '41 Satchel got his arm back, and that was the worst break I got. I actually hit my peak, too, in '41. I was to the place then that I could just do anything, I felt that good. I thought I could go out there and get *anybody* out. I won 25 games and lost one that year. A semipro team in Dayton, Ohio, beat me 1–0 after I had relieved Satchel. We struck out 18 between us. They got one hit off Satchel and one off me but beat me on an error. It was the only game I lost that year.

[That October] I pitched one game against Bob Feller's All-Stars. Walker Cooper was catching. Stan Musial [.426 in 12 games] and Johnny Hopp [.303] in the outfield. They hit Satchel pretty hard in the first four innings, and I came in and relieved in the fifth. I held them, struck out six of them, didn't give but one hit, but they beat us 4–3. Feller [25–13 with a fourth-place team] pitched three innings. Kenny Heintzelman [11–11 with the fourth-place Pirates] pitched the last six. He really broke off some jugs that day, because I doubled with nobody out and didn't score. It would have been the tying run.

Sports editor Bob Burnes of the St. Louis *Globe-Democrat* covered the game and agreed. "Smith showed the best speed and the sharpest curve of the quartet," he reported.

Paige's known record in league games for the year: 5–1, with a low 2.21 TRA. Smith topped him with a league-leading 7–0, 2.01, and two saves. Frank Bradley was 6–1, and rookie Connie Johnson 2–2.

At any rate, with Willard Brown hitting .337, and leading in just about everything, the Monarchs won again. (The league leader was Birmingham's Lyman Bostock Sr., with .412. In 1981 his son would be shot to death accidentally while playing for the Minnesota Twins.)

Gibson, meanwhile, spent the summer in Mexico again. Posey had signed him for $500 a month for four months, "the largest salary ever given to a colored ballplayer," but at the last minute Mexico's Jorge Pasquel came in with an even better offer—$800 a month for eight months. Josh took it, leaving Posey to fume and sue him.

Josh—or "Yosh Hibson" as the Latins called him—joined Pasquel's team, Vera Cruz, with Willie Wells and Ray Dandridge of Newark, first baseman-pitcher Lazaro Salazar of the Cubans, plus pitchers Ray Brown, Johnny Taylor, and Ramon Bragana. The Mexicans consider it the greatest team in their history, sort of the 1927 Yankees of Mexico. But when Gibson rapped out a triple, double, and two singles in a game, Pasquel scolded him: "I got Wells and Dandridge for doubles and singles; I got you for home runs."

So home runs is what Pasquel got. Josh was the first man to drive one over the fence at Chihuahua, Taylor said. Gibson did it three times in one game, the second time that he had hit three in one game in Mexico. In all, he had 33 homers in 94 games, plus 124 RBIs and a .374 average. He even led in triples, three times. Those RBIs equaled 213 in a 162-game schedule!

Mexico, incidentally, gives us a rare chance to examine Gibson's strikeouts and walks. Amazingly, he got few walks, and fewer strike-outs, much like Joe DiMaggio. Here is his two-year record in Mexico:

	AB	SO	BB	HR
1940	92	6	16	11
1941	358	25	75	33

Gibson is one of a handful of hitters—Williams, DiMaggio, and Musial are among the others—to record more homers than strikeouts.

Cool Papa Bell, Sammy Bankhead, Bill Wright, and others also jumped to Mexico, decimating the black teams at home. In the States, Leonard took over Gibson's home run crown with eight. He also led in batting with 380, and the Grays won again, their fifth straight flag.

That winter Josh headed to Puerto Rico. His buddy Dick Seay recalled:

Did I tell you about him lifting an ox cart? That's right. We got to this one little town, all the cars were stopping. We wanted to know what happened. They said, "One of the cart's wheels went into the ditch."

Gibby was sleeping when they told him. He said, "Man, them little bitty carts up there?" He went up there, put his arm under that damn big wheel, set that damn thing back on that road. He was strong—powerful.

With Stearnes retired and Suttles at the end of his career, Gibson had only one rival left as the premier black slugger in the land— Willard "Home Run" Brown of the Monarchs. When I met Brown in 1972, he was working as a furniture refinisher in Houston, and his arms were still as thick as two mahogany tree trunks. Reggie Jackson had similar biceps. About three years younger than Josh, Willard was also hurt by a large park in Kansas City, where the left field wall was 350-some feet away. That summer, in addition to leading the league in batting, Brown had topped the western league in homers for the third time (data are sketchy for 1939 and '40, or he might have led two more times). Brown would lead at least seven times in all.

Even Gibson's teammate, Grays pitcher Wilmer Fields, was eloquent about Brown's devastating power. "Brown hit some shots off me," he winced. "You generally remember the ones who hurt you. Brown could hit them to left field, he could hit them to center field, he could hit them to right field." If Fields had a vote, Brown would join Gibson in the Hall of Fame.

A swift center fielder, Brown even led the league in stolen bases twice. "This guy could jet when he wanted to run." Quincy Trouppe wrote:

Brown is the one who challenged the feats of Josh Gibson. He could hit the ball out of the park, but he swung at a lot of bad pitches. Who knows? Brown might have been as great, or greater, than Gibson if he had been a little more patient and waited for strikes. He could hit a bad ball but frequently went at pitches he couldn't hit with a ten-foot pole.

Most of the Monarchs, such as Newt Allen, insisted that Willard was a better player than Jackie Robinson. "He could outhit and outrun anybody in our league," Renfroe said. "But he'd only play hard on Sunday; he'd loaf the rest of the time."

That may have been the reason Brown didn't stick in the American league, in 1947; but he went on to establish home run records in the white Texas league and especially in Puerto Rico, where fans adored him and hailed him simply as *Ese hombre,* "That man."

In the winter of '41, Gibson and Brown met head-to-head for the first time. On January 12, Willard was leading the league with .441; Josh trailed in ninth place with .355.

"Heh, Trouppe," Gibson said, "I'm not going to try to hit any home runs, I'm just going to try to bat .500." A week later Gibson had moved into third place with .412 to Brown's .456. By February 9, Josh had shot into first place, .460 vs. .402 for Brown.

"You know what he ended up batting?" Trouppe demanded. "Four-seventy-nine! He was hitting screamers through the infield there." Josh's record still stands, having withstood the challenges of such great latter-day hitters as Willie Mays, Roberto Clemente, Tony Oliva, and Orlando Cepeda. (Some other batting averages that winter: Irvin .297, Campanella .295, Dandridge .288.)

And Gibson still ended up with 13 homers, also tops in the league—Brown hit four. Josh batted in 41 runs in 31 games. Naturally they named him MVP.

How did Gibson hit against Satchel Paige? a radio reporter asked. Josh answered that he could hit Satchel the same as any other pitcher, a bit of hubris that would come back to haunt him.

1942

Manila, Singapore, and Rangoon fell. MacArthur retreated to Bataan, then Australia, vowing, "I shall return." Jimmy Doolittle bombed Tokyo. The battles of Stalingrad, Guadalcanal, Midway, El Alamein. Rationing. Blacks complained of discrimination in the Navy.

"Praise the Lord and Pass the Ammunition," "Onward Christian Soldiers," Beethoven's Fifth, "White Christmas," "Serenade in Blue," "That Old Black Magic," "Don't Get Around Much Any More," "Don't Sit Under the Apple Tree," "Sleepy Lagoon," "Strip Polka," "I've Got a Gal in Kalamazoo," "Paper Doll," "As Time Goes By."

Mrs. Miniver, Casablanca, Pride of the Yankees.

Radio: "People Are Funny."

Joe Louis was drafted. Feller enlisted. Williams won the triple crown. The Cards beat the Yanks 4–1.

The season opened prophetically with the White Sox giving a tryout to a UCLA football star named Jackie Robinson, along with pitcher Nate Moreland of the Elite Giants. Robinson reported with a charley horse. Marveled manager Jimmie Dykes: "I'd hate to see him on two *good* legs! . . . He stole everything but my infielders' gloves." Jackie was worth $50,000 of "anybody's money." Apparently not the White Sox' money, however, and Dykes wistfully watched him go. "Personally," he shrugged, "I'd welcome them [blacks], and I believe every one of the major league managers would do likewise." The White Sox, with Joe Kuhel (.249), Don Kolloway (.273), Luke Appling (.262), and Bob Kennedy (.231) in their infield, finished sixth.

The publicity lavished on Satch the previous two years, plus the booming wartime prosperity, combined to give the black leagues their first two-million dollar gross. Paige complained that he had to find new ways to spend his money, like antique collecting. He bought Wedgwood, Royal Vienna, and Sèvres French china and Chippendale and Queen Anne dining room suites. Mrs. Wilkinson, wife of his owner, was a shrewd antiquer, and the pitcher's home was liberally furnished with some of her finds.

At 38, Paige found a new romance, a drugstore clerk named Lahoma, who swept him off his feet.

Josh Gibson, 30 years old and 4-F in the draft because of bad legs, also had a new girl friend—Grace, the wife of a Washington gambler with a reputation for violence. Luckily, he was safely away in the service. Coincidentally, teammates caught Josh sneaking drinks in the clubhouse more and more.

The new love interest may have been one reason Gibson decided not to return to Mexico. A delegation of Mexican owners traveled to the States to lure him back, and Posey replied by taking a swing at the Mexicans' snoots. Subdued, they left without Josh.

In May, Paige faced his old buddy, the now retired Dean, who led a team of servicemen, including Washington favorite Cecil Travis, who had topped Joe DiMaggio the year before with .359. Satchel and Hilton Smith combined to win it 3–1, giving only two infield hits, before 31,000 fans in Chicago. Meanwhile across town, the White Sox and Browns drew only 19,000 to their doubleheader. (How many more would they have drawn with Robinson in the Sox lineup?) Some papers once more demanded to know why Paige and other blacks couldn't play in the white leagues.

Declared Dean: "I've pitched 31 games against that Satchel Paige. . . . If that guy pitched in the majors, he'd be worth a million dollars."

Again the *Daily Worker* was leading the agitation for equal opportunity in baseball, with an open letter to Commissioner Kenesaw Mountain Landis. The paper quoted Leo Durocher, manager of the defending champion Dodgers, as saying, "I'll play the colored boys on my team if the big shots give the OK. Hell, I've seen a million good ones." Only a "subterranean" rule was keeping them out, Leo said.

Commissioner Landis called Leo in, then told the press Durocher had denied making the statement. Then Landis added what he thought was a *pro forma* disclaimer:

There is no rule, formal or informal, no understanding, subterranean or otherwise, against hiring Negro players.

The black press seized on it. LANDIS CLEARS WAY FOR OWNERS TO HIRE COLORED the Washington *Afro-American* banner proclaimed. WAS THE JUDGE JIVING? the Pittsburgh *Courier* asked and apparently decided he wasn't:

NEGROES WILL SOON PLAY IN THE BIG LEAGUES,
ACCORDING TO THE OWNER OF THE CHICAGO CUBS
Wrigley Thinks Public
Must First Support Move

The *Courier* rushed to interview the legion of white stars who had played against blacks.

"I've seen any number of Negro players who should be in the major leagues," the Pirates' Hall of Fame coach, Honus Wagner, said.

Another Pirate immortal, Paul Waner, said he'd played against "countless" Negroes who were good enough for the majors.

"Satchel Paige threw me the fastest ball I've ever seen in my life," Dodger first baseman Dolph Camilli said.

If Negroes were allowed in, "there'd be a mad scramble" for them, Cubs manager Gabby Hartnett said.

The *Afro* reported that for three weeks, owner Jerry Nugent of the last-place Phillies had been scouting home town boy Roy Campanella, who rushed to Shibe Park to practice every off-day. He could presumably replace Phils first-string catcher Benny Warren (.209) or his backup, Mickey Livingston (.205). Roy reportedly also planned to try out with the Athletics, whose catcher, Hal Wagner, was hitting .236 with one home run.

"I've played against many white big leaguers," Campy said. "I'm sure I'd do OK if given the chance. I've played against many southern whites" and never had any trouble. "All we ask is an opportunity."

Next, *Daily Worker* sports editor Nat Lowe sent wires to three players—Campanella, Elite second baseman Sammy T. Hughes, and pitcher Dave Barnhill of the Cubans—saying he had arranged a tryout for them with the Pirates. Their competition: 35-year-old catcher Al Lopez (.256, one home run), second baseman Frank Gustine (.229, two), and a pitching staff with only one winning pitcher, Rip Sewell.

Pirate owner Bill Benswanger reportedly met in a top secret confab behind locked doors with the editors of the *Courier,* who informed him that the entire Homestead Grays team, including Gibson, Leonard, and Brown, was available either collectively or individually! There was only one key man missing from the meeting—Cum Posey, who owned the Grays and had nursed them through the long Depression with his own life savings. No one thought to consult him about the generous gesture of giving his lifetime investment away.

Benswanger listened carefully. Then he announced:

> We will give any man, white or colored, a chance when asked. . . .
> Colored players are American citizens with American rights. I know
> there still are many problems of traveling and playing to be ironed out,
> but after all, somebody has to make the first move.

The idea has "interesting facets," Benswanger said, "and it is a
daring innovation," but first he wanted to consult manager Frankie
Frisch.

The Cleveland Indians also talked of giving tryouts to three
members of the Cleveland Buckeyes.

Everybody was ducking. Benswanger said it was up to manager
Frankie Frisch. Frisch said it was up to Benswanger. Phillies manager
Hans Lobert said it was up to owner JerryNugent. Nugent said it was
up to Lobert: "I'm just the president." Cleveland manager Lou
Boudreau said it was up to owner Alva Bradley. Bradley had no
comment.

Dr. J. B. Martin, owner of the Negro American (or western)
league, gave his blessing to the idea and listed a long litany of qualified
blacks, beginning with pitcher Verdell Mathis of Memphis.

What did the black players themselves think about the news
reports?

"A lot of bunk," scoffed Grays manager Vic Harris.

"A bunch of hot air"—Grays outfielder Jerry Benjamin.

But Gibson couldn't believe the owners weren't sincere. "Aw," he
said, "I don't think they'd kid about a serious thing like that."

Paige sneered that "they couldn't pay me enough to play in the
majors." He was probably right; with Tiger MVP Hank Greenberg in
the Air Corps, Satchel was probably the highest paid player in America.

Satch found himself in the middle of the controversy when he
was quoted as saying he was against integration. In the middle of the
East–West game, he left the bull pen to climb to the announcers'
booth and make an extraordinary statement to the fans.

"Ladies and gentlemen," he began:

> I want you to know that I did not say anything against the use of
> Negro players in the big leagues. A reporter came and asked me what I
> thought about Negroes playing on major league teams. I told him I
> thought it was all right.
> He said, "Satchel, do you think the white players would play with the
> colored?"
> I told him I thought they would, but that if they wouldn't, it might be
> a good idea to put a complete Negro team in the majors.

White columnists took up the campaign. Bill Cunningham of the Boston *Herald* shrugged off his Texas background and wrote, "Let's give them a chance—let 'em up here and let's see if they can hit."

Hy Turkin of the New York *Daily News* conceded that hotels and trains would present problems. "But these are insignificant in face of the larger and more vital issues of 'equal opportunity.'"

Later, Shirley Povich of the Washington *Post,* columnist Bob Considine, and sports editor John Kieran of the New York *Times* added their support—though Kieran's *Times* continued to close its news columns to black teams.

Some white columnists ducked the issue. When Ric Roberts wrote to Grantland Rice for a statement, his secretary said Mr. Rice was on his way to Los Angeles to a football game. She promised to bring the letter to his attention, but she must have forgotten; Grantland never replied.

Others were downright hostile. Baseball's "bible," *The Sporting News,* editorialized that

> There's no law against Negroes playing with white teams, nor white with colored teams, but . . . the leaders of both groups know their crowd psychology and do not care to run the risk of damaging their own game.

Joe Louis and Jesse Owens were "different," the paper said. Suppose a white fan booed a Negro for striking out?

> Clear-minded men of tolerance of both races have realized the tragic possibilities and have stayed clear of such complications, because they realize it is for the benefit of each and also for the game.

Washington Senators owner Clark Griffith suggested that, instead of joining the white leagues, blacks should put together their best team and challenge the white champions, an idea advocated 20 years earlier by black pioneer Rube Foster. The *Daily Worker* went to the Grays players with a petition aimed at Griffith: "At a time when we are engaged in a great war for democracy and freedom, it is necessary that we fight for such democracy on the home front as well as on foreign battlefields."

Buck Leonard recalled:

> There were some people used to come around in New York, especially from the *Daily Worker* and other papers: "Don't you think

Negroes should be playing in the majors? Don't you think Negroes should be doing this or that?"

We said, "We're going to leave that to you all to discuss, we're going to play ball."

They used to say, "We're going to arrange for you to get a tryout."

We said, "All right, arrange it. We'll try out any time you arrange it."

They said, "Wouldn't you agree to sign this paper?"

"We're not signing anything, we're not making a statement. Any writing you want done, go ahead and do it. We're out here to play ball, we're not out here to demonstrate or anything like that." You know, they wanted us to put on some kind of exhibition, demonstrate, but we just wanted to play ball.

Griffith called Gibson and Leonard into his office. As Buck told the story:

He said, "You all played a good ball game today. You fellows got good size on you and you looked like you were playing to win. Sam Lacey and Ric Roberts [of the *Afro*] and a lot of other fellows have been talking about getting you fellows on the Senators team." He said, "Well, let me tell you something: If we get you boys, we're going to get the best ones. It's going to break up your league. Now what do you think about that?"

We said, "Well, we'd be happy to play in the major leagues and believe that we could make the major leagues."

They never heard from him again.

In a column at the time, Roberts wrote that "the older school of baseball men, Clark Griffith, Connie Mack, etc., declare it to be a communistic plot to overthrow baseball"—maybe even the government.

But in later years, Roberts thought Griff, always strapped for money, was thinking of the rent he took in from the Grays. The team would draw 102,000 fans in ten games there that year, a rent of $100,000. "He wouldn't think of taking black ballplayers from the Grays," Roberts said. "I don't call that prejudice. He just had a yen for making money."

If not prejudiced, Griffith was shortsighted. If Josh, Buck, and the others had bolstered his sagging Senators, Griffith might have fielded a pennant contender and made much more money at the turnstile than he got in rent from the Grays. Since its last pennant in '32, Washington had become the butt of jokes ("first in war, first in peace, and last in the American league").

Actually, in '42 they had the core of a good team—outfielders George Case and Stan Spence were .300-hitters, and Mickey Vernon was a coming star at first base. Cecil Travis was a great hitting short-stop and would be back after the war. Meantime, they were weak at shortstop (Sammy Bankhead?) and pitching (Brown?), while catcher Jake Early batted only .204 (Gibson!). If Griffith had added these men and traded Leonard for another pitcher, the Senators might have forged a dynasty to challenge the Yankees—they might still be in Washington today.

Connie Mack had another explanation for baseball's timidity. When Judy Johnson asked him why blacks couldn't play in the white majors, Mack replied, "To tell you the truth, Judy, there are just too many of you."

Paul Robeson, the singer-actor-athlete, made an appeal to Landis and the owners to "have a heart." It was met with silence.

Brooklyn owner Larry MacPhail snorted that the whole thing, beginning with Landis' statement, was "100 percent hypocrisy." No colored players will play with the Dodgers, he vowed. The campaign is being pushed by "groups of political and social-minded drum beat-ers." All this Jim Crow propaganda is just "talking through their hats." A major league player must have something besides natural ability, MacPhail said. He must also have a competitive attitude and discipline acquired "only after years of training in the smaller leagues." Mac-Phail favored a limited number of blacks each year "after they show their ability and character."

In the end, all the white owners backed down. The Pirates finished fifth, 36½ games behind the Cards. The Senators finished seventh, 39½ behind the Yanks. And the Phils and A's each finished last, the A's 48 games behind, the Phils 62½.

The Grays finished first again, and Posey could heave a sigh. His investment was safe, at least for another four years.

HOPES FOR COLORED PLAYERS IN MAJOR
LEAGUES FADE WITH WANING '42 SEASON

the epitaph in the *Afro* read.

Honus Wagner shook his head sadly. Josh Gibson was "one of the best natural hitters I've ever seen," he shrugged, "but it's too late for the big leagues now."

Should Gibson and Paige have raised black fists and spoken out in protest, as Muhammad Ali or the Olympic athletes of 1968 would do? I don't think so. The 1930s were not the 1960s. Jim Crow was deeply entrenched, both north and south. A demonstration would have set off a backlash that might have set back the goal of integration a decade or more. Did Josh and Satch, with their silence in 1942, buy Jackie Robinson his big opportunity three years later?

(That winter Bill Veeck, a minor league executive in Milwaukee, hatched a scheme to buy the Phils, "a major league franchise by definition only," stock them with blacks who were safe from the draft—he later mentioned Paige, Gibson, Leonard, Bell, and Campanella, among others—and "we'd have won the pennant by 30 games." But when he told Landis of his plans, the commissioner quickly found a new buyer. "I realize now," Veeck grinned later, "it was a mistake to tell him.")

If Josh was hurt and angry, he seemed to pound the ball with even greater savagery. That summer he led the league in both batting and homers.

He also unloaded one of his mightiest blasts, a reported 540-footer in Cleveland's cavernous Municipal Stadium. Some say it went into the center field bleachers. If true—and many doubt it—it would be the only ball ever to reach that distant target. Leonard could not remember Josh hitting one into that inviolate area, and presumably he would know, so perhaps the report is another case of apocryphal hyperbole.

In other news: Two members of the Cleveland Buckeyes were killed when their bus broke down and a car crashed into them as they stood on the roadside. Pitcher Eugene Bremer suffered a fractured skull.

In August, the Washington *Afro-American* made history by sponsoring the first known radio broadcast of a Negro league game, the Grays and Elites at Baltimore's Bugle Field.

And Leon Day of Newark hurled a one-hitter with 18 strikeouts.

There were plenty of white scouts in the stands in the big East–West game that year. Paige (8–5, 2.28) led the vote of the fans for pitcher, although his teammate, Hilton Smith (8–3) was named to start the game.

Josh singled to right in the first. In the third, he drove a high fly deep to the scoreboard for an out. In the fifth, underhander Porter Moss was pitching, and Gibson hit a scorcher through short to knock in a run.

Just before the seventh inning, Paige made his dramatic statement over the public address, then put down the mike, picked up the ball, and took the mound to pitch with the game tied 2–2. Lenny Pearson (.295) lifted a fly and got a double when the outfielder lost it in the sun. The next batter bunted for a hit. Bankhead (.248) scored Pearson with a fly to Bell in center. Wells, the league leader at .344, hit through the infield, then pulled a double steal, not a very bright move because it left first base open with Gibson and Bill Wright (.325) up next.

So Josh, the black game's most famous power hitter, stepped up against Satch, its most famous power pitcher, renewing one of the unforgettable duels of black ball annals. "It was always beautiful to see those two tangle up," Grays pitcher Wilmer Fields said. "I guess I can tell you just about every pitch Satchel threw—fastballs up here at the letters. Dangerous? No, no, no—not when *he* was throwing them!"

But this time Paige chose not to duel: Without hesitating, he put Gibson on. The strategy proved wise when Wright slapped into a double play to end the inning.

In the ninth, losing 3–2, Paige threw two ground balls, but both were booted for errors. Bankhead's ground out again put men on second and third with Gibson and Wright coming up once more. Again Paige refused to take a chance on Josh and walked him. But this time Wild Bill lined a two-run single to put the game on ice.

When the players went back to the pennant races, the Grays were in a close fight with the Elites, though most of the Homestead hitters were suffering yearlong slumps. Bankhead and Harris hit .248, Wilson .247, rookie Howard Easterling at third hit .224, while Leonard suffered a broken finger and hit only .184.

Josh was forced to carry the major load offensively, and the pitchers could now safely pitch around him. Still, he hit a league-leading 11 homers, almost twice as many as runner-up Willie Wells, with six. Josh also batted .323. Incomplete and unverified stats published by the *Afro* show Gibson walking 14 times in 19 games, though he also knocked in 16 runs. One wonders that he found anyone on base to knock in.

On the mound, Ray Brown also overcame the feeble support of most of his hitters and posted another fine year with a 12–4 mark, leading the league in almost everything, including a 2.83 TRA. The other pitching bright spot was lefty Roy Partlow, who hurled a seven-inning no-hitter.

Thanks to Gibson and Brown, the Grays just beat out the Elites and Campanella (.279) by half a game.

In the West the Monarchs won again, their fourth straight pennant. Strongman Willard Brown led at bat with .365, topping the league in both homers (six) and steals (four), although many games went unreported. Barney Serrell and Harlem Globetrotter Ted Strong hit .323 and .333.

On the mound, Paige and Smith led the league in wins—Satch 8–5 and Hilton 8–3, though Paige had the better TRA—2.88 to Smith's 4.85. Paige also led the league in strikeouts for the second straight year. He was being used more and more to draw a crowd, starting 20 games and completing only six of them. Two KC rookies also had fine years—Booker McDaniel (6–0) and Jack Matchett (6–1). McDaniel could throw "just about as hard as Satchel," Buck Leonard said. "Ruined his arm from it."

Another young fastballer, Connie Johnson, came in at 3–0. According to Richard Wilkinson, son of the Monarchs owner, "for two years he was the best of anybody on the Monarchs. Before he hurt his arm, there wasn't anybody could touch him. He was another Satchel Paige." Even with a sub-par arm, Johnson would go on to the white majors and compile a 40–39 record.

Except for Smith, the Kansas City pitchers were stingy with the runs. Paige was 2.88, Matchett 2.63, Johnson 2.03, and McDaniel a low 1.76.

So Josh and Satch prepared to face each other once again, this time in the first black World Series since 1926. It set up another showdown between the black game's two greatest stars, a spectacle that always produced electricity. Each was sure he could whip the other.

Several years earlier, in a preseason interview with Cum Posey for the Pittsburgh *Courier,* Posey was about to close when Josh interjected, "Why don't you ask me how I think I will come out when I face Satchel Paige this year?"

So Posey did ask: "What do you figure?"

"I look to get an even break, two out of four. [They were in different leagues and might play only one exhibition against each other.] One thousand in a pinch, providing Charleston don't say, 'Put him on.'"

When the two had played together in the winter of '39–40, Satch remembered wryly:

> He and I was playing in Porta Rica. He said, "One of these days I'm gonna be against you," and he says, "and shame on you. I'm gonna have my family there," and blab-blab-blab. And that went on for two years.

Gibson returned to Puerto Rico alone in '41–42, and Kansas City's catcher, Joe Greene, heard a radio interviewer ask him how well he did against Satchel. "I hit him about like every other pitcher," Gibson replied. Joe came home and reported the remark to Satch, who replied drily that Josh was the best hitter in baseball with only one weakness—"he can't hit what he can't see."

Before the series, O'Neil says, he saw the two great gladiators at opposite ends of Greenlee's Crawford Grille bar, trading taunts of what each was going to do to the other.

Paige was a tenacious competitor, O'Neil said. He played any-thing—from whist (an early version of bridge) to pitching pennies. He threw half dollars, but the other guys said, "No, no half dollars, you have to throw with a quarter or less," because the lighter the coin, the harder it was to toss. But Satchel "got deadly with the quarter," so they dropped it to a nickel, then a dime, then a penny. Buck added:

> He wanted to pitch to Josh in a tough situation, so all the focus would be on Josh and Satchel. He lived for these situations. He was a great, great competitor. My only criticism of Satchel was getting light hitters out.

The Grays entered the series confident—they had beaten KC four games straight on the year.

The light-hitting Monarch shortstop, Jesse Williams, whom many considered better than Jackie Robinson in the field, though not at bat, sidled up to Josh before game one. Later blind and living in Kansas City, Williams recalled telling the older star, "Heh, come here, Josh, sit down beside me." He offered to bet a steak that he'd get more hits than Josh would.

> He'd look at me and laugh. He say, 'You see that bat there?"
> I say, "Yeah."
> He say, "That's my bat. I don't break 'em, I *wear* 'em out!"

But, Jesse says, "Josh didn't know what I knew: We had better pitching than they did."

In the first game, in Washington, Satchel established his mastery right away. As Greene told the story:

> When Josh came up in the first game of the series, Satchel said, "You talkin' about the way you hit me. Come up here, you big so-and-so, see how you can hit my fast one."
> Naturally Josh was looking for a curveball, but Satchel blazed number-one, fastball, down the middle. Josh looked at it. Strike one.

Manager Frank Duncan said Paige taunted Gibson: "Look at you, you're not ready up there. Come on up to the plate, don't be scared."

"I'm ready," Josh replied testily. "Throw it."

Greene resumed the story:

Satchel waved his hand at Josh, and on the next pitch he threw him another fastball. Josh made an attempt to hit it, but he was too late. He just barely tipped it, and I caught it for strike two.

Satchel came walking halfway in, said, "Get ready to hit; you can't hit with your bat on your shoulder. I'm not gonna waste anything on you, get ready to hit." He threw another fastball, and Josh looked at it for strike three. All the time he was looking for the curveball, he was crossed up by the way Satchel was talking to him. And the crowd just roared.

Next time Josh came up, Satchel says, "Get ready, I'm gonna throw you one belt-high, so don't crowd the plate." Then, "I'm gonna throw you one outside and low on the corner. You better swing."

I noticed Josh set his left foot closer to the plate, to hit that outside pitch, and I told him, "You know you don't hit like that. Get your foot back." And the people just roared. They wanted to see those two tangle up.

Satch pitched five innings of two-hit ball; then Jack Matchett came in to pitch four perfect innings. Josh and Buck both went 0 for 3. KC's Willard Brown drove a triple 435 feet into the center field corner to help win it 8–0.

Two nights later, on a rainy night in Pittsburgh, 5,000 damp fans were on hand to see Satch and Josh square off again. They would witness one of the great pitching dramas of black ball history.

The story has been retold by many eyewitnesses—Greene, O'Neil, Leonard, Duncan, and Satchel himself. Each story differs in details, but all agree on the essentials. (One report says the incident happened, not in the World Series, but on July 21 of that year. However, there is no record that the two teams played each other on that date. And at least one reporter, Sam Lacy of the Washington *Afro-American* and Pittsburgh *Courier,* in a spartan account does confirm a very similar incident in the second series game. I therefore believe it is probable that the face-off did indeed take place then.)

Hilton Smith started against Partlow, who was 3–0 against the Monarchs for the year. Smith went five scoreless innings and left with a 2–0 lead. He and Paige pulled a switch on their usual routine. "You've been relieving me all year," Satch told Hilton. "Let me relieve you."

In the seventh, Paige was still nursing that 2–0 lead. Grays' lead-off man Jerry Benjamin singled, with Harris, Easterling, and Josh to follow. "Heh, Nancy," Paige yelled to O'Neil at first base, I'm gonna put Harris on base; I'm gonna put Easterling on base. I'm gonna pitch to Josh!"

According to writer Donn Rogosin, O'Neil replied, "Oh, Satchel, you got to be crazy."

But Satch calmly went ahead and loaded the bases. In Paige's words, this is what happened next:

> It took me about 20 minutes to start the game again, because my owner, Mr. Wilkinson, he come out on the field and wanted to know what was wrong with me. "Are you losing your mind? What in the world is going on here, you pitching to Josh?"
> "I'll get Josh out."
> And my manager, Frank Duncans, he didn't know *what* to say. The people all thought I was crazy. They said, "Man, don't you know that's Josh Gibson up there?"
> I said, "Yeah, but he told me once in Porta Rica that he was gonna have his family out to the park, and it was gonna be 'shame on me' if he could get up there with some men on." I said, "So I fixed it like that today."
> When I told them that, they just laughed, they said, "Well, this is your funeral, you know who you got up here." And the bases was drunk. And the score was leadin' 5–3 [actually 2–0], and there was Josh up there.

Rogosin's version in *The Sporting News* quoted Satchel as calling to Josh: "Now I'm gonna throw you a fastball, but I'm not gonna trick you. I'll tell you what, I'm gonna give you a good fastball."

According to Paige, "I wound up and stuck my foot way up in the air. It hid the ball and almost hid me too. Then I fired."

It was knee-high, wrote Rogosin. A called strike.

"Now I'm gonna throw you another fastball, but I'm not gonna trick you. Only it's gonna be a little faster than the other one." Strike two.

The *Afro* said Josh fouled off the first two pitches. Paige's version to me: "He didn't swing one time. He didn't swing at *no* pitch. All of them was in there sidearm."

Paige wrote:

> One more to go. I knew it. Josh knew it. The crowd knew it. It was so tense you could feel everything jingling. . . . The last one was a three-

quarter sidearm curveball. He got back on his heels. He was looking for a fastball.

It was knee-high on the outside corner. Strike three. "Josh threw that bat of his 4,000 feet and stomped off the field."

I had learned that he couldn't hit a sidearm pitch. I never did tell anybody that, until I pitched to him that day. They found out. I guess the fans thought I was crazy, but I knew Josh better than I knew Easterling.

(Anticlimactically, the Grays pounded Paige for four runs in the eighth and ninth, but the Monarchs got six more themselves to win 8–4.)

Next, the two teams went to Yankee Stadium, where Paige started against Partlow before 30,000 fans. Easterling's homer into the right field stands scored two quick runs off Satchel in the first. After two innings, Paige came out, losing 2–0, and Jack Matchett went in. The Monarchs got the two runs back on a homer by Willard Brown, and went on to rout the Grays 9–3. Josh and Buck were held to one single apiece.

(A second game, counted as an exhibition, was also won by the Monarchs 5–0).

Greene told us:

> We had the weakest man on the team, Jesse Williams, who was ragging Josh. They had a bet between themselves, the one who outhit the other each day would get a steak. Jesse got about two steaks from Josh and was teasing him too. This just had a psychological effect.

The series moved to Kansas City. On the way, Posey stopped off in Newark to sign Eagles pitcher Leon Day, third baseman Ray Dandridge, and outfielders Ed Stone and Lenny Pearson to Grays contracts. Thus fortified, they arrived to find Paige on the mound again, his fourth straight appearance in the series. He held Josh and Buck hitless, but the other "Grays" hit him—nine hits and four runs. Meanwhile, Day pitched a five-hitter and fanned 12 to win 4–1. Of course the Monarchs protested, and the game was thrown out.

Back in Philadelphia two nights later, 15,000 chilly fans turned out to see Paige start and perform the iron-man feat of pitching in every game of the series. But at game time Satchel was nowhere to be found, so Jack Matchett hurriedly warmed up to face Partlow.

In the second, with two out and one on, Gibson hit a high fly that right fielder Ted Strong let fall for a hit. Leonard's hard smash to first scored one run, and a passed ball and double scored two more.

In the third, Easterling singled, but Gibson popped to O'Neil on first. Leonard followed with a single to center, Ray Brown walked, and Chester Williams singled two more runs in, making it 5–2, Grays.

That was all for Josh, who had gone 2 for 13 for the series. Harris pulled him and sent Bob Gaston out to catch. "We just ran him out of the lineup," Greene said. "He just never had had this kind of carrying on, you see."

In the fourth, the missing Satchel came hurrying into the dugout. "Where *you* been?" Duncan demanded. As Satch sheepishly explained, he had spent the last two days in Pittsburgh, because "there was a mighty nice gal over there I just had to see." On the drive to Philadelphia, he was "clipping right along" in Lancaster, Pennsylvania, when a policeman's siren pulled him over. Ignoring Paige's protest that he had to pitch that night, the cop took him to the local barbershop, where the justice of the peace was getting his hair cut. While Satchel waited, the barber snipped. At last the JP heard Paige's case. "That'll be three dollars," he said and let the pitcher go. Satch broke all records getting to the park, where he "jumped into a uniform and ran out there."

As Satch dashed up, panting, the Grays proceeded to put men on second and third with two out and Gaston up, and Duncan rushed the truant out to the mound. Satchel hadn't even had time to warm up. He said he warmed up by throwing about ten pick-off tosses to first, which would be a great story if there had been a runner on first. Perhaps he meant third base. Anyway, he added correctly, "I looked in at my catcher, got my signal, and started firing. I struck out the batter for the third out."

For five more innings Satch held the Grays scoreless, striking out five more of them, while his teammates rallied to overwhelm the mighty Grays 9–5 and claim the black world championship.

It was Paige's fourth straight series game—five counting the protested game—a feat no white pitcher has ever accomplished. Two Japanese have done it. In 1959, Kazuhisa "Iron Arm" Inao pitched six games of the Japan Series, lost the first two and won the last four. The next year, Tadashi Sugiura pitched and won all four contests. Like Paige, both Japanese relieved as well as started.

Paige left no doubt who was cock of the walk in the black baseball world that year. Josh hit just .152 for the series, Buck .166, and the

Grays as a team .204. Against Satch the Grays hit .115. Meanwhile, the Monarchs hit a combined .364. Serrell hit .555, Williams, .470, Greene .444, Brown .411, and Strong .400.

Satch struck out more than one man per inning, while winning two and saving one:

Game	Score	IP	H	R	SO	BB	W–L–Sv	TRA
1.	8–0	5	2	0	5	1	W	
2.	8–4	4	4	3	4	0		Sv
3.	9–3	2	2	2	3	1	—	
5.	9–5	5.1	0	0	6	1	W	
Total		16.1	8	5	18	3	2–0–1	2.76

If one adds the disputed fourth game, Paige's totals are:

	IP	H	R	SO	BB	W–L–Sv	
Total	25	16	9	—	—	2–1–1	3.24

At the end of game five, Satch just couldn't help razzing his old teammate, Josh. "How's that, big man?" he yelled, but Josh wouldn't reply.

Satchel didn't mind. "Sometimes," he wrote, "it seems to me like that was the best day I ever had pitching."

1943

Germany was bombed. The marines took Guadalcanal, the Allies took North Africa, the Russians took Stalingrad, Patton took Sicily (and slapped a GI), Clark took Naples. Italy surrendered, Mussolini was slain. Troops quelled a Detroit race riot. Marian Anderson sang at DAR Constitution Hall. Meatless days.

"Oh What a Beautiful Mornin'," "The Surrey With the Fringe on Top," "As Time Goes By," "All or Nothing at All," "Besame Mucho," "Pistol Packin' Momma." In New York 30,000 rioted to hear Sinatra.

For Whom the Bell Tolls.

Broadway: *Oklahoma.*

Radio: "Amos 'n Andy" canceled.

Books: *A Tree Grows in Brooklyn, The Human Comedy. Esquire* was called lewd.

Baseball held spring training in the north. Most stars were in the service. The Yanks beat the Cards 4–1.

In 1943 Josh Gibson enjoyed probably the finest season any Negro league hitter ever had—and went through one of the worst hells any player has ever suffered.

The year began prophetically on New Year's day, when Josh fainted, went into a coma, and was rushed to the hospital, where he stayed for ten days. Doctors said it was a nervous breakdown. Posey said he was "completely run down." His biographer, William Brashler, said Josh told his sister Annie that he had a brain tumor but had refused to permit an operation.

It was a summer of nervous breakdowns, severe alcoholism, and possibly drug addiction that kept Gibson going in and out of Washington's St. Elizabeth mental hospital. Gibson was committed for ten days of heavy sedation, but was so strong he literally ripped a straitjacket off. He had to be recommitted, and he played for the Grays on weekend furloughs chaperoned by hospital orderlies. He was in and out of the hospital "like a drunken monkey," in Leonard's phrase.

Yet on the field that summer, Gibson hit an amazing .521, second highest average in black history, surpassed only by Pop Lloyd's .564 in 1928. Gibson powered 14 homers to Lloyd's 11, including one of the longest ever hit in Griffith Stadium. A comparison of the two men shows:

	G	AB	H	2B	3B	HR	SB	BA	SA
Lloyd	37	149	84	4	1	11	10	.564**	.826*
Gibson	—	190*	99*	32**	8*	14*	0	.521*	.995*

* = League-Leading Record. ** = Negro League Record.

It was almost as though Josh were taking out on the ball all the rage and frustration of the year before.

Reporter Ric Roberts supplied his own data on Gibson's games at home. Although the newspapers, including Roberts' own Pittsburgh *Courier*, did not print box scores to corroborate all the games, it is not inconsistent with the games we have verified and is printed below as a matter of interest:

G	AB	R	H	2B	3B	HR	RBI	SB	BB	BA	SA
40	149	49	75	21	6	10	59	6	28	.503	.926

The RBI figure, if correct, means Josh would have knocked in about 227 in 154 games and 237 in 162. The ten home runs in Griffith Stadium must impress anyone who remembers those distant left field bleachers. In Fenway Park or Ebbets Field, Gibson might have smashed twice as many out of the playing field. Oddly, given that crushing power, he walked surprisingly few times.

The white press recognized Gibson at last, with a one-page story and a picture in *Time* entitled "Josh the Basher." In a fairly straight-forward journalistic report, *Time* said a large following of white fans watch the Negro teams and "like their fancy windups, their swift and daring base running, their flashy one-handed catches." It described Newark owner Effa Manley as "a hula-hipped Harlem beauty," who, it said, directed the team from the dugout.* And it said the Grays often drew larger crowds than the Senators.

"The idol of these happy fans is Josh (for Joshua) Gibson, a

---

*Mrs. Manley did not direct the players from the dugout, although she did dictate frequently their behavior off the field. *Time* was apparently misled by a famous photo of her in an Eagles cap and jacket, posing prettily on the dugout steps.

hulking 215-pounder with features suggestive of a very dark Babe Ruth." It said Josh has a peculiar habit at bat of rolling up his tongue "and sandwiching it, like a hot dog, between his lips" before swatting the ball a country mile. It reported his Monessen 513-foot homer and a 485-footer in Griffith Stadium, and said he was hitting .541.

Time contrasted Josh to "the famed but fading" Satchel Paige (5–9 that year), noting that Gibson

> is no gaudy eccentric. He drives no cerise roadster, makes no startling statements about a strict diet of fried food [they got that backwards], and receives no $40,000 a year salary. Josh's salary is $750 a month plus bonuses.

The magazine did not mention his emotional problems. Josh's behavior remained erratic. He picked fights with bartenders, and in one game, Leonard said, he urinated on the field. He climbed nude onto a window ledge six stories high and threatened to jump.

Birmingham first baseman Jim Canada recalled:

> I've seen him when he was drinking all that wine and got kind of doped up on it—I've seen him come up there and tell the manager that he wanted to pinch-hit. He pushed his cap bill up and hit the ball over the fence and ran around the bases the third base way. That's when they knew he'd been drinking.

Leonard questioned the reports of Josh's heavy drinking. "They say he drank whiskey, but I never did see him. He did drink beer, which I didn't think was too bad, because all of us were drinking beer, especially after a ball game."

Wilmer Fields was in the army that year, but he knew Josh intimately before and after the war. Later, as a professional counselor of alcoholics, he told us:

> I never saw Josh drunk. I've been around alcoholics, and I know what they look like. The only time I saw Josh drink was after a ball game. He might go to a bar and have a few beers. Josh used to sit next to me on the bus, and I never saw him look hung over. We never had to push him on the bus or anything like that.

Fields' theory: "I think it was dope." The players were guests at parties in every city they visited, and Gibson, as the star, was feted more than any of them. That's where Fields believed Josh may have begun the fatal habit.

Bankhead told Brashler that Grace was on narcotics. "And what she was taking, Josh was taking."

Gibson was not the only black star to suffer severe psychological trauma. Rube Foster, the single greatest figure in the formation of the Negro leagues, died in a mental institution. Cannonball Dick Redding, a great speedball artist before World War I, also died in an insane asylum, as did Toussaint Allen, a first baseman of the same era. Jud Wilson, Josh's teammate on the Grays, would die of epilepsy from being beaten on the head in his many fistfights.

And of course, alcohol abuse, and more recently drug abuse, have attacked many an athlete, black and white, from Rube Waddell and Grover Alexander to Dave Parker and LaMarr Hoyt. The pressure of being a professional athlete makes it a dangerous occupation. And the frustration of being a black athlete in an era of apartheid must have made the burden even weightier.

But through all his problems, Gibson kept swinging and connecting. It was a hitters' year. Tetelo Vargas was second to Josh with .518. Pancho Coimbre of Puerto Rico hit .419, while on the Grays, Easterling hit .438. It suggests that the ball may have been livelier that year, although the white major league averages remained about the same as in '42.

Homestead's Jerry Benjamin hit .385, Harris .380, second baseman Lick Carlisle .344, the newly-acquired Cool Papa Bell .331 and Leonard .278. With all that support, rookie Johnny Wright had a splendid season, 15–3. It would help win him a contract with the Dodgers' Montreal farm team two years later, along with Jackie Robinson.

If anything, playing conditions were even worse than before, Leonard said:

During the war we couldn't go but 700 miles a month in the bus, because of gasoline rationing. Now from Pittsburgh to Washington was 263 miles, back to Pittsburgh was 263. Well, that was over 500 miles for just one trip. Had to put your bus up the rest of the month and take the train. One time the conductor told us, "We don't have room on the train for you, and we're not going to let you stand up." So we stayed in the baggage car. That's right. And played that night. . . .

And we had portable lights that we put up in the parks. We'd install them on poles all around in the field. A big dynamo out there in the outfield generated the electricity. We used to have trouble with outfielders running into poles. Jerry Benjamin ran into one of the guy ropes while chasing a fly ball up in Niagara, New York and broke his ankle.

Sometimes we thought the belt was slipping on the dynamo. The lights would dim and get bright, dim and get bright. We had to stop the game about five minutes and put some belt dressing on the belt that turned the wheel to keep the belt from slipping. Some people said they were giving us about as much light as we were paying for. They said we must have owed them some money. Teasing us, you know.

One speedballer had a record strikeout one night under those lights.

Al Gipson of Birmingham, a perennial loser, whiffed 20 Philadelphia Stars, breaking the record of 18 shared by Paige and Leon Day.

Of Gibson's 16 homers, 10 came in Washington—more than all the sluggers in the American league could hit in 77 games there. One of the blows soared over the left field bleachers about where Mickey Mantle's 565-foot tape measure drive left the park ten years later.

The Grays drew 150,000 fans to their games in Washington, almost a 50 percent increase from 1942. Posey gratefully threw a "night" for his star, called Josh "the greatest player I ever saw," and presented him with a piece of luggage—white stars were getting automobiles on their nights.

Sweetest of all, Gibson got his revenge against Paige in Chicago. As Satch said:

I got two strikes on him and got my fastball a little too high, and he hit it so hard, it hit the top deck, and it bounced back in the park, and the boy tried to make a play on him at second—he didn't know it had gone out of the park.

Then he hit the clock in Comiskey Park.

Who was the hardest hitter for me to pitch against? That's him: Josh Gibson. He could hit home runs around Babe Ruth's home runs. You look for his weakness, and while you're looking for it, he's liable to hit 45 home runs.

Ted Page observed that "people love to talk about how Satchel struck out Josh in Forbes Field, but they fail to bring up the times Josh hit the fences against Satch. Of course, Satchel is around, and Josh isn't."

"I've seen Satchel get Josh," Fields summed up. "But I believe over the long run they got each other."

Paige was not having a good year. He was 5–7 on the season, leading the league in losses for the second year in a row, though he also led in strikeouts for the third straight year. Smith was 4–3, and young Johnson was in the service. Luckily, McDaniel had a fine sophomore year, 9–1, but the Monarchs fell to fourth. Offensively, the team was as potent as ever. Brown led the league in homers, six, and batted .383. Rookie Hank Thompson, who would play for the New York Giants hit .328.

One of Satchel's wins was a 1–0 gem while on loan to the Memphis Red Sox for a big Satchel Paige Day before 25,000 fans in Chicago's Wrigley Field. The fans crowded around for autographs, and Paige said, before he knew it he had signed his name to his own divorce summons brandished by Janet's lawyer. The settlement was a painful one (for those days)—$1,800 in cash. But he raced back to Kansas City to tell Lahoma joyfully, "I'm free!"

Of course Gibson led the vote for catcher in the East–West game. In spite of his so-so record, Paige was, as he wrote, "still the biggest name in the Negro leagues." He easily led the poll for pitchers in the West, as the fans ignored the Monarchs' lesser known McDaniels and even Eugene Bremer, who posted an 8–2 with the third-place Cleveland Buckeyes. Neither of them placed in the top three vote-getters.

With wartime prosperity, Negro league attendance had finally left the Depression behind. As Paige said, "Even the white folks was coming out. They'd heard about Josh Gibson and me." That got Satchel to thinking. "Without me, the East–West game wouldn't draw two-third the people it would if I was playing." He didn't have to make the owners richer, he reasoned. "The only person I had to make richer was me." The usual pay for a player appearing in the game was $50. Paige approached Gibson with his plan: "They got to come through with some extra money for us if we both hold out." Satch suggested $200, a month's pay for many players. Josh hesitated, then agreed.

When Paige announced the news to Dr. J.B. Martin, the western (American) league president, Martin "almost fell out of his chair." But he finally nodded a grudging OK.

By game time, 51,000 persons were jammed into the park, not counting some of Paige's friends who had snuck in, nor 10,000 others who had to be turned away. So Snatch put on a real pre-game show, playing pepper ball and flipping the ball around in infield practice.

In the game, Paige breezed through three hitless innings, and by the ninth, the West was leading 2–0 on a one-hitter. Then Leonard homered off Theolic "Fireball" Smith, and Josh smashed one to short-stop Jesse Williams that tore his glove off. If Gibson had gotten under it a little more, the game would have been tied, Paige said. Easterling also singled, but Porter Moss rushed in to get pinch-hitters Vic Harris and Jerry Benjamin and end the threat. (Soon after that, Moss was shot to death in a Pullman. The reason was never made public.)

Once more the Grays won the pennant, their seventh in a row, counting 1939. In the West, the Monarchs fell to fourth. Birmingham won the play-off over Chicago, thanks to a one-hit 1–0 victory by John Huber.

In the World Series, Birmingham's Alfred Saylor held the mighty Gibson to one hit to win the first game 4–2.

The Grays' Partlow and Brown won the second, and Wright won the third 9–0.

The fourth game was a free-for-all. The Barons led 11–6 in the ninth when Gibson smacked a grand slam to pull within one run, but his mates couldn't get the tying run and lost 11–10.

Wright beat Saylor in game five 8–4, but Birmingham tied the series three-to-three with a 1–0 win in game six.

In the final game, in Montgomery, Wright was losing 4–2 in the eighth in spite of Josh's single and double. Then Leonard walked, Gibson singled, and Easterling singled for one run, Harris singled for another and stole, and Bankhead singled two more runs home for the winning margin.

For the series Josh hit .263, Leonard .272, and Easterling, .313. The Grays were back on top of the black baseball world, thanks to a magnificent year by their brooding, troubled star.

Brashler writes that Josh's teammates found him that summer sitting alone by his rooming house window, mumbling to himself:

C'mon, Joe, talk to me. Why don't you talk to me? Hey, Joe DiMaggio, it's me. You know me. Why don't you answer me? Huh, Joe? Why not? C'mon, Joe, you know me. You ain't gonna answer me?

1944

The Leningrad siege was broken. Mass air raids on Berlin. Rome fell. D-Day at Normandy. Paris fell. MacArthur in the Philippines ("I have returned"). Roosevelt won a fourth term, over Tom Dewey. The Battle of the Bulge. The Supreme Court said color is no bar to voting in primaries.

"Accentuate the Positive," "Don't Fence Me In," "I'll Walk Alone," "Time Waits for No One," "This Heart of Mine," "Rum and Coca Cola," "Moonlight in Vermont," "Mairzy Doats."

Going My Way, Double Indemnity, Gaslight, Meet Me in St. Louis, See Here, Private Hargrove.

Broadway: *Harvey.*

Radio: "Life Can Be Beautiful," "When a Girl Marries," "Portia Faces Life."

Books: *The Razor's Edge, A Bell for Adano.* Boston banned *Forever Amber.*

The St. Louis Browns won their only pennant, lost to the Cards 4–2. Hockey's Maurice Richard scored 50 goals.

Gibson stayed in Pittsburgh that winter. His old teammate, Ted Page, was operating a Pittsburgh bowling alley:

> He didn't go to South America for some reasons, money problems or whatever it was. He wanted so much money, and he didn't get it, so he just stayed around town. This was definitely after he started to drink. Cum Posey knew Josh and I were friends, so he asked me to see if I could talk to Josh. I was teaching him to bowl, and I had him on my volleyball team at the YMCA, and we played all winter. We played handball and volleyball, and we did a lot of bowling.

In May Gibson was in trouble again for "breaking training." He was unfit for duty in one Saturday exhibition, receiving a "final admonition" from Posey. The next day the Grays played Newark in a doubleheader in Ebbets Field, Brooklyn, a park out of which Josh should have been able to bunt home runs. He was in no shape to play, but Posey put him in the lineup anyway because, he said, the fans demanded it. Poor Josh went 1-for-9. Even the partisan pro-Newark fans there were begging him for a hit.

Satch married Lahoma, explaining that "you don't find good business managers that look as good as Lahoma too often." He gave up his galivanting ways and settled into his house in downtown Kansas City with his guns, fishing poles, cars, antiques, dogs—and a flock of chickens. Eventually he added a cow. When a zoning board officer came to ask if it were true that Paige was keeping a chicken ranch, the pitcher looked innocent. "No, sir, not Ol' Satch," he said. Just then the cow "came wandering around the side of the house." That was the end of Paige's lucrative milk and egg business.

Satch went out to California after the 1943 season to join an All-Star team that included outfielder Bob Kennedy, later his teammate on Cleveland, and managed by the immortal Ty Cobb. Typically, Paige didn't arrive until the third inning. "Heh, Satchel," Kennedy called, "Cobb's looking for you."

"Who's Cobb?" Satchel asked.

He also faced a team of wartime white big leaguers—Andy Pafko, Vern Stephens, Peanuts Lowrey, George Metkovich, Lou Novikoff, Jerry Priddy, and Johnny Lindell—and struck out 14 of them. Upset, Judge Landis ruled that the whites could barnstorm for only ten days after the end of the World Series. Pafko defied him and was fined $400.

While Paige was out there, he visited some wounded GIs from the Pacific. Both white and black, they lay on their stretchers, felt his pitching arm, and peppered him with questions. Some of them were just "pieces of men." One of his old opponents on the House of David couldn't even lift his head to talk to Satch, and Paige had to lift it for him.

Satch hatched an idea to play the 1944 East–West game as a benefit for those fighting men. He told the owners the game had "growed up. Our leagues have got big." They can afford to play charity games like the white leagues did. Twenty years ago there were almost no white faces at Negro league games. Now in some towns, half the fans were white.

The owners turned the idea down flat. "I'm gonna lead a walk-out," Satch warned, but when he asked the other players to join him, the men refused. They were more interested in their own campaign to get more pay for the game, as he and Josh had already done.

Each of the 12 owners sent three men to the game, paying them $50 each, plus $15 per diem, Newark outfielder Johnny Davis said, then the owners split the receipts from up to 50,000 fans. Would it hurt them to pay the players $200 each, or $600 per team? he demanded.

Chicago third baseman Alec Radcliff, Double Duty's brother (though without the e), had already negotiated a raise to $300 for himself the year before.

The West players met in the clubhouse and refused to take the field. "The players do all the work, and the owners make all the money," a player spokesman said. The owners hurriedly huddled and finally agreed to $150 minutes before the game was to begin. In fact, it wasn't until Cool Papa Bell stepped into the batters' box to lead off that the owners could be certain that the game would actually go on.

Even Radcliff agreed to take a pay cut to preserve the unity of the players:

> The owners really pushed us around. It's bad to say, but they gave us a hard way to go. Mmmm-hmmmm. I guarantee, if we were making the kind of dough they are today, I don't believe we would have struck. We'd have been too glad to get that kind of money. I may be wrong, but I think the players are hurting the public today by striking.

The newspapers conceded that Paige's proposal for a benefit game had helped win the raise. But the game went on without him. Josh and Buck played, however. Gibson got two hits, one of them "the longest ball I ever saw Gibson hit," according to third baseman Ray Dandridge. "He hit a line drive right into the microphones in center field [440 feet away]. It went 'round and 'round in that thing and dropped back onto the field. He got two bases on it." But the West won 7–4.

Actually, Paige was not having a big year, mainly because almost all the Monarchs were overseas. Brown, Thompson, O'Neil, Greene, and Johnson were gone. The club was last in team hitting and last in the standings, 23–42. Only shortstop Barney Serrell hit .300. Many Monarchs considered Serrell a better big league prospect than Jackie Robinson, and when Jackie was chosen by the Dodgers over him a year later, Serrell, deeply hurt, fled to Mexico.

Satchel, who turned 40 in July, compiled a record of 5–5, though he had a fine TRA of 1.28. (That includes interleague games; his published league marks were 4–2 and 0.75.) In 48 league innings, he whiffed 47, and those years of pitching over match books continued to pay off, as he walked only five men. (Counting interleague games, Satch walked eight and whiffed 70.)

Satch had only himself to blame for one of those losses. Beating Philadelphia 1–0 with two out, he gave up a triple to catcher Bill "Ready" Cash. The next three men were the pitcher, center fielder Gene Benson, and Jimmy Austin, the little Panamanian who led the league in hitting that year with .390. Satch was up to his old tricks. He deliberately walked the pitcher and Benson so he could face Austin. Only this time he also walked Austin, letting the tying run score. He went on to lose the game 2–1.

Cleveland's Sam Jethroe led the league with .353 and also led in steals. He would go on to hit .261 with the Boston Braves and lead the National league in steals twice. Second, at .346, was Birmingham's Artie Wilson. In 1951 he would get a cup of coffee with the New York Giants but was sent to the minors to make room for another Black Baron graduate, Willie Mays.

Gibson's average fell to "only" .373. His home run output was cut in half, from 17 to eight, but still enough to lead the league. The drop can be explained, partly at least, by the inferior wartime materials that went into the balls—the white big leaguers also experienced a fall in batting. Elsewhere, published statistics gave Campanella a .350 average, and Newark's rookie pitcher, Don Newcombe, broke in with a 1–3 mark.

The Grays finished first again for the eighth time in a row and faced the injury-riddled Black Barons once more in the World Series.

The first game was in Birmingham's spacious Rickwood Park, with one of the longest outfield fences in America. In the fourth, with the score tied 1–1, Josh lashed a homer over the fence in left. An inning later, Buck followed with one to right. In the eighth, Grays newcomer Dave Hoskins homered, Josh doubled, Bell tripled, and the Grays went on to win 8–3.

In game two, in New Orleans, the Barons started the league's best pitcher, Al Saylor (14–5). Josh got two hits off him in a 6–1 victory.

Back in Birmingham, the veteran Ray Brown shut the Barons out 9–0, as Josh got another hit.

Birmingham's Johnny Huber threw a three-hitter at the Grays (one of the hits was by Gibson) for the Barons' first win.

But at home in Washington, the Grays scored three quick runs against Saylor in the first inning, to wrap the series up.

Josh had redeemed himself after several sub-par series, hitting an even .500.

Two months later, in November, Judge Landis died. The game was about to witness perhaps the greatest revolution in its history.

1945

Yalta. FDR died. Truman was sworn in ("the buck stops here"). Hitler killed himself. Germany surrendered. The flag-raising on Iwo Jima. Okinawa. Hiroshima. Japan surrendered on the USS *Missouri*. New York passed an antidiscrimination law.

"It's Been a Long, Long Time," "Spring Is Bustin' Out All Over," "It Might As Well Be Spring," "April Showers," "Let It Snow," "I Love You for Sentimental Reasons," "Sentimental Journey," "On the Atchison, Topeka and the Santa Fe."

Lost Weekend, National Velvet, They Were Expendable, Children of Paradise.

Broadway: *The Glass Menagerie.*

Radio: "Arthur Godfrey Show," "Information Please," "Ma Perkins." Mayor LaGuardia read the comics during newspaper strike.

Books: *Animal Farm, The Thurber Carnival, Up Front* by Bill Mauldin, Richard Wright's *Black Boy*.

One-armed Pete Gray. Greenberg and Feller returned from the war. Detroit beat the Cubs 4–3.

In April, the major leagues announced the name of the new commissioner, Senator A.B. "Happy" Chandler of Kentucky. Chandler had led a wartime Senate committee that made a trip to the South Pacific and was shaken by the suffering he found among the troops. The day after the story of his appointment broke, Ric Roberts remembered:

> We went right down to see him. Chandler came out immediately, shaking our hands, and said, 'I'm for the Four Freedoms. If a black boy can make it on Okinawa and Guadalcanal, hell, he can make it in baseball." And he told us, "Once I tell you something, brother, I never change. You can count on me." I always thought that was a pretty stout thing for a southerner to say.
>
> The *Courier* headlined that! [Branch] Rickey couldn't have made a move but for that. The moment Rickey read that in the *Courier*, he began to move. And Chandler paid for it. Mr. Griffith was outraged. He was outraged! They never forgave Mr. Chandler for that. The first time he

stubbed his toe, he was a goner. And it broke his heart. [Chandler was fired by the owners after one term.] None of those people could have done a doggone thing if they hadn't gotten a green light from the commissioner. And he never got credit for it. I think he's long overdue for what he deserves.

While Rickey planned his bombshell, Gibson negotiated the best contract of his life from Posey. Josh and Leonard both had lucrative offers to play in Latin America that summer and took them to Posey, similar to the double holdout that Sandy Koufax and Don Drysdale later pulled successfully on the Dodgers. Posey got the point. He gave Leonard a contract for $1,000 a month, for four and a half months and Josh $1200 a month. It made Gibson, after Paige, the highest paid black star in the game.

The two men earned their raises.

Josh hit .375 and again led the league in homers with eight, in spite of his continued heavy drinking. His old Crawford pal, Jimmie Crutchfield, told William Brashler that he and Josh spent a night reminiscing while Gibson downed shots of straight whiskey without a chaser.

Satchel, meanwhile, was having his worst year since his sore arm. He appeared in only six league games, only one of them complete, and his record, as published by the Howe News Bureau, was 2–2, with a 4.50 Total Run Average. Again his control was sharp, however— only six walks and 30 strikeouts in 33 innings. Jim LaMarque (pronounced La Mar), 8–2, and Hilton Smith, 5–2, led the staff. The Monarchs finished fourth. In interleague games, Paige was again 1–2, giving him a losing record overall of 3–4.

The Monarchs still suffered from the military call-ups and were limping along as best they could. "About the best of the lot," said Satch, "was a college boy, a kid named Jackie Robinson. I'd never heard of him before, but he was pretty good—quick on his feet and a good hand at the plate."

Robinson had been an Army lieutenant but was discharged early for causing a commotion over segregated seating on an Army bus. Jesse Williams voluntarily moved to second base to make a spot for him at short.

Jackie could hit. In June, the Monarchs journeyed east and met Gibson and the Grays in a doubleheader. In the first game, Robinson went 4 for 4, with two doubles, two singles, and a walk. But he was shaky in the field. In the sixth inning, Satchel was tied up 2–2 with the bases loaded and Gibson up. Josh drilled one to shortstop; Jackie fielded it and whipped the ball home—over catcher Double Duty Radcliffe's outstretched glove. Two men scored on the play, and five more followed them before the inning was over.

In game two, Robinson tried to atone at bat. He had another perfect game, 3 for 3, making 7 for 7 on the day. But the Monarchs lost anyway 10–6.

After his tryout with the White Sox before the war, and another with the Red Sox, Jackie had his eye set on the white majors. One night, with scouts in the stands, Robinson reported with a bad shoulder and asked manager Frank Duncan to play him at first. He kept telling the other fellows to hustle. "He was always so *serious*," said infielder Chico Renfroe.

The Monarchs' traveling secretary, old-time pitcher Dizzy Dismukes, feared that Jackie didn't have the arm to make it at short, so Dizzy asked Cool Papa Bell to hit them to Jackie's right side to prove the point. Bell considered Monte Irvin the Negro leagues' best young prospect. Robinson reached the balls, Cool said, but he couldn't plant his foot and throw, he had to take an extra step or two before he stopped. Bell beat them out easily.

Cool said he also stole second four times with hook slides around Robinson's tag. After the game he told the rookie, "See, they got a lot of guys slide like that. You can't get those guys out like that." Bell also urged him to switch to one of the other infield positions. "If he missed his chance," Bell said, "I don't know how long we'd have to wait until we got another chance." Indeed, second base is where Robinson would spend most of his Dodger career. In his entire career there, he played only one game at short.

Paige was reduced to a few spot pitching assignments, got into only seven league games all year, and won only a single game against three losses.

In the East–West game in August, neither Josh nor Satch was on the squad. Josh was benched for "breaking training," while Campanella caught in his place and went 2 for 5. For the West Robinson went 0 for 5.

Robinson batted .387 overall and .345 in league games, sixth best in the league, and was fifth in stolen bases. Once again the batting leaders were Jethroe (.393) and Art Wilson (.374), with Jethroe tops in steals as well.

Although hobbled by a leg ailment, as well as his various chemical ones, Gibson hit .375 with eight homers, the sixth straight year he'd led the league. (He came to bat 104 times, so that was about 43 per 550 at bats.) According to researcher Tim Joyce, the last one came in the Polo Grounds against little Dave "Impo" Barnhill of the Cubans, who later went to Minneapolis with Willie Mays and Ray Dandridge. With the score tied in the ninth, two on and two out, Barnhill elected to pitch to Josh. That was a mistake. Gibson walloped it over the roof, a drive estimated at 500 feet, one of the longest of his career.

The Grays won an amazing ninth straight pennant. One big factor of course was that both Gibson and Leonard were exempted from the draft, while other teams were decimated of their stars— principally third-place Newark, which lost half its infield, Monte Irvin and Larry Doby, and its two top pitchers, Leon Day and Max Manning.

In the West the upstart Cleveland Buckeyes won with a squad of young unknowns. Jethroe, of course, led their hitters, and the two Jefferson brothers, Willie and George, led the pitchers. Willie was 10–1 with a 1.57 ERA and George 11–1, 1.75.

In game one of the World Series in Cleveland, Willie beat the Grays 2–1; Josh got one single.

In game two at Pittsurgh, veteran Eugene Bremer (8–4) beat them 4–2, limiting Josh to another single.

George Jefferson won game three in Washington 4–0 as Gibson went hitless.

And Frank Carswell (5–2) stopped them 4–0 in Philadelphia, again shutting Gibson down without a hit. It was something like the Mets' humiliation of the proud Orioles in 1969, or the Dodgers shocking the mighty A's in '88. But the Buckeyes were a young and hungry squad, while the Grays were complacent and aging. Poor Josh hit only .133.

Brooklyn scouts were quietly joining the crowds. Rickey had told them to keep their eyes out for "a man that possesses more than talent, a man who could carry the burden of abuse on the field, a man to wear the badge of martyrdom, a man whose humility and courage would force the press to accept him."

Unbeknownst to them, Paige had already been considered and rejected as too old and Gibson as too unstable.

That winter, the news was out. Robinson had signed with the Dodgers.

Paige was on the West Coast when the news hit. "'I hadn't thought it would ever happen," he said. But if it did, "somehow I always figured it'd be me. . . . It was my right. I got those white boys thinking about having Negroes in the majors, but when they got one, it wasn't me."

He consoled himself that the white owners knew they couldn't start him in the minors, and that "those high-priced white boys" wouldn't stand for him going directly to the parent club. Still, signing Jackie "hurt me deep down." The pain was like "when somebody you love dies or something dies inside of you."

"They didn't even look at me," he told Lahoma.

"He's young, Satchel. Maybe that's why."

"He's no Satchel Paige."

Yet, realistically, Paige was no big league prospect in 1945. Rickey would have been a fool to put all his chips on a 40-year-old who hadn't had a really outstanding year in more than a decade.

Gibson got the news in Puerto Rico and reacted with the same hurt and bewilderment as Satch did. He batted a despondent .190 with no home runs. Police arrested him wandering nude in San Juan and committed him to a sanitarium.

Said Ric Roberts:

> Most people don't realize what pride Josh took in being "Mr. Black Baseball." It was a challenge to him to sustain that. He thought, if they're going to pick a black man, it had to be Josh Gibson. He was so sure that he was the greatest black player. How they could pick Jackie Robinson was something he never could understand. To find his kingdom in a shambles at the age of 33 was too much for him. He turned to anything he could find—dope and everything.

Many players agreed with Gibson. "We thought Josh should have gone at the same time as Robinson," Israel said.

Indeed, Gibson had the credentials. He was still a solid 300-hitter and the home run champ. But his severe personal problems would have scared any wise investor away.

And, Leonard warned: "Josh wouldn't have taken the heckling Jackie took. He would have blown his top. He was happy-go-lucky among us black ball players [only]."

In later years, a more philosophical Paige also saw the rationale behind the Robinson decision. "Jackie was the right guy," he would say. "I'll say it a thousand times: I'm glad it wasn't me, because I couldn't have taken it either."

Jackie had signed with Brooklyn the night before embarking for Venezuela with Leonard, Campanella, Jethroe, and others. It wasn't until they arrived that Buck got the news. On the tour Leonard hit .425, Jethroe .339, Robinson .281, and Campy .211. Buck recalled:

> At that time we didn't think too much of Robinson. He had played a few games with Kansas City; he was a hustler, but other than that he wasn't a top shortstop. We said, "We don't see how he can make it."
>
> When we got down to Venezuela, Robinson didn't look too good, because he hadn't been playing as long as some of us. Of course now we see what he really could do. You know, you can be wrong about a ballplayer. You can't always tell what a person's going to do in the athletic world.
>
> One thing though, a fellow with a college education is just a little better than a fellow you pick up on the sandlot. Now I see that they got the right man in Jackie Robinson, because he had the education. There were other players we thought were better players, but they had to find the ideal ballplayer to start. And they finally got him. I can't think of anybody that could have been better than Robinson. A lot of things that he took, a lot of other ballplayers would not have taken. They got the right man after all.

Jackie was worried that he couldn't make the grade in Brooklyn and confessed his fears to his roommate, outfielder Gene Benson of the Philadelphia Stars. They sat up one night, as Gene tried to talk Jackie's doubts away. He told Robinson of how much tougher the Negro pitching was, with all sorts of illegal and knockdown pitches that are outlawed in the white majors.

"Jackie," Benson said, "just remember one thing: Where you're goin' ain't half as tough as where you been."

1946

The United Nations. Truman seized the coal mines. Top Nazis were hanged after Nuremberg. Churchill's "Iron Curtain" speech. The Cold War began. Blacks voted in Mississippi.

"The Gypsy," "They Say that Falling in Love Is Wonderful," "To Each His Own," "Doin' What Comes Natur'ly," "Tenderly," "Prisoner of Love," "Dancing in the Dark," "Sioux City Sue," "Shoo-fly Pie and Apple Pan Dowdy."

The Best Years of Our Lives, The Postman Always Rings Twice, Henry V, The Killers, The Outlaw ("What are the two great reasons for Jane Russell's rise to stardom?").

Books: Dr. Spock.

Feller struck out 348. The Cards beat the Dodgers 2–0 in the play-off and the Red Sox 4–3 in the series on Slaughter's run. Louis KO'd Conn in a rematch.

Josh and Satch were virtually forgotten men, as even the black papers filled their pages with Jackie Robinson in Montreal. The Dodgers had also signed the Grays' Johnny Wright, Baltimore's Campanella and the Eagles' Newcombe. Rickey, of course, didn't pay a cent for any of them.

Cum Posey died in March, raving at the effrontery of Rickey in "coming into a man's store and stealing the merchandise right off the shelves."

Gibson had wintered in Puerto Rico, where he suffered the most disastrous season of his life, hitting a sickly .193 with no home runs. The presumption is that he must have been using drugs heavily.

When he returned to Washington, Brashler says, Gibson's two children by his first wife, now teenagers, and their grandmother often came to the park to beg money from him.

Grace's husband also returned from the service, and she left Josh, which may have contributed to his increased drinking. "He loved this girl in Pittsburgh," his old mentor, Judy Johnson said. "He loved her dearly, and I think that was the first trouble that started the decline of his health. I think he was down in Puerto Rico playing, and when he got back, he got some bad news about her, and I think that started it. Because he was a touchy guy."

A photo of Josh at bat that summer shows an almost obese figure, and indeed, he had ballooned to an estimated 230 pounds. "He couldn't bend his knees," Newark pitcher Max Manning recalled. "Instead of getting all the way down [to catch], he would be in a half crouch. It was just a pitiful thing to see."

Half a Pint Israel agreed. "His legs were so bad he couldn't catch a foul ball. I've seen him hit a double, and he just did get to first."

And yet this overweight, arthritic, alcoholic shell of the old Josh had the greatest season of his life, surpassing even his heroic 1943 production. As in '43, he seemed to smash the ball with a savagery that released the pent-up frustration and anger seething inside. But almost nobody paid any attention.

The headlines were all about Robinson. Nothing about Jackie was too trivial for the black papers to seize on, while Josh and the Grays were relegated to the bottom of the sports pages.

50,000 SEE ROBINSON SPARKLE IN FIRST 6 GAMES the headline screamed on April 27 above a three-column picture of Jackie scoring on his first home run in the International league.

On May 11 another banner cried: MONTREAL FANS GREET JACKIE WITH WILD ACCLAIM, this time accompanied by a two-column cut of Robinson shaking hands with the mayor of Montreal. Lower down the page a modest one-column head noted that GIBSON HOMERS AS GRAYS WIN, LOSE.

Josh had opened the season with a first inning blast against Baltimore to lead the Grays to a 9–8 victory. He would keep blasting them for the next four months.

A week later fans learned that CAMPANELLA SHINES IN DEBUT, along with a shot of Roy in his Nashua uniform, and that NEWCOMBE SHUTS OUT PAWTUCKET.

Amid this adulation of Robinson, Gibson arrived in Pittsburgh and pounded the ball over the 457-foot center field fence—about 100 feet over it, according to the papers. This was the second time Josh had conquered it and the first time since the play-off against the Lincolns in 1939 when "Sampson Gibson" was an 18-year-old rookie. The papers scarcely noticed.

ROBINSON LEADS INTERNATIONAL LEAGUE BATTING the *Afro-American* reported on June 8, again with a two-column photo of Jackie.

In Yankee Stadium meanwhile, Gibson replied by smashing another monstrous drive, this one into the center field bleachers 440 feet away, a spot that few other men have ever reached. But there were no headlines or picture to mark the feat, only a small box midway down the sports page.

Next Josh faced another rival—Joe Louis. The Louis–Billy Conn rematch, which had been awaited for five years, dominated all the sports news on June 15, along with reports of the death of exchamp Jack Johnson. A week later JOE KEEPS TITLE, the *Afro* shouted in two-inch letters on page one, and filled its sports pages with photos and stories of the fight.

No one seemed to notice or care that Josh had driven a ball over the double-deck stands at Philadelphia's Shibe Park (Connie Mack Stadium): Birmingham outfielder Ed Steele said it came in the teeth of a stiff wind.

"What about *me?*" Josh seemed to be crying out. But it was in vain.

In Sportsman's Park, St. Louis, he cleared the bleachers to the right of the center field scoreboard. Normal "Tweed" Webb, who was scoring the game for the black St. Louis *Argus,* estimated the drive went 540 feet. Bob Burnes of the St. Louis *Globe Democrat,* was more conservative; he said the ball traveled between 450 and 500 feet. "It's probably the longest ball I've seen hit at that ballpark. It was a line drive, just kept rising; it was still on its way up when it went out of the park."

The *Afro* ignored the blow. PITCHER ROY PARTLOW RELEASED BY MONTREAL ROYALS it declared on July 20. And a week later: TAN PITCHER PROVING SENSATION FOR DODGER FARM over a story about Don Newcombe. Even the East–West game in August merited only a two-inch story plus box score. The *Afro* editors had their eyes on Canada: JACKIE'S STICK HELPS TO TAKE FLAG and HAIL JACKIE AS ROYALS GREATEST KEYSTONER OF ALL TIME.

Finally, Louis knocked Josh out of the headlines again, as Joe KO'd Tammy Mauriello in a September brawl.

A week later Josh Gibson drilled his final home run, against the Cubans. It gave him the amazing total of 18 in only 119 at bats—one

	HR	AB	AB/HR	HR/540 AB (Ruth)	HR/590 AB (Maris)	BA
Maris	61	590	9.7	56	61	.269
Ruth	60	540	9.0	60	66	.356
Gibson	18	119	6.6	82	89	.361

every 6.6 times up. In 1927, Ruth had averaged a homer every nine at bats; in 1961, Roger Maris' average was 9.7. To put it another way, if Josh had come to bat as often as Roger did, he would have socked 89 over the wall!

What's more, Josh's .361 was second only to Larry Doby's .386.

Cool Papa Bell taped up his tired 43-year-old legs and hit .435, though he came to bat 100 times less than Josh.

Wilmer Fields, who had been waiting for four years in the Army for his big chance on the Grays, pitched brilliantly; our figures show him with a 12–2 record, although he said he won 16 in all, and it may well be that four more wins will some day be found.

Still the Grays were an overaged club, and they fell to third behind the younger, hungry Eagles of Doby, Irvin (.333), Day (9–4) and Manning (10–0)—the only team in the league with a winning record. The Cubans also finished strong with a rookie third baseman named Orestes Minoso (.309).

Out West the 40-year-old Paige, meanwhile, was also enjoying a great season after his mediocre 1945 season. He sported a 5–1 record with an unbelievably low TRA of 0.47. His five wins included three shutouts, one a 1–0 victory over the Grays.

He probably would have won more, but Wilkinson bought a Cessna light airplane, christened it "The Satchel Paige," and ferried his star around the country accepting pitching dates. Wilkie's son, ex-Air Force Captain Dick Wilkinson, did the piloting. Dick had flown 27 combat missions before getting shot down over the Ploesti oil fields in Romania. He liked to buzz the other team before the game "for the psychological advantage." But after one stormy trip with him, Satchel announced, "I ain't ever flying in one of those little birds again."

There were two East–West games that year, and Paige didn't get the call to pitch either one. A young hard thrower from Memphis, Dan Bankhead, Sam's baby brother and the league strikeout leader, started the first game. Gibson did play both games and was held to a single in five at bats.

The Monarch vets had returned from the service—Willard Brown (.348), Hank Thompson (.287), Buck O'Neil (.350), and Connie Johnson (9–3). A holdover, Hilton Smith, was 8–3.

Word was going around that Paige couldn't go nine innings any more. He didn't want the big league scouts to be scared away, so he went nine innings against the Indianapolis Clowns to clinch the pennant.

So the Monarchs prepared to play the Eagles in the World Series. A good trivia quiz question is: Name five men who played in both the black and white World Series. Four of them played in 1946.*

The series opened in New York's Polo Grounds before a crowd that included a dozen big league scouts.

Smith got the honor of starting the first game against Newark's Leon Day. In the first, Thompson singled and scored the first run, but Day whiffed the dangerous Willard Brown to end the inning. For the Eagles, Doby bunted safely with two outs and stole, but Smith got Irvin on a fly for the third out.

Smitty nursed the lead until the sixth, when Doby walked and stole, and Duncan called Paige in from the bull pen to a mixture of cheers and boos. Satch gave up a single to Johnny Davis (.307) that tied the score. But Paige atoned an inning later by getting a hit, a rarity for him, and scoring the game winner on an error and another single. In four innings, Satch gave four hits and whiffed eight.

Two days later in Newark, heavyweight champ Joe Louis threw out the ceremonial first ball, a silver ball honoring 90-year-old Ben Holmes of the old Cuban Giants, winners of the first black World Series way back in 1888. Ex-infantry Captain Ford Smith started for the Monarchs, and again Paige came in in the seventh after Newark had tied it. This time however, the Eagles kept right on hitting, scored three more runs off Paige, and defeated Satchel 7–4.

In Kansas City for game three, Hank Thompson went 4 for 5 to lead the Monarchs to victory behind Jim LaMarque by 15–5.

The Eagles tied it in game four 8–1. Again Satch came on in relief, losing 4–1, and gave up a three-run homer to Irvin. In five innings, Paige gave up eight hits and four runs. Monte had a great day, four for four, and Doby hit a double and a triple. But what Monte remembered most vividly was this play:

> We had a rally going, scored a couple of runs. Men on first, second, two out. Jimmy Wilks was off the bag at second, thinking of trying to steal

---

*Paige of the Monarchs and 1948 Indians; Thompson of the Monarchs and 1954 Giants; Doby of the Eagles and 1948 Indians; Irvin of the Eagles and 1951 Giants; and Willie Mays of the 1948 Black Barons and the 1951, '54, and '61 Giants.

third. Satchel goes into the stretch and throws behind him [without looking]! You know how difficult it is to throw a strike like that? I'd never seen it before! He was an innovator.

"Satchel used to do it with ease," his catcher, Chico Renfroe, agreed.

Smith won game five 5–1 over Manning—Max's only loss of the season—as Thompson got two more hits to put the Monarchs ahead three games to two.

Newark took the must-win sixth game in a slugfest 9–7. Brown and O'Neil hit homers for KC, but Irvin topped them with two for Newark to win it.

That brought the two teams down to the seventh game at Newark two days later, and manager Duncan named Satchel to clinch it. The Monarchs went into the contest without their big men, Brown and Ted Strong, who had been lured into an early departure for Puerto Rico. That meant moving a catcher and a pitcher into the outfield.

And on the afternoon of the game, Paige was missing too! "It can't start till I get there," Satchel said. "I'm gonna pitch, they're gonna wait for me. They want to see me."

But they didn't wait. Ford Smith hastily took the mound and pitched magnificently, holding the Eagles to only three hits. An error and Irvin's hit scored Newark's first run. O'Neil countered with a homer to tie it 1–1. Kansas City went ahead 2–1 in the seventh. But in the eighth, Doby and Irvin walked, and Johnny Davis hit a double to score them both and win the game and the Series.

Paige had not been particularly effective—one win, one loss, and a 5.40 TRA. And, the players demanded, where the hell had he been in game seven?

O'Neil's theory: He had been busy discussing business details with Bob Feller for their forthcoming transcontinental barnstorming tour.

Feller, the strikeout champ with 348 that year, put together a truly all-star squad. American league bat champ Mickey Vernon (.353) played first. Johnny Berardino, who later starred on the TV hit soap opera "General Hospital," played second (.265.) Phil Rizzuto (.257) played short. Ken Keltner (.241) was on third. The outfield was Sam Chapman (.261), Jeff Heath (.278), and Charlie Keller (.275, 30 homers). Frankie Hayes (.256) and Jim Hegan (.236) caught. Pitching were Feller (26–15), Spud Chandler (20–8), Johnny Sain (20–14),

Dutch Leonard (10–10), and Bob Lemon (4–5). Later, NL bat king Stan Musial (.365) joined the team after the World Series.

Satch's team included Jethroe, Johnny Davis, and Gene Benson in the outfield; O'Neil, Thompson, Art Wilson, Easterling, and Herb Souell in the infield; the pitchers were Paige, Smith, Gentry Jessup, Manning, Neck Stanley, and Barney Brown, while young Renfroe and old-timer Quincy Trouppe (later with the Cleveland Indians) did the catching. Gibson was not invited, it's not clear why.

The two teams played 13 games that October. The Paiges won six, the Fellers seven. Said Renfroe, who later became an Atlanta sportscaster:

> I'll be honest with you: We played against the cream of the big leaguers, and we weren't the best in our league. The team Satchel Paige was supposed to put together, a lot of them left and went to Puerto Rico. [Others, such as Irvin and Doby, joined Jackie Robinson's All-Stars.] If Satchel had put *that* team together, Bob Feller and them would have caught hell. In fact, I never would have been able to go.

Not all the newspaper accounts of the series have been found—some apparently do not exist. But a partial summary of those that are known follows:

The teams opened in Chicago, where the crowds were so great, Smith said, Feller himself had to help man the turnstiles to handle all the customers. Bob and Satch each pitched one-hit ball for three innings before Sain took over and beat Jessup 6–5.

In New York's Yankee Stadium, Chandler of the Yankees faced Barney Brown. Reliever Bob Lemon's homer broke a 1–1 tie in the eighth, and the Fellers won it 4–2 in the tenth.

The next night Paige and Feller each went five innings in the Stadium. Thompson's long home run in the fifth put the Paiges ahead, as Satch got relief from emeryball artist Neck Stanley and beat Bob 4–0. Paige whiffed four and Feller none. As O'Neil put it:

> Satchel really rose to the occasion when he was pitching against Charlie Keller or someone who was oustanding. It looked like he would reach his greatest peak, seemed as though it was more of a challenge to him.

In Baltimore the following night, Feller demanded that Satch drop Stanley from the team. So Jessup pitched and beat Feller, Sain, and Lemon 7–4.

In Pittsburgh, the two stars, Feller and Paige, left the game tied 1–1, but the Paiges won it 3–1 as Satch and Barney Brown combined on a two-hitter.

Manning lost a close one in Dayton.

At Columbus, Feller and Paige started again, but again Lemon lost it in relief 4–3.

In Kansas City Davis's home run beat Chandler in the ninth 3–2.

Stan Musial, the big league bat champ with .365, joined Feller's club in Los Angeles after the World Series against Boston. Bob and Satch each worked the first five innings, and Satch stopped Stan without a hit. He and Feller left with Bob winning 4–3, which was also the final score. One sportswriter warned Feller that he would lose his arm trying to match Paige three or five innings every night.

The white World Series had been played that year in the two bandbox parks, Boston and St. Louis, and the players' winning shares came to only $6,000 a man. Musial gleefully chortled that he made more money playing Paige than he had playing the Red Sox: "I should have been here all the time!" a statement that made commissioner Chandler blanch. What if players deliberately tried to evade the series, or take a dive to get it over quickly? In the future, Happy ordered, no barnstorming would begin until the Series was over.

By tour's end, Paige led the pitchers with two victories and one loss. Box scores sometimes did not give complete data or even enough data to assign a pitcher of record, but, as far as can be determined, the pitching line was:

	W–L		W–L
Feller	1–1	Paige	2–1
Sain	1–1	Jessup	1–1
Lemon	1–2	Brown	1–1
Chandler	0–1	Manning	0–1

In their personal duel, Feller and Paige came out like this:

Feller	W–L	IP	H	R	SO	BB	Paige	W–L	IP	H	R	SO	BB
Chicago		3	1	0	1	2			3	1	0	3	0
New York		—	4	—	0	4		W	5	3	—	4	1
Baltimore	L	5	4	2	0	—		W	5	4	0	4	—
Baltimore		1	1	0	3	0			didn't pitch				
Pittsburgh		3	2	1	3	0			3	2	1	3	0
Columbus		3	—	—	—	—			3	—	—	3	1
Wichita		3	3	1	5	0			2	2	0	2	0
Los Angeles	W	5	5	3	7	0		L	5	3	4	4	7
Totals		23	20	7	19	6			26	15	5	23	9

TRA 2.73; PA* .235   TRA 1.73; PA .159

---

*Pitching Average (Opposition Batting Average)

That winter, in a dark Pittsburgh bar on The Hill, Josh Gibson drank and brooded. His weight had fallen alarmingly, down to 180 pounds. Ted Page found him on a bar stool, shaking another customer by the collar. "Tell him who hit the longest ball any place," he called to Page. "Tell him!"

On a cold Saturday night in January, Page bumped into Josh again, this time on a windy street corner. "He was like always, full of play and kidding around," Ted recalled. "I think we kind of rassled a little bit and punched one another on the arm, some kind of boyish gesture."

Gibson returned home, half drunk and with a headache. His sister Annie told Bob Peterson in *Only the Ball Was White* that he was put to bed, where he laughed and talked among his trophies until he was suddenly seized by a stroke.

Brashler reports a different story, that Josh was stricken in a movie theater and taken home unconscious.

Whatever the circumstances, the next day Posey's old partner wired the other players the news:

Pittsbugh Penna Jan 20 1947
    Josh Gibson passed Monday 1 am funeral Friday 1 pm 2712 Bedford Ave Pgh
                    Rufus Jackson

Judy Johnson heard the news on radio 300 miles away in Wilmington and was stunned. He blamed himself:

> He was the biggest kid you ever saw in your life. Like he was 12 or 13 years old. Oh, he was jolly *all* the time. When he got sick, it hurt me, it hurt me real bad. I couldn't get around to help him. I only wish I could. I think I could have helped him a whole lot, because he thought the world of me. I started him off. Anything I'd say: "OK, Jing . . . OK, Jing." I could almost make him cry just talking to him. That's the truth—I could. He'd just sit there, never say a word, never argue back, he'd just sit there and listen.
>
> But he got sick. I never got the right story about his illness. I don't know whether it was the drugs.

Today, over four decades later, the death is still a mystery. Was it a stroke, a brain hemorrhage, or a drug overdose?

"Drugs? No way!" insists Buck O'Neil.

> Josh died of a tumor on the brain. He was just a shell of a man. I think he had what [Kansas City Royals manager] Dick Howser did. He couldn't remember things, just like Howser. The last time I saw him he was calling me Buck, but he was thinking of Buck Leonard. We said, "Josh is going crazy." Actually, he probably was.

"He just drank himself to death," Johnny Taylor believed. "I think (Robinson's signing) just gnawed away at him. Bankhead destroyed himself the same way." (Sam Bankhead also became an alcoholic and never went to see his youngest brother, Dan, pitch for the Dodgers. Sam was shot to death in a barroom fight.)

Bill Yancey, who played against Gibson in that famous Yankee Stadium play-off in 1930, also subscribed to the alcohol theory.

But Fields disagreed. "Strong as he was, it would take more than liquor to kill him."

Whatever the cause, "I refuse to say that Josh destroyed himself," Page said. "Some people say Josh Gibson died of a brain hemorrhage. I say he died of a broken heart."

"Josh just might have died of grief," O'Neil agreed.

If he didn't die *of* a broken heart, he died *with* one, Larry Doby believed. Gibson "was the king," said Ric Roberts. "He just couldn't recover when he saw they picked Jackie Robinson over him."

Gibson's death was more than a personal tragedy. It was also a loss to all baseball fans, especially those who never saw him. Sug Cornelius said:

> The American people were denied the right to see a superstar perform. Had he been given the chance to participate in the American or National league, I bet he'd have hit 75 home runs a year. I mean, with his strength and power, and the way the average pitcher pitches today—if he throws you a fastball the first time, you can bet his next pitch is going to be a curveball. If you're out there every day, you're going to think baseball every day. Josh would have easily been a .400-hitter—.400-plus.

"He would have been a superstar in the majors," Page nodded.

"If Josh had been in his prime and come along when Roy Campanella did, you'd never have heard of Campanella," said old-time pitcher Bill Holland.

Campy cheerfully agreed. "I couldn't carry Josh's glove," he told reporters who came to congratulate him on his own election to Cooperstown. "Anything I could do, Josh could do better."

Gibson was buried in a numbered grave in Pittsburgh's Allegheny cemetery. Twenty-eight years later, Puerto Rican promoter Pedrin Zorilla and Ted Page located it covered with weeds and began a fund drive to buy a headstone. Willie Stargell was the first to contribute, and commissioner Bowie Kuhn's office covered the rest.

> The time you won your town the race
> We chaired you through the market-place;
> Man and boy stood cheering by,
> And home we brought you shoulder-high.
>
> To-day, the road all runners come,
> Shoulder-high we bring you home,
> And set you at your threshold down,
> Townsman of a stiller town. . . .
>
> Eyes the shady night has shut
> Cannot see the record cut,
> And silence sounds no worse than cheers
> After earth has stopped the ears. . . .
>
> A. E. Housman
> *To an Athlete Dying Young*

1947

Palestine was partitioned. The Truman Doctrine aided Greece and Turkey. The Marshall Plan. Indian independence. The House Un-American Activities committee. The GI bill. Truman ordered the armed forces desegregated.

"Peg O' My Heart," "Bongo, Bongo, Bongo, I Don't Want to Leave the Congo," "Open the Door, Richard," "How Are Things in Glocca Morra?," "That's My Desire," "Near You," "I'm Looking Over a Four-Leaf Clover," "Everything I Have Is Yours."

Miracle on 34th Street. The Hollywood blacklist.

Broadway: *A Streetcar Named Desire.*

TV: "Howdy Doody," "You Bet Your Life."

Books: *The Diary of Anne Frank, Gentleman's Agreement, Inside USA;* Mickey Spillane's *I, the Jury; Tales of the South Pacific.*

The Yankees spoiled Bill Bevens' series no-hitter, beat the Dodgers on TV 4–3. Rocky Graziano KO'd Tony Zale, Sugar Ray Robinson won the welterweight title.

The Grays got Luke Easter to replace Gibson as their power hitter. He batted .311 with ten home runs, but the team still finished only fourth. The New York Cubans, with Minoso (.294) and Luis Tiant Sr. (10–0), won the pennant and World Series over Cleveland.

The fans, however, had lost interest. They would rather take a train 300 miles to see the Dodgers and Robinson play than to take a trolley across town to see the Negro leagues. "We couldn't draw flies," Leonard said.

Bill Veeck, the owner of the Cleveland Indians, signed the first black in the American league—22-year-old Larry Doby, who had hit .414 that year and tied Monte Irvin for the league in homers, 14.

Hopefully, Paige wired Veeck, asking, "When are you going to bring me in?"

"It will happen," Bill wrote back. "Let's take our time." Veeck already had a reputation as a circus showman and knew there would be an outcry if he hired a 41-year-old legend known to the white world mostly for his clowning. The Indians were stuck in fourth place with no hope of winning a pennant. Why cause a hullaballoo for nothing? Bill reasoned.

Veeck may have been a little bit disingenuous to Satchel. Author Joseph Thomas Moore said Bill had instructed his scouts not to look for aging stars but for younger men who had a future, such as Doby.

The lowly St. Louis Browns also hoped to cash in on the new-found drawing power of black stars and took Paige's two teammates, Willard Brown and Hank Thompson, from the Monarchs. But the Browns were in last place, and the St. Louis fans went to see the Cardinals instead. Brown's old Monarch friends said the 34-year-old Brown had the talent but not the temperament to be a pioneer, while Thompson at 21 was still too young. Brown hit only .179 in 21 games with only one home run. Thompson hit .256 in 27 games. The Browns, strapped for cash, sent them back to Kansas City in return for a refund. Back on the Monarchs, Willard hit .336 and Hank .344. They would go on to star in the Texas league and the New York Giants, respectively.

Branch Rickey, meanwhile, signed Dan Bankhead, who had struck out 113 men in 197 innings for a weak Memphis team, and rushed him into the Dodgers' pennant race. In the World Series against the Yanks, Dan was inserted as a pinch-runner, entering baseball's trivia world as the first black pitcher to play in a World Series.

Paige saw only limited action for the Monarchs. He pitched only two games, both of them the seven-inning second games of dou-bleheaders, when the shadows, plus the hitters' fatigue, would make his fastball even more effective. He won one and lost one, though he sported a low 1.64 TRA. Again Smith topped him with 7–3.

O'Neil had replaced Duncan as manager.

> How did I manage Satchel? I don't think anybody ever managed Satchel. He was a very agreeable fellow, he was a fun-loving man, but you had to let him have the reins. The little things you wanted him to do, you could kid him into doing. But just putting down a demand—that would never be met.
>
> "We want you to be on time"—you say that, he's never on time. But you say, "I bet you we'll be in Cleveland before you get there; I'll bet you a dollar."

Paige didn't ride the team bus, he drove his own car. He also liked to sing with his ukulele. Often O'Neil and the rest of the team would find Satch's car pulled off the highway and the pitcher lolling under a tree strumming. "I just thought of this song," he'd tell them, "let's sing."

> Satchel couldn't hit, but he had a lot of fun. I left him in a ball game to hit over in East Chicago. Satchel said, "Nancy, I can hit this guy," and he hit the ball over the center fielder's head. Anyone else would have made a home run, but he laughed all the way to second base, said, "You can take me out now." He talked about that till the day he died.

But Satchel had a serious side too. He and O'Neil went fishing in Buck's home state of Florida, and when water moccasins began swimming around their boat, O'Neil reached for a gun. Paige stopped him. This is their home, he said; the men were the intruders.

On another occasion they were in Charleston, South Carolina, and went to see the old block, where slaves had been auctioned a century before. After a couple minutes of silence, Satch said, "I feel like I been here before, roomie."

"Me too," Buck nodded.

That autumn Paige was on the coast, facing Feller and his All-Stars as a member of Chet Brewer's Royals team again.

Satchel was backed by Monarch catcher Joe Greene, Charlie Neal, who later went to the Dodgers, and Lorenzo "Piper" Davis, the Birmingham playing manager who was about to give a teenage rookie named Willie Mays his first push toward stardom.

This time Feller added home run champ Ralph Kiner (.313, 51 homers) and Andy Pafko (.302). The rest of the cast included Ferris Fain (.291), Ken Keltner (.257), Eddie Miller (.268), and Gerry Priddy (.214). Pitching was Feller (20–11 with Cleveland), Eddie Lopat (16–13 with sixth-place Chicago), and Bill McCahan (10–5 with the fifth-place A's).

Paige must have thrown all his pent-up anger into the games, as he made Bob's squad look like amateurs.

In game one, Satch struck out seven in five innings (Feller whiffed two) but lost 2–1. Kiner doubled and singled, though it's not clear whether it was against Paige or his relief.

Paige's contract called for 15 percent of the gross, but Brewer said he discovered that Satch was receiving only 15 percent of the net after expenses. They owed him another $2400.

"Sure enough, Dooflackem?"

"Yeah."

"Come on, let's go." They barged into the office and demanded the rest of the money. Back at the hotel, Satch tossed Chet a tip: "Here, Dooflackem, here's $30." Brewer said he threw it back in Paige's face.

A week later Satch whiffed eight in five innings, including Kiner two times, and was leading 1–0 when he came out, but his relief lost it 2–1 again.

Next Satch faced Ewell "The Whip" Blackwell, who had had a spectacular season—22–8 with fifth-place Cincinnati, including 16 straight victories. Paige whiffed nine more in four innings, gave two hits and was leading 2–0 when he retired, though the Blackwells tied it before losing in the 13th.

In a rematch with Blackwell, Paige struck out five in four innings and was losing 2–0 before his teammates rallied to win.

Finally, the promoters begged both Feller and Paige to go nine innings against each other, which they did. Bobby was raked for 11 hits and eight runs, as Davis and Greene homered and Satch pitched a four-hit shutout with 15 more K's.

Both Feller and Paige ended with 1–1 records, but Satch had completely dominated Bob. He struck out 44 big leaguers in 27 innings, walked only one, held them to one run per nine innings, and had them hitting a mere .144 against him. A comparison of the two pitching totals follows:

	IP	H	R	SO	BB	K/9 IP	TRA	PA
Feller	18	18	9	7	1	3.5	4.50	.261
Paige	27	13	3	44	1	14.2	1.00	.144

What more did Paige have to do to prove he was a major league pitcher? Still, no one made a move to sign him.

Disheartened, Satch sailed to Puerto Rico, where he was battered for an 0–3 record. Was the old man washed up?

1948

G andhi was assassinated. The Berlin airlift. Israel was born and came under attack from the Arabs. Tito broke with Stalin. Tojo was hanged. Truman upset Dewey ("Give 'em hell"). The bikini.

"Now Is the Hour," "A Tree in the Meadow," "Buttons and Bows," "On a Slow Boat to China," "Baby, It's Cold Outside," "Nature Boy," "It's Magic," "My Happiness," "Bouquet of Roses."

The Red Shoes, The Treasure of Sierra Madre, Key Largo.

TV: "Douglas Edwards and the News," "Arthur Godfrey's Talent Scouts," Ed Sullivan's "Toast of the Town," "The Milton Berle Show," Perry Como's "Chesterfield Supper Club."

Radio: "Duffy's Tavern"

Broadway: *A Streetcar Named Desire.*

Books: *The Kinsey Report.*

Babe Ruth died. The Olympics resumed; Harrison Dillard, Mal Whitfield, and Bob Matthias won golds. Citation (Arcaro up) won the Triple Crown.

The Grays with Easter (.363) won a play-off against Baltimore with Jim Gilliam and Joe Black (10–5). Out west Birmingham, with rookie Willie Mays (.262), defeated Kansas City and Willard Brown (.394) for the pennant. The Grays won the series in five, holding Mays to one hit.

But nobody much cared any more. The black papers wrote about nothing but Robinson and Campanella. Black attendance plummeted as Griffith's dark prediction of 1942 came true.

As Paige put it 33 years later: "The majors broke us up. Then they took whoever they wanted to."

In 1948, however, they didn't want Satchel Paige. He was 41 and back to bouncing around the prairies barnstorming—the sharp decline in Negro baseball attendance meant a sharp decline in Paige's earning power as well. As far as we can find out, he didn't pitch an inning for the Monarchs.

Satch and Lahoma sat down at their dining room table to talk about the future. Satchel had decided to pack it in for good. "My mind was made up," he said. "I was sick of hopping around, and things weren't going too well."

Then Satch got a letter from Abe Saperstein, owner of the Black Barons and Harlem Globe Trotters and special scout for Indian owner Veeck. It told him to report to Cleveland for a tryout. "Lahoma and me danced all over the house," Satch rejoiced.

Paige reported on July 7, his 42nd birthday. He wrote that he asked Veeck not to forget Wilkinson and Tom Baird, the two who had picked him up when his arm went dead in 1938 and put him back in the money. Veeck reportedly gave them $5,000 to split.

How much did Veeck pay Paige? Some reporters say $25,000, a bargain considering how crucial he would be to the team. Five years earlier, Satch had been taking home a reported $40,000 a year. But by '47 he was happy to be making anything.

Gibson would have been 37 years old. Roberts believed:

> If Josh had had the patience to wait—as Satchel Paige waited—18 more months, it is certain that he would have gone to the Indians as special receiver for Paige. I look at Dave Winfield with all that money he's making, and Josh got $1200 a month. Winfield got $120,000 a month to go 1 for 22 in the 1981 World Series.

(In June, a year and a half after his father's death, Josh Jr. had broken the Organized Ball color line that his father had died assaulting; he became the first black to play in the Middle Atlantic league. The younger Gibson wasn't the athlete his father had been, however; he went 0 for 6 in his debut. Years later, he developed kidney trouble, and friends raised $20,000 for a dialysis machine and transplant.)

Paige joined young Larry Doby, Cleveland's center fielder, who had preceded him by a year as the first black in the American league. It was the first time they had met since the '46 Eagles–Monarchs World Series.

As Veeck had anticipated, *The Sporting News* accused him of "demeaning the standards of baseball" by signing Paige as a publicity stunt.

But this was different from '47. Now the Indians were in the midst of a four-way pennant fight with Boston, New York, and Philadelphia. Veeck was ready to take the heat for signing Satch if it could mean a pennant.

Paige's first game came July 9, a week after he reported, against the sixth-place St. Louis Browns before 35,000 in Cleveland. Bob

Lemon was losing 4–1 when Satch was waved in from the bull pen. "I just shuffled along, and every time I shuffled, the stands busted loose," Paige wrote. Photographers' flashbulbs popped in his face.

The first batter was Chuck Stevens, a .260 hitter with one home run. Satch admitted that his nerves "were jumping every which way." Stevens singled.

Then the nerves disappeared. "I was just as calm as could be." The next batter was Gerry Priddy (.296), and Satch got him out on four pitches—overhand, sidearm, underhand, and hesitation. The Browns' best batter, Al Zarilla, a left-hander batting .329, flied out to end the inning. Satch pitched shutout ball in the seventh inning too, before leaving for a pinch-hitter.

Soon thereafter, AL president Will Harridge banned the hesitation pitch. It wasn't illegal, Paige insisted; he'd never thrown an illegal pitch in his life, only some "that haven't been seen by this generation." He decided not to show them his other pitches—the Midnight Creeper and Bat Dodger, for instance—for fear that Harridge would ban *them* too.

On July 14, Paige pitched an 11-inning exhibition against the third-place Dodgers of the National league before 65,000 people who came to see Paige and Doby play Jackie Robinson and Roy Campanella. The Indians won it 4–3, as Satch faced three men in the seventh—pitcher Hugh Casey, Pee Wee Reese (.274), and Tommy Brown (.241)—and struck them all out. Jackie Robinson would have led off the eighth, but he had already left the game, spoiling the hopes of a confrontation. So Satch got his replacement, Eddie Miksis (.213), plus Gene Hermanski (.290) and Marv Rackley (.327) on pop-ups.

Robinson considered Paige a minstrel show comedian, who was making it difficult for serious blacks to win respect on their talent. "Jackie detested Satchel," Doby said in his biography, *Pride Against Prejudice* by Joseph Thomas Moore. "I don't see how the hell you could stay with a guy like Satchel Paige," he told Larry.

Doby himself kept his distance from his roommate—the white teams usually hired blacks in multiples of two so they could room together. On the road, Paige liked to fry himself catfish on a hot plate, and Doby, who grew up in urban New Jersey, hated even the smell of it. Before long, the two blacks were living in different rooms.

Larry was embarrassed that Satch seemed to be playing the buffoon for the whites, and when Paige began to spin his tales in the dugout, Larry would "ease" away.

The problem didn't seem to be jealousy between the old master and the young upstart who had beaten him to the white majors. Instead, it sounded like the North–South prejudice Paige had run into from his black teammates when he had first joined the Crawfords 16 years earlier. Then, too, there was a 21-year age difference between the two men. In addition, the introverted Doby was the direct opposite of the ebullient Paige, who referred to Larry as an "old lady." For whatever reason, Doby said, "Satch and I didn't spend too much time together."

But one night Paige was burping on the mound, when pitcher Bob Lemon ran out with a bicarbonate of soda, and even Doby admitted he had to laugh in spite of himself.

Moore reports, however, that Larry and Satch did join teammates Jim Hegan and Eddie Robinson in one of Satchel's favorite pastimes, quarteting. With Satch singing bass, they harmonized on "Old Black Joe" and other old standbys.

Sometimes it was Satchel who undertook to instruct the younger man on how to behave. In St. Louis one day, fans behind home were riding Doby, who challenged them with a bat, and one fan leaped over the railing ready for combat. The players rushed to intervene, and afterwards, outfielder Bob Kennedy said, old Satch took Larry into the dugout alone and "chewed him out" for jeopardizing blacks' gains.

The day after the Brooklyn game, manager Lou Boudreau again called on Satch in relief of Lemon against the A's, who were making their last pennant run for Old Connie Mack (they eventually finished fourth). Hank Majeski (.310, 12 homers) smashed a Paige pitch over the roof to tie it, but Cleveland's Ken Keltner replied with one for the Indians, and Satch had won his first major league game, giving up three hits in 3.1 innings.

Paige pitched his first Yankee stadium game as an Indian on July 21, pitching one inning of hitless relief. One senses that the *New York Times'* John Drebinger shared *The Sporting News'* opinion of Paige's signing. In his report, he hardly mentioned Paige at all, as if trying to ignore the whole embarrassing business.

The next day, after Joe DiMaggio's grand slam had driven Bob Feller out of the game, Paige pitched two more innings of relief, gave one hit, and whiffed two. One of the strikeouts, reportedly, was DiMag, although Drebinger didn't mention it. In fact, this time Drebinger didn't mention Paige at all!

Finally, on July 30, Satchel lost a game on two bad plays by his outfield. The rampaging Red Sox, winners of 18 games in their last

20, had KO'd starter Gene Bearden with four runs in two innings, and Ted Williams knocked in two or more in the fourth with a double off Don Black to make the score 7–6, Cleveland, when Satchel was hurried in from the bull pen to face Vern Stephens (.269, 29 homers) and Bobby Doerr (.281, 27). He got them both and left Ted stranded on second.

In the fifth, Satch retired Stan Spence (.235), the hot rookie Billy Goodman (.310), and Birdie Tebbetts (.280).

Paige opened the sixth by getting pitcher Denny Galehouse out. Then lead-off man Dom DiMaggio (.285) hit a bloop single to the opposite field. Right fielder Allie Clark let it get through him for two bases, then threw wildly to the infield, as Dom scampered to third, whence Johnny Pesky (.281) scored him with a fly to tie the game. The menacing Williams (.369, 25 homers) went out to end the inning.

In the seventh, Stephens and Doerr both singled, putting men on first and second, Spence popped up, and Goodman hit a low line drive to left. This time Dale Mitchell let it get through him as Stephens scored the tie-breaking run. Needing a DP to get out of the inning, Satchel got it. He then pitched hitless ball in the eighth. As Frank Gibbons of the Cleveland *Press* wrote, except for Mitchell's misplay, "the game might still be going on."

Satchel had pitched better than either Bearden (20–7) or Black, but he got the loss, not them. Those are the breaks of the game.

On August 3, Satchel drew his first starting assignment, against the seventh-place Senators, as the Indians clung to a three-way tie for second, one game behind the A's. To be safe, manager Lou Boudreau sent Feller and Bob Lemon down to the bull pen to be ready to rescue Satch if need be. "They're still down there yet," Paige said drily years later.

In the first inning, Satch gave up two walks plus a triple to Ed Stewart (.279), but he told Boudreau not to worry. By the sixth, the Indians had gone ahead 4–3, and Paige had his second victory, a seven-hitter for six innings. He had also pitched the Indians into first place.

On the 7th, Satch faced the Yankees again in relief, this time with the score tied in the eighth. He held them for two innings and won his third game.

Satchel got another starting call on August 13 against the last-place White Sox in Comiskey Park, a park that held a lot of memories for him. Officially, there were 51,000 fans in the stands. Unofficially, some 71,000 stormed the turnstiles. Eighteen persons were hospitalized in the rush. There was standing room even *under* the stands, Veech laughed. Paige pitched nice and easy for eight innings. Larry Doby's triple gave him a lead, and he never lost it, winning 5–0, his first big league shutout, on five hits and no walks.

Eight days later, Satch played to his third sell-out crowd in a row—78,382 at Municipal Stadium, the largest crowd, till then, ever to see a night game. It brought his three-game total to 202,000 and edged the Indians closer to baseball's first 2-million mark. "I should be working on percentage," Paige sighed.

Again he faced the White Sox, and, after a pre-game tribute of fireworks and taps to Babe Ruth, who had just died, for the first three innings Satch gave up only one tainted hit—Pat Seerey (.229) fell away from an inside pitch in the second and blooped a hit to right.

In the fourth, Tony Lupien walked, and Luke Appling (.314) singled to center, but Doby whipped a throw to third to nip Lupien for an out. In the bottom of the inning, Larry knocked in the only run Satch would need.

Two innings later Lupien (.246) doubled. In the seventh, Doby went back to the fence to catch Seerey's blast—if Pat had pulled it, it might have been a homer, Satch admitted later. In the eighth, Paige threw his only curve of the evening and struck out a surprised Don Kolloway (.273). At last Satchel shuffled off the mound to a loud ovation after a quick (one hour, 50 minutes) masterpiece, his second three-hitter in a row. It gave him a run of 20 straight scoreless innings, and gave the Indians their fourth straight shutout as a team—they would break the record, 41 straight scoreless innings—the following night. Most important, it left the Indians three games ahead of the Red Sox.

After the game, Paige sat on a locker room stool, pulling on a beer, and told reporters how close he had come only a couple of months earlier to packing baseball in forever.

In three starts Paige's record was three wins and over 200,000 tickets sold.

A gleeful Veeck wired Spink: PAIGE PITCHING—NO RUNS, THREE HITS. HE DEFINITELY IS IN LINE FOR SPORTING NEWS 'ROOKIE OF THE YEAR' AWARD. REGARDS.

Did Satchel think he would get it?, a writer asked. Paige looked a long time before replying, "Twenty-two years is a long time to be a rookie."

When he was announced to pitch in Boston, fans lined up at ten A.M. for tickets, and 18,000 of them had to be turned away. He got

through the first two innings without a run against Ted Williams
(.369), Bobby Doerr (.285), Dom DiMaggio (.285), Johnny Pesky
(.281), etc. But in the third, he nicked pitcher Joe Dobson on the
sleeve. DiMaggio smacked a triple for one run, Pesky hit a long fly for
another, Williams lined a single, Vern Stephens (.269) lined another,
and that was all for Paige. The Indians rallied to win, however,
rescuing him from the loss.

Finally, on August 30, Satch whipped seventh-place Washington
7–1.

Then Satch lost his effectiveness. The Brownies, of all teams,
twice knocked him out of the box. In addition, Jules Tygiel writes,
Paige was caught coming in after curfew and once was fined for not
showing up at the park because, he said, he "thought it was going to
rain." An exasperated Boudreau pulled him from the rotation for the
stretch race. Cleveland finished the season in a dead tie with Boston,
and one wonders if Satchel could have added at least one more victory
to make a play-off unnecessary. On the other hand, they needed every
one of Paige's six victories to get into the play-off.

Veeck took great glee in wiring *Sporting News* editor J.G. Taylor
Spink that Paige had "demeaned" baseball with a 6–1 record, plus one
save—not bad for an old man who had been 1–1 in the Negro league
just a year before. Spink sniffed that it just proved that the caliber of
the big leagues wasn't what it used to be.

But by year's end even *The Sporting News* had to recognize Satch as
Rookie of the Year. When asked to comment on receiving the honor,
Paige asked which year they were talking about.

Satch grew eager at the prospect of his first World Series, against
the Boston Braves of "Spahn and Sain and two days of rain."

In the opening game, Feller (19–15) lost a heart-breaking two-
hitter 1–0.

Bob Lemon (20–14) started game two. When he ran into trouble,
Boudreau signaled for Paige to warm up. Satch said his stomach was
churning with excitement, but Lemon pitched himself out of trouble,
and Paige dejectedly sat down.

Rookie Gene Bearden (20–7), the hero of the play-off, started the
third game and won it.

Satchel coyly waited to be announced to start game four. Instead,
a journeyman named Steve Gromek (9–3) got the call against the
Braves' ace, Johnny Sain, who had beaten Feller in game one. Gromek
said he was picked as a sacrificial lamb so Feller would be rested to
start game five. If Boudreau had needed a "lamb," wouldn't Paige

have served as well as Gromek? But Satchel was probably still being punished for his past antics in missing workouts and bed checks. "I felt sick," he wrote. But Gromek surprised everyone by pitching a fine game, and Doby's homer beat Sain 2–1.

Would Satchel get his big chance in game five? I was in the stands that Sunday, along with 86,288 other fans, the largest crowd till then ever to see a big league game. With the Indians ahead three games to one, the well-rested Paige was a natural choice to start.

But Feller, who had never pitched in a World Series before, sensed that this would be his last chance to win a Series game. He wanted revenge for the first game loss, which, but for an umpire's blown call, should have been his victory. Manager Lou Boudreau gave Bob the ball, and once more Satchel trudged to the bull pen and sat down. He didn't exactly want Feller to lose, but he was hoping Bob would at least get into enough trouble to need a fireman like Paige to rush in and save the game.

Feller did get into trouble fast, yielding a three-run homer in the first. After six innings, he was still gamely struggling 5–5, but a sentimental Boudreau patiently left him in. Then two singles and a sacrifice scored another Boston run, and Lou finally pulled him. Three men—Satch, Ed "Specs" Klieman (3–2), and Russ Christopher, the Indians' top reliever with 17 saves—were all furiously throwing. "This is it," Satch thought.

Boudreau waved to the bull pen, but Satch did not come out. Instead, Klieman appeared, and Satchel, deeply wounded, for the first time in his life, didn't even want to throw the ball any more. Klieman gave up another run-scoring hit and two more walks, and Boudreau went to the bull pen again, while the fans chanted, "We want Satchel."

But again it was not Paige who responded. Christopher came in, faced two more men and gave up two more singles and two runs. It was 10–5 with men on first and third, one out, and pitcher Warren Spahn at bat.

At last Boudreau called on Paige to stop the hemorrhaging. Satchel ambled in, spit on his hands, gave the old double-pump windup, and fired. Umpire George Barr, a National leaguer, inspected the ball and apparently found it acceptable. On the next pitch, Satch took his stretch and paused, while Barr ran out again, complaining of the pause. Finally Paige threw a satisfactory pitch, which Spahn, a good hitter, hit in the air to center for a run-scoring out.

With left-handed Tommy Holmes (.325) up, Satch reached up

high—and wiggled his fingers. Barr ran out to the mound again, gesticulating balk, as the runner on first base trotted to second. Satchel was so mad, he threw Holmes his trouble ball, which Tom slapped on the ground for a double play, and the inning was over.

Satch's big World Series moment was over too. He was lifted for a pinch hitter in the eighth, having pitched just two-thirds of an inning.

As the huge crowd filed silently out of the stadium, I watched general manager Hank Greenberg stare glumly down. A banquet had been prepared to celebrate Cleveland's first victory in 28 years, and Greenberg had wanted to clinch it at home. Now he would have to go to Boston to do it. If Satchel had started the game instead of Feller, Hank might have gotten his wish.

Two days later, Bob Lemon (20–14) wrapped the series up.

Paige's two-thirds of an inning was all he would pitch. He thought that was small thanks for pitching them into the series to start with. Why hadn't Boudreau started him? "There was something wrong with my skin, I guess."

After he left the American league, Paige pointedly never went back to Cleveland.

1949–1982

B y this point, Satchel Paige's career has left the realm of black legend entirely behind and has entered the world of documented white history. His story is chronicled in his own *Maybe I'll Pitch Forever*, Bill Veeck's *Veeck as in Wreck*, Jules Tygiel's *Jackie Robinson and His Legacy*, and other books. Rather than recount the familiar, I prefer to offer a few anecdotes that may not be well known to most fans.

After the '48 series, Paige went back to Los Angeles for some games against his Cleveland teammates, Lemon (20–14) and Bearden (20–7), plus outfielder Al Zarilla of the Browns. Paige's club included Hilton Smith, Charlie Neal, and 45-year-old Cool Papa Bell.

Satch's most memorable moment, however, came not on the mound but at bat. With Pittsburgh's Murray Dickson pitching and Bell on first, Satch dropped a bunt—the old hit-and-run sacrifice that Rube Foster had been playing 30 years before. Bell got a big jump and tore around second without stopping. When the third baseman, a minor leaguer named Lang, came in to field the bunt, Bell kept right on running to the unguarded third. Catcher Roy Partee of the Browns ran down the line to cover third, so Bell brushed past him, too, and crossed the unguarded home, while Partee vainly hollered, "Time!" It was the first run of the game, which Satch's Royals won 4–3. Hilton Smith, catcher Chico Renfroe and Dickson himself confirm the play.

In 1969, I attended a luncheon in Washington along with Jesse Owens and others, when Ted Williams was honored with a Brotherhood Award by Howard University for urging Cooperstown to open its doors to Satch and Josh. Ted recalled his first sight of Satch back in San Diego in 1935 and his impression of him 14 years later in the American league of 1949:

> Well, I want to tell you, he still had a nice easy windup, and a nice easy hesitation pitch, and good control. Paige would give you all that easy motion, he'd stop—and there it was! All the time I was hitting up there, he's moving rhythmically, and all the time I'm saying, "Boy, this guy must have been some kind of pitcher—boy, this guy must have been some kind

of pitcher." Meantime, I had gone to the plate six times and had gotten one hit off him. I said, "To hell with this, I've got to go to work."

And then again, he was smart. He was smart. I can give you an example. I was up to the plate one time, I had the count 3–2. He gives me that double windup, got right up here, with his hands back of his head, and turned his wrist like this. Everybody in the park saw it—he made damn sure *I* saw it. I said, "Jesus—curve ball." And whoom! Fastball. Strike three.

Next day—he was always late getting to the park—just after they played the National Anthem, here comes Satchel. He comes in the dugout, says, "Where's Ted? Where's Ted?"

I said, "Right here, Satch."

He said, "You ought to know better than to guess with old Satch."

Joe DiMaggio "couldn't touch him" either, Veeck wrote. "Satch handled Joe with such ease that he'd drive us all nuts by deliberately walking a man to get to him."

Satch scoffed at the major league hitters. "Who they had up there for hitters? No one 'cept Ted and Joe. Outside, that's how I pitched to Ted and Joe and Yogi, and they never gave me no trouble with that long ball hitting."

Satchel's old friend, Ted Page, came to town to see him pitch and bumped into him in the lobby of their hotel. "Heh, Satch, what you say?" Ted greeted him. Paige, who was talking to the room clerk, looked up absentmindedly and said a quick "hi." Ted replied with a shrug and a "hi" himself and went out.

Later at the game, Ted went over to the bull pen and whistled a secret whistle they had once shared. "Heh, roomie!" Satchel, instantly recognizing his old friend, cried out and motioned Ted to meet him under the stands. While Satch kept one eye on the game to see if he was being called, the two old buddies spent the rest of the game gabbing.

Unfortunately, Satchel's stomach was "disputin'" him that year, and before he could pacify it with cool thoughts, he was 4–7 and the Indians were in third place. (Paige also saved five games, and had a good 3.04 ERA.) The Indians' troubles can't be blamed on Satch, however. Bearden had been driven out of the league, as the batters solved his knuckleball. Joe Gordon and Ken Keltner both lost 30 points off their batting averages. And outfielder Jeff Heath never recovered from a broken leg.

That winter Veeck sold the club, and Paige was unemployed again. His old boss, Tom Baird, gave him a job pitching for the Monarchs, who were just a shell of the former strutting kings of black baseball. Satch's record was 1–2 with a high 5.88 TRA.

When Veeck acquired the Browns in 1951, he sent for old Satch to return.

Paige "was still overpowering people," said Brownie pitcher Ned Garver. "The guy I compare him to more than anyone else is Nolan Ryan."

Garver became Paige's closest buddy on the team and won 20 games for the last-place club. He had seen Satchel pitch back in 1944 in a barnstorming game against Dizzy Dean in Ohio. "Oh, baby, he could hum that ball!" Garver said. In '51 Satch couldn't throw as hard as in '44,

> but he was still able to psych people out and still able to overpower people.
> Paige threw a lot of different pitches. He threw breaking balls from every different angle. He varied his motion and knew more about attacking the hitter from the pitching mound than anyone I ever saw. Paige didn't match his strength against theirs. That isn't pitching. Paige knew that hitting is timing and pitching is breaking that timing up. He didn't throw two fastballs at the same speed.

Brownie catcher Matt Batts agreed that Satch was still fast, had that legendary control, and knew the pitching art. If he lost his control, he'd move around on the rubber, trying different footholds, until he got it again. Against right-handed power hitters, Paige moved all the way to the right—he'd be off the mound entirely if they didn't watch him—then he'd come sidearm and drive the hitter off the plate.

Satch's motion was deceptive, Garver added. He could turn his back and look at second, and could still pinpoint the ball wherever he wanted to. "Today's coaches tell you to be consistent in your motion, and it's probably good advice. But they've never pitched as much as Satchel Paige did."

Paige was still a showman. In one game against a farm team in York, Pennsylvania, Garver said, Satch deliberately walked the bases loaded. After each walk, he'd stomp around on the mound, slam the resin bag down in disgust, etc. Then, said Garver, "he throws nine pitches, strikes out three people."

In St. Louis, Satch fielded a two-out grounder and started ambling to the dugout while the runner raced to first. Without breaking stride, at the last second Paige threw the ball across his body and threw a strike to first base for the out. "To me," said Garver, "that's colorful."

Satch didn't use the team trainer; he rubbed himself with his private snake oil, telling Garver that the secret formula involved going into the woods to find a hollow tree stump and scooping the water out. And "people from the different islands also sent him different ingredients," Garver said.

In his book, Veeck recounted one game against the Yankees: Paige had a no-hitter going after seven, when Phil Rizzuto spiked him covering first, and Satchel limped to the dugout. As was his custom, the peg-legged Veeck was sitting with his crutches in the bleachers, chatting with the fans about conditions in the restrooms and other matters of interest to general managers. He was also already mentally reading the next day's headlines: PAIGE PITCHES NO-HITTER, RETIRES WITH INJURY.

Then, to Veeck's horror, he realized that manager Zack Taylor was sending Satch back out to pitch the eighth! Bill broke all records for the 100-yard hobble to get to Taylor and tell him to call Satch back. But he was too late. Paige limped to the mound, gave up two hits, and the headline went up in smoke. It was the only time, Veeck said, that he seriously considered strangling a manager.

Satch was still using his hesitation pitch, Batts said: "He sure did." Facing his old teammate, Doby, one day, Paige called Batts to the mound. "Give me any signal you want to," Satch said, "I'm gonna throw my hesitation pitch and strike that so-and-so out." The Indians had a runner on second, who was presumably relaying Batts' signs to Doby, so Batts gave all sorts of fancy finger signals. Satch raised his big foot up high and brought it down, as Doby strode to meet the pitch. Then Satch released the ball. Doby cussed all the way to the bench.

Always the showman, Veeck staged a gala celebration one night. Satch and three other players formed a fife and drum corps—Satchel on the drums—and marched onto the field ahead of a giant cake, out of which popped a midget, Eddie Gaedel, in a Brownie uniform. A few moments later, the diminutive rookie strode up to the plate to pinch-hit in one of the legendary moments of baseball history. The occasion was doubly historic—the only time Paige was upstaged by anyone, especially a four-foot midget.

Satch spent three years 1951–53 as relief ace on the tail-end Browns, who finished eighth, seventh, and eighth.

He said he ran into surprisingly little race prejudice. In the

Pullman on day, he silently watched his teammates dealing the cards. When no one invited him, he leaned over and asked, "Did you all call for the porter?" They laughed and made room for him.

Batts said at first Satchel waited for the other players to take their showers before he went in, but later he showered with the others— and nearly scalded anyone next to him.

Louisianan Clint "Scrap Iron" Courtney caught Satch in '52 and '53 and struck up a friendship. They were as different as could be, said shortstop Billy Hunter—"the tall black man and the real short stubby white guy." Manager Marty Marion called Courtney "the bull-dog." Clint and Satch enjoyed riding each other.

Once, shagging flies in the outfield, Hunter remembered Court-ney taunting his buddy: "You only have to throw 60'6″. You couldn't throw the ball from here to home plate."

"I have $50 says I can," Satch smiled back. Runners were sent to the clubhouse to get the stakes, which Hunter held. They were about 320 feet from home, he estimated.

Clint says, "I'll give you three throws."

"I'll tell you what I'll do, Scrappy. I won't even take a step." He stood flat-footed and threw the first ball against the screen behind home plate. "That's just one warm-up. You said I could have three."

"Give him the goddam money," Clint growled; and, adds Hunter, "Satch threw the next one into the upper deck behind home."

When Courtney's unreconstructed father announced he was com-ing for a visit, Clint said they better cool the friendship, then changed his mind. He figured that together "Satch and me can whup pap."

Paige said he never got thrown out of a game in his life. "But I came close once." Jimmy Piersall, the erratic Red Sox outfielder, called him a "black so-and-so," and Satchel asked him how he'd like to hit with the ball in his mouth. Next time, "when he came up, he went down. He chased his hat and belt for half a block."

In 1952, Paige's manager was his old antagonist, Texan Rogers Hornsby, who called Satch in from the bull pen so often he won 12 games, the most by any 46-year-old in history.

Dizzy Dean, by then broadcasting games on TV, said Satch would make a better starting pitcher: He could win 15–20 games a year just pitching every Sunday, "and think of the drawing card you'd have." Hornsby must have been listening; he named Satch to start against the last-place Tigers, and Paige amazed everyone by going 12 innings to win it 1–0. The Tigers loaded the bases in the tenth with no outs, but Paige got Johnny Pesky (.254) and Johnny Groth (.284) on two ground balls, and Neil Barry (.228) on three straight "trouble ball" strikes.

By 1953 Paige, 47 years old, wasn't very fast anymore, his new manager, Marty Marion, said. "He was just a showpiece, he wasn't a good pitcher any more." But Marion admitted that Paige's control was still razor fine.

Brownie pitcher Harry Brecheen said Satch could still put his hat on home plate and bet the other fellows he could knock it off. On good days Satch could still throw the fastball. If he wanted to pitch, Brecheen said, "he'd go out there and get you out." But if he didn't feel good, "he'd throw a lot of breaking balls, and he wasn't a breaking-ball pitcher."

For the second time in his three years with the Browns, Satchel watched someone else steal the spotlight. The thief was an ancient rookie as screwy as Satchel himself, a character known as Alva Lee "Bobo" Holloman. After a few unimpressive relief stints, Bobo begged Marion to let him start. Poor Marty, with a second whacky pitcher to torture him, finally relented. That night, as the baseball gods directed every line drive into a Brownie glove, Bobo hurled a no-hitter, a goal that had eluded Satch in his five years in the majors.

Bobo didn't have another good game left and was gone by mid-season.

But Paige was named to the All-Star squad for the second time and finally got to pitch an inning at the age of 47. He faced perhaps the toughest lineup of his life, including four future Hall of Famers:

Gil Hodges	.302	31 homers
Roy Campanella	.312	41 homers
Eddie Mathews	.302	47 homers (league leader)
Duke Snider	.336	42 homers
Enos Slaughter	.291	6 homers

The old man got Hodges on a line drive. Campanella singled through the box. Mathews popped up for the second out. Snider walked. Slaughter singled over second for one run, and pitcher Murray Dickson—of all people!—singled to short left for another run but was thrown out trying to take second.

Satchel still entertained the Brownies with his stories. He'd keep the players up all night on the train spinning tales, Marion said. "But a team person? Nope. No team person. He was a strange person, made his own rules."

But Paige put people in the park. One time we had an exhibition in Hartford, a night game. He was advertised to pitch, and he didn't show up. The sportswriters were giving me hell. I said, "If you find him, I'll pitch him." [The crowd was getting nasty.] We got out of there fast. The next morning there was old Satchel sitting in the lobby in Boston. I said, "You almost got us lynched. That'll cost you five grand." But you know, Bill wouldn't take it [out of his pay].

The story with the Browns was the love affair with Bill Veeck. Satchel could do no wrong. If you fine Satchel for doing something wrong, it went in one ear and out the other, because Bill would never take [the money].

Old Satchel did things he wanted to do, didn't listen to anyone. My players were always saying, "Why don't you make Satchel do this? You're making us do it." I'd say, "When you get that old, you can do anything you want to, too."

I recall going out to say, "Pitch this guy high and outside." He'd say, "I like to pitch low and outside." He liked to defy you. You couldn't tell Satchel what to do no way.

Hunter recalled one game when Satchel did follow orders. Red Sox outfielder Tommy Umphlett (.283) was up with two out, two on, and the Brownies leading 4–3. Marion trotted to the mound. "I want you to throw him a fastball up in his eyes," Marion said.

"Skip, that's the only ball he can hit," Paige protested. But he obeyed orders, and Umphlett drove it against the fence to score two runs and win the game.

In the clubhouse after the game, Hunter said, Marion pounded the table to get attention. "I just want everyone to know I take the responsibility for that loss," he said.

"Will you be the losing pitcher too, Skip?" Satch asked wryly. Satch needed the win; he ended up 3–9 for the year, his worst showing in the white leagues.

That was the end of the line for Satch. Veeck sold the Brownies to an outfit that moved them to Baltimore and renamed them the Orioles.

Nevertheless, Paige's career in the American league, spanning ages 41–47, had been remarkable. In four of his five years his ERA was better than the American league average, usually much better:

Year	AL	Paige
1948	4.28	2.48
1949	4.20	3.04
1951	4.12	4.79
1952	3.67	3.07
1953	4.00	3.53
Average	4.05	3.29

Pete Palmer points out in *Total Baseball* that Paige's career ERA was 24 percent better than the average AL pitcher of his era.

Palmer also says that in four of Satch's five years, he was tougher to hit than the average American league hurler. (I call this the Pitching Average, the mirror of Batting Average; Palmer calls it Opposition Batting Average.):

Year	AL	Paige
1948	.266	.228
1949	.263	.230
1951	.262	.276
1952	.253	.226
1953	.262	.257
Average	.261	.241

Paige ended with a decent lifetime won–lost record of 28–31, plus 32 saves, not bad considering that three of the five years were with the Browns. Here is how Satchel did compared to his teams, year by year:

Year		W – L –Sv		Pct	Rank
1948	Cleveland	97 – 58		.626	(1)
	Paige	6 – 1	1	.857	
1949	Cleveland	89 – 65		.578	(3)
	Paige	4 – 7	5	.364	
1951	St. Louis	52 –102		.338	(8)
	Paige	3 – 4	5	.429	
1952	St. Louis	64 – 90		.416	(7)
	Paige	10 – 12	10	.545	
1953	St. Louis	54 –100		.351	(8)
	Paige	3 – 9	11	.250	
	Total	356 –415		.462	
	Paige	28 – 31	32	.475	

Paige's relief record was 18–23. Perhaps Dean was right about Satchel being more valuable as a starter. His record there was 10–8—5–3 in Cleveland and 5–5 with the wretched Browns.

For the next two years, Baird found Satchel some barnstorming gigs. Marion, meanwhile, moved to the White Sox and finished third twice in a row behind the Yankees. He made his best run for the pennant in '55, when the Sox finished five games behind. Veeck phoned Marion. "Why don't you get Satchel?" Bill asked, "He'd help you win the pennant."

Marty suppressed a hysterical laugh. "I couldn't control him with the Browns," he said, "how can I control him here?" Yet Satch just might have done it. It's intriguing for Chicago fans to think that one or two more victories here, another two or three more saves there, and the Sox just might have knocked Casey Stengel's Yanks out of the flag.

What was the secret of Paige's longevity? He couldn't have done it in the Negro leagues, Satch admitted—they would have bunted him right out of the league. Why the whites didn't, he never could figure out.

In 1956, Bill Veeck called Satch back to pitch in Triple-A minor league ball at Miami. His record: 11–4, 1.86. One of his wins was a one-hitter. Another came before 51,000 people at the Orange Bowl, second largest crowd in minor league history. He was 50 years old.

One of Paige's teammates was young Whitey Herzog, later famous as manager of the Royals and Cardinals. In a distance-throwing contest, Whitey wrote, he was throwing two-hoppers to home plate. Paige ambled out to center field and flipped sidearm throws to the plate on the fly.

The outfield wall had a small hole, just big enough for a ball to squeeze through, with a sign challenging batters to hit a ball through and win a thousand dollars. Could Satch throw one through the hole at 60'6"? Herzog asked.

"Wild Child, do the ball fit the hole?" Paige replied. Just barely, he was told. They bet a fifth of whiskey, shook hands, and Satch took aim and fired. The ball rattled around for a second, then dropped out. On the second pitch, it disappeared cleanly without even touching the sides. "Thank you, Wild Child," Satchel said and ambled away.

After a stint as pitching coach for the Atlanta Braves to help him qualify for a pension, Satchel pitched his last big league game for the Kansas City A's in 1965. He was 59, the oldest man by far ever to play in the majors, white or black. A's owner Charlie O. Finley signed him up, again to give him one more year toward his pension.

The organist played "The Old Gray Mare," "Ol' Rockin' Chair's Got Me," and "Silver Threads Among the Gold." Then Satchel pitched three legitimate innings of one-hit shutout ball against the Red Sox, the second-best hitting club in the league, with Carl Yastrzemski (.312), home run champ Tony Conigliaro, and others. He faced ten men and got nine out. The only ball hit out of the infield was a double by Yaz on a 3–0 count. In all, Satchel threw only 28 pitches.

Finley had invited as many of Satchel's old friends as he could find. Satch laughed that "Cool Papa Bell loved it so much, he pretty near had a heart attack."

Paige's career had now spanned 40 years, 1926–65.

He next embarked on a new career, this one in Hollywood, making a western with Robert Mitchum. Except for riding the horse, there was nothing to it, Satch said. "I've been in show business all my life, you know."

In 1971, Paige was elected to Cooperstown, the first Negro leaguer so honored. At first he was going to be put in a separate section, sort of "the back of the bus," as many quickly pointed out. The idea was hastily abandoned, and Satch's plaque went onto the same wall as Mathewson, Johnson, Alexander, Feller, and all the rest. I went to Cooperstown to be present at the historic occasion. Ted Page and Buck Leonard were there. So were Judy Johnson, Roy Campanella, and Monte Irvin, members of the special committee that had named Satch.

"Well, Mr. Veeck," Satchel told the crowd, "I got you off the hook today." He recalled the hardships of the old-timers ("I learned to pitch by the hour"), the high salaries of the moderns ("In my day, *banks* didn't have that much money"), and the contribution of blacks ("Who put the big leagues back on their feet after World War II?").

The next night Leonard and I had supper a block away from the Hall of Fame, and over coffee Buck grew philosophical:

> I stayed awake almost all night last night thinking about it. You know, a day like that stays with you a long time. It's something that you never had any dream you'd ever see. Like men walking on the moon.
>
> I always wanted to come up to Cooperstown. You felt you had a reason, because it's the home of baseball. But you didn't have a *special* reason. We never thought we'd get in the Hall of Fame. It was so far from us, we didn't even consider it. We didn't even think it would some day come to reality. We thought the way we were playing was the way it was going to continue. I never had any dream it would come. But last night I felt like I was part of it at last.

A year later I returned to Cooperstown to watch Josh Gibson and Leonard himself get inducted. They were followed by Bell and Irvin, Johnson and Oscar Charleston, Pop Lloyd and Martin Dihigo, Rube Foster and Ray Dandridge.

From his home in Kansas City, Satchel often went out to Harry S. Truman Stadium to see the Royals. He usually ended up in the dugout before the games, keeping Amos Otis and other players laughing at his tales of the old days on the road.

The last time I saw Paige was in 1981 at Ashland, Kentucky at a reunion of black old-timers. He had also been invited, along with 100 other top athletes, to the White House to lunch with Ronald Reagan on the same day and couldn't decide which invitation to accept.

"Ashland is a reunion of old black ball players, isn't it?" Lahoma asked.

Satchel admitted that it was.

"Well," she said, "that's you. Have you looked in the glass lately?"

He went to Ashland.

The expense account he turned in was, treasurer Nancy Dickinson told me, a masterpiece of its genre and brought tears of laughter to the eyes of all who were privileged to read it.

Suffering from emphysema, Satchel had to sit and rest most of the time, wheezing through a tube in his nose connected to his own portable oxygen machine. But he was glad to be there, he told his old friends and the townspeople. "At my age, I'm glad to be anywhere."

Oldsters Clint Thomas, almost blind; Double Duty Radcliffe, cherubic and lisping; Judy Johnson, Page, Bell, Webster McDonald, Chet Brewer, and Happy Chandler were there. So were youngsters Leonard, Dandridge, O'Neil, Hilton Smith, Willard Brown, Feller, Irvin, Johnny Taylor, Dave Barnhill, Leon Day, dapper Jimmie Crutchfield, a new Kentucky colonel; Gene Benson, bewhiskered Pint Israel, Piper Davis, Connie Johnson, Artie Wilson, Wilmer Fields, Chico Renfroe, Willie Mays, Ernie Banks, and Joe Black, plus Smokey Joe Williams' daughter, and Turkey Stearnes' widow.

They banqueted, joked, slapped hands, signed autographs, gave interviews to young white writers, hung out in motel rooms swapping tales both true and tall, and milled around the motel parking lot until almost dawn, taking their old stances at bat, taking their old stretches on the mound, fielding grounders, and turning double plays.

Irvin recalled a young kid who hung around the park in Havana, hoping to make the team—Fidel Castro. "If we knew he wanted to be a dictator," Monte said, "we would have made him an umpire."

Cool Papa recalled Satchel's famous story that Bell was so fast he could turn out the light and jump in bed before the room got dark. One night, he said, they shared a room on the road, and while Paige was out galavantin', Bell discovered that the light switch was faulty. There was a few-second delay before the lights went out. When Paige returned, Bell was waiting for him in his pajamas. "Sit down, Satch," he said. "I want you to watch something." He flipped the switch, strolled over to bed and pulled the covers up. Bing! The lights went out. "See, Satch," he called in the dark. "You been tellin' people that story 'bout me for years, and even *you* didn't know it was true!"

Feller, now gray but still dimple-chinned, told the group, "You did a lot for baseball, but baseball hasn't done much for you."

Chandler, 80, said he still played 18 holes of golf and offered his biceps to admirers, saying, "Feel these, pardner." Happy said he made his historic decision "because some day I'm going to meet my Maker. If He asks me, 'Why did you keep those people out?' and I say, 'Because they're black,' that just might not be a good enough answer."

Mays remembered hitting a double off Satchel in 1948, when Willie was 17 years old. "Who's that young fellow there?" Paige demanded of O'Neil. "Let me know when he comes back up."

"I come to the plate," Mays said. "The first baseman says, 'Here he is.' You know, I didn't come *close* to hitting him again."

Satchel remembered the game. But as he recalled it, Mays had not hit a double, he had robbed Paige of a double to center. Satch was very proud and sensitive about his hitting.

Willie said he once got beaned in Birmingham, and as he lay at the plate groaning, manager Piper Davis trotted out. "Can you see first base?" Davis asked, leaning down. Willie nodded weakly. "OK, get up and get on it," Davis said and trotted back to the dugout.

"You taught me to survive," Mays said. "You were the pioneers. You made it possible for us."

Diminutive Dave Barnhill took a lot of kidding from the others about throwing a cut ball. Satchel came to his defense. "That little man didn't have to cut no ball," Satchel declared.

"That made me feel bigger," Dave beamed. "I grew up. Satchel's the one and only. He made me feel good."

Satch told the group:

They said we couldn't play ball. They said we had tails. But we showed 'em we're people just like anyone else.

I got in trouble in Cooperstown for saying we had players in our league who didn't have to go to a farm club before they went to the major leagues. They told me to sit down. That's why I don't go back to Cooperstown. And I'm not going back either.

Did he look back on his career with bitterness? "Listen," Satch said, "if I had to do it all over again, I would. I had more fun and seen more places with less money than if I was Rockefeller."

In 1982 they wheeled Satchel out to dedicate Kansas City's new Satchel Paige Stadium.

Four days later, on June 8, the city had a power outage. Paige complained of chills. Lahoma put a blanket around his shoulders and asked, "You feeling OK, honey?" He died in his chair.

Epilogue

B uck O'Neil delivered the eulogy at the grave:

> Everyone was saying, "Isn't it a shame Satchel didn't play with all the great athletes of the major leagues [when he was younger]? But who's to say that he wasn't, playing with us? We played the white teams, and we won most of the time. I don't know that we were that much better, but we had something to prove. Maybe we played a little harder. We thought we were the best, but nobody else knew it but us.
>
> Our lives have been beautiful, but it could have been better. I was cheated. Yeah, all of these men were cheated. This is America, and that shouldn't have happened. I do think that our baseball did so much toward changing public accommodations.
>
> But don't feel sorry for us. I feel sorry for your fathers and your mothers, because they didn't get to see us play.

Satchel's old catcher, Joe Greene, wasn't at the grave. He was in ill health in Stone Mountain, Georgia and couldn't be there. But he would have understood Buck's remarks. As Greene told me once:

> I still say we did a lot for baseball, even if nobody knows about us any more. They say Jackie paved the way. He didn't pave the way. We did.

Today's millionaire black players don't know this. But the generation before them—the Mayses and Campanellas and Irvins—do. As Minnie Minoso, who went from the New York Cubans to the Cleveland Indians and Chicago White Sox, said, "Everything I had, I owe to you guys."

Baseball, and the world at large, had undergone profound changes since Paige and Gibson had picked up their first baseballs almost eight decades earlier.

"I'm writing a 'Memo to Josh Gibson,'" Ric Roberts told me.

> He's been dead over 30 years, but we used to talk a lot about blacks going into the major leagues. Josh said to me, "I'll believe it when I see it."

219

I'm writing about the things that have developed since the mid-'40's when he was roaring toward his end.

Roberts' mind wandered back to the day I had seen Josh and Satch play on that summer night of my boyhood. "Satchel Paige led us to the promised land," Ric said. "He was the guy that gave black baseball its first real economic solvency. We won't see his like again in our lifetime."

Or as Satchel himself would have put it: "If you want to know the truth, wasn't any mebbe so."

Appendix

Negro League Record Holders

The following were compiled by Dick Clark from data gathered from original box scores by Jim Riley, Paul Doherty, Jim Holway, John Holway, Jr., Tim Joyce, Neil Lanctot, Larry Lester, Jerry Malloy, Mona Peach, Bill Plott, Diane Walker, Edie Williams, the author, and many others. Totals are low compared to white major league leaders, because the Negro leagues played between 40 and 80 league games a year. The following are based only on Negro league games or against other top black teams; the Latin American winter league games are not included, nor are the innumerable barnstorming games against semipro and white major league opposition.

LIFETIME BATTING LEADERS
Batting Average

Player	AB	H	BA
* Pop Lloyd	1769	651	.368
John Beckwith	1739	637	.366
Dobie Moore	1393	509	.365
Heavy Johnson	1347	489	.363
Turkey Stearnes	3372	1186	.359
* Oscar Charleston	2992	1069	.357
Willard Brown	1787	635	.355
* Josh Gibson	1700	599	.352
* Monte Irvin	908	314	.346
Jud Wilson	3007	1036	.345
. . .			
* Cool Papa Bell	3952**	1335**	.338
* Ray Dandridge	824	276	.335
* Buck Leonard	1587	514	.324
* Martin Dihigo	1435	453	.316
* Judy Johnson	2692	816	.302

*Hall of Fame
**Leader

Home Runs

Player	AB	HR	HR/550 AB
Turkey Stearnes	3372	185	30
Mule Suttles	2962	183	34
* Oscar Charleston	3372	151	28
* Josh Gibson	1700	142	46
Willie Wells	3442	123	20
John Beckwith	1739	104	33
Edgar Wesley	1577	82	29
Frog Redus	2063	80	21
Dewey Creacy	3069	73	13
* Buck Leonard	1587	71	25

*Hall of Fame

Doubles		Triples	
Willie Wells	212	Turkey Stearnes	106
* Cool Papa Bell	203	* Cool Papa Bell	68
Turkey Starnes	199	Mule Suttles	63
Mule Suttles	184	* Oscar Charleston	63
* Oscar Charleston	167	Willie Wells	49
Jud Wilson	146	* Josh Gibson	47
Newt Allen	135	Bullet Rogan	47
George Scales	132	Clint Thomas	47
* Judy Johnson	135	Hurley McNair	47
Clint Thomas	122	Mackey, Torriente, Creacy	46

*Hall of Fame

SINGLE SEASON
Batting

Player	Year	AB	H	BA
* Pop Lloyd	1929	149	84	.564
* Josh Gibson	1943	190	89	.521
John Beckwith	1930	200	96	.480
Jud Wilson	1927	196	92	.469
Chino Smith	1929	229	104**	.454
Howard Easterling	1943	164	74	.451
Turkey Stearnes	1935	149	64	.430

*Hall of Fame
**Leader

Home Runs

Mule Suttles	1928	27
Willie Wells	1929	27
Turkey Stearnes	1928	24
Dewey Creacy	1926	23
Willie Wells	1927	23
Frog Redus	1928	21
* Oscar Charleston	1925	20
Chino Smith	1929	20

*Hall of Fame

Home Runs/550 AB

		AB	HR	HR/550 AB
* Josh Gibson	1939	72	16	122
* Josh Gibson	1937	42	7	92
Mule Suttles	1938	55	9	90
* Josh Gibson	1946	119	18	83
* Josh Gibson	1936	75	11	81

*Hall of Fame

Doubles			Triples		
* Josh Gibson	1943	32	Mule Suttles	1926	19
Willie Wells	1930	31	Turkey Stearnes	1923	15
* Cool Papa Bell	1925	29	Biz Mackey	1922	13
Mule Suttles	1929	29	Turkey Stearnes	1924	12
Ed Rile	1928	27	Turkey Stearnes	1924	12
Dobie Moore	1924	26	Turkey Stearnes	1930	12
* Cool Papa Bell	1929	25	Dobie Moore	1925	12
Mule Suttles	1926	25	* Buck Leonard	1943	11
* Cool Papa Bell	1926	24	* Oscar Charleston	1921	11
Dewey Creacy	1926	24	Riggins, McNair	1925	9

*Hall of Fame

LIFETIME PITCHING LEADERS
Victories

	W	L	Sv	Pct
Bill Foster	137	62	12	.688
Andy Cooper	123	58	30**	.674
* Satchel Paige	123	79	8	.609
Bill Byrd	115	72	7	.615
Bullet Rogan	113	45	15	.715
Ray Brown	109	34	2	.762**
Bill Holland	99	81**	5	.550
Nip Winters	95	54	3	.638
Ted Trent	94	49	3	.657
Webster McDonald	92	60	2	.605

*Hall of Fame
**Leader

Strikeouts

	IP	SO	SO/9 IP
* Satchel Paige	1584	1177	6.7
Bill Foster	1659	734	4.0
Bullet Rogan	1337	677	4.6
Bill Byrd	1283	577	4.0
Bill Holland	1356	575	3.8
Chet Brewer	1110	552	4.5
Ted Trent	1139	505	4.0
Andy Cooper	1455	476	2.9
Bill Drake	1098	446	3.6
Rube Currie	1146	442	3.5

Shutouts

Bill Foster	34
* Stachel Paige	26
Ray Brown	18
Bullet Rogan	18
Ted Trent	16
Andy Cooper	15

*Hall of Fame

SINGLE SEASON PITCHING RECORDS
Victories

	Year	W	L	Pct
Ray Brown	1940	24	4	.857
Slim Jones	1934	22	3	.880
Bill Foster	1927	21	3	.875
Ted Trent	1928	21	2	.913
Nip Winters	1925	21	10	.677
Connie Rector	1929	20	2	.909
Bill Drake	1921	20	10	.667
Leroy Matlock	1935	18	0	1.000

Strikeouts

	Year	IP	SO	SO/9 IP
* Satchel Paige	1929	196	184	8.4
Bill Foster	1930	199	134	6.1
Sam Streeter	1924	208	127	5.5
Bill Drake	1921	231	123	4.8
Bill Foster	1928	208	118	5.1
* Satchel Paige	1928	120	112	8.4
Dan Bankhead	1947	113	109	8.7**
* Satchel Paige	1932	120	109	8.2

*Hall of Fame
**Leader

Total Run Average (TRA)

	Year	IP	TRA
Slim Jones	1934	195	1.69
Laymon Yokely	1928	113	1.90
Bill Foster	1926	137	1.98
* Satchel Paige	1934	154	1.99

*Hall of Fame

Career Statistics

Paige, Leroy "Satchel" BR TR 6'3½" 180 lbs.
B. 7/7/06 Mobile, Ala.   D. 6/8/82 Kansas City, Mo.
Hall of Fame 1971

Year	Team	W-L	Pct	TRA	G	GS	CG	IP	H	BB	SO	ShO
1927	Bl Barons	8-3	727	3.27	20	9	6	93	63	19	80	3
	Playoff	0-0	.000	2.54	2	1	0	7	4	0	5	0
1928	Bl Barons	12-4	.750	3.07	26	16	10	120	107	19	112	3
1929	Bl Barons	11-11	.500	5.28	31	20	15	196*	191	39	184**	0
	Cuba	6-5	.545		15		8					
1930	Bham/Balt	11-4	.733	2.84	18	13	12	120	92	15	86	3
1931	Cle/Craws	5-5	.500	4.47	12	6	5	60	36	4	23	1
1932	Crawfords	14*-8*	.636	3.79*	29*	23*	19*	181*	92*	13	109*	3*
	California	No Record										
1933	Crawfords	5-7	.417	3.68	13	12	10	95	39	10	57	0
	Bismarck	No Record										
	California	18-1	.947					140			229	
1934	Crawfords	13-3	.813	1.99	20	17	15	154	85	21	97	6*
	Denv Post	3-0	1.00	2.20	4	4	3	28	22	1	44	
1935	Crawfords	0-0	.000	0.00	2	2	0	7	0	0	10	0
	Bismarck	No Record										
1936	Crawfords	7-2	.778	2.70	9*	9*	9*	70*	54	11	59	3*
	Denv Post	3-0	1.00	0.90	4			30	18	9	50	
1937	Dom Repub	8-2	.800									
	St L/Stars	1-2	.333	3.46	3	3	2	26	22	6	11	0
	Denv Post	0-1	.000	4.50	1	1	0	8	7	3	14	0
1938	Mexico	1-1	.500		3	1	1	19		12	7	
1939		Sore Arm, on Monarchs' 'B' Team										
	P Rico	19-3	.864	1.93#	24			205			54	6
1940	Monarchs	1-1	.500	4.50	2	2	2	12	10	0	15	1
1941	Monarchs	7-1	.875	2.21	13	11	3	67	38	6	61*	0
1942	Monarchs	8-5*	.615	2.88	20	18	6	100	68	12	78*	1
	W Series	2-1	.667	324	5	3	0	25	16	3	18	0
1943	Monarchs	5-9	.357	4.26	24*	20	4	88*	80*	16*	54*	0
1944	Monarchs	5-5	.500	1.28	13			78	47	8	70	2
1945	Monarchs	3-5	.375		13	7	1	38	22	2	23	0
1946	Monarchs	5-1	.833		9	9	1	68	65	12	48	0
	W Series	1-1	.500	6.30	3	0	0	10	16	1	13	0
	Vs Majors	2-1	.667	1.00	3			26	15	9	23	0
1947	Monarchs	1-1	.500	1.64	2	2	2	11	5			0
	Puerto Rico	0-3	.000	2.91#				40	5			
	Vs Majors	1-1	.500	1.73	5	5	1	27	13	1	44	0

Career Statistics (continued)

Year	Team	W-L	Pct	TRA	G	GS	CG	IP	H	BB	SO	ShO
1948	*Indians*	*6–1*	*.857*	*2.59*	*22@*	*7*	*3*	*75@*	*61*	*25*	*45*	*2*
	W Series	0–0	.000	0.00	1	0	0	1	0	0	0	0
1949	*Indians*	*4–7*	*.364*	*3.14*	*31*	*5*	*1*	*83*	*70*	*33*	*54*	*0*
1950	**KC/Phil**	**1–2**	**.333**	**5.88**	**8**		**0**	**26**	**28**			**0**
1951	*Browns*	*3–4*	*.429*	*5.66*	*23*	*3*	*0*	*62*	*67*	*29*	*48*	*0*
1952	*Browns*	*12–10*	*.545*	*3.33*	*46*	*6*	*3*	*138*	*116*	*57*	*91*	*2*
1953	*Browns*	*3–9*	*.250*	*3.92*	*57*	*4*	*0*	*117*	*114*	*39*	*51*	*0*
1954		No Record										
1955		No Record										
1956	Miami	11-3	.733	2.35	37			111	101	28	79	
1957	Miami	10-8	.556	2.65	40			119	98	11	76	
1958	Miami	10-10	.500	3.20	28			110	94	15	40	
1959		No Record										
1960		No Record										
1961	Portland	0-0	.000	4.32	5			25	28	8	12	
1962		No Record										
1963		No Record										
1964		No Record										
1965	*Athletics*	*0-0*	*.000*	*0.00*	*1*	*1*	*1*	*0*	*3*	*1*	*0*	*1*
1966	Peninsula	1-2	.333	9.00	1			0	2	5	0	0

Boldface entries indicate Negro league teams
Italic entries indicate Major League teams
\# ERA
@ Includes two hitless innings against Dodgers
*Led league
**Negro league record

Recap:

League	W-L	Pct	G	GS	CG	IP	H	BB	SO	ShO
Negro Lg	**123-79**	**.609**	**279**	**207**	**122**	**1548**	**1142**	**241**	**1177**	**26**
Latin Am	36-14	.720							241#	6#
Minor Lg	31-22	.585	111			367	320	59	214	
Major Lg	*28-31*	*.475*	*179*	*26*	*7*	*476*	*429*	*183*	*290*	*4*
Vs Maj Lg	*4-2*	*.600*	*7*	*7*	*2*	*62*	*34*	*13*	*76*	*0*
Californ	18-1	.944				150			229	
Denv Post	6-1	.857	9	9		66	37	13	108	0
W Series@	3-1	.750	11	4	0	43	37	18	36	0
East-West@	2-1	.667	6	1	0	12	11	4	13	0
Totals	251-152	.623	622	257	142	3032	1960	602	2398	37

Boldface entries indicate Negro league teams
Italic entries indicate Major League teams
incomplete
Vs Major Lg: includes 1936, 1946-47 only
@ Includes white majors World Series and All Star games
*Led league
**Negro league record
Denver Post tourney figures courtesy of Jay Sanford

Career Statistics

Gibson, Josh BR TR 6'2" 217 lbs.
B. 12/21/11 Buena Vista, Ga. D. 1/20/47, Pittsburgh, Pa.

Year	Team	G	AB	H	2B	3B	HR	HR/550 AB	SB	BA	Psn
1930	Grays	10	33	8	1	0	1	17	1	.242	c
	Playoff	9	38	14	2	1	3	45	0	.368	c
1931	Grays	32	128	47	8	4	6*	26	0	.368	c
1932	Grays	46*	147	42	3	5*	7*	26	1	.286	c,of
1933	Grays	34	116	42	8	1	6	28	1	.362	c,p
	Cuba		No Record								
1934	Crawfords	50	190	56	13**	4	12*	35	0	.295	c
1935	Crawfords	49	191	58	11	2	13*	35	8*	.304	c
	Playoff	5	9	4	0	1	2	122	0	.444	c
1936	Crawfords	23	75	27	3	0	11*	81	0	.360	c
	Denv Post	7	30	13			4	125		.433	
1937	Domin Rep	13	53	24	4	5	2	21		.453	c
	Grays	12	42	21	0	4*	7	92	0	.500@	c
	Cuba		61	21	3	2	3	27		.341	c
1938	Grays	18	60	21	2	0	4	37	1	.350	c
	Cuba		186	66	11	3	11*	33		.355	c
1939	Grays	27	72	24	2	2	16*	122	0	.333@	c
	P. Rico		150	57			6	22		.380	c
1940	Grays	1	6	1	0	0	0	0	0	.000	c
	Mexico	22	92	43	7	4	11	66	3	.467	c
1941	Mexico	94	358	134	31	3	33*	51	7	.374	c
	P Rico		123	59	12	4	13*	58		.479*	c
1942	Grays	40	121	39	8	1	11*	50	3	.323	c
	W Series	4	13	2	0	0	0	0	0	.154	c
1943	Grays		190*	99*	32**	8*	14*	41	0	.521*	c
	W Series	6	20	5	0	0	1	28	0	.250	c
1944	Grays	48	165	57	8	5	8	27	2	.345	c
	W Series	5	15	6	0	0	1	37	0	.400	c
1945	Grays	49*	161	64	6	4	9	31	0	.398	c
	W Series	4	15	2	0	0	0	0	0	.133	c
	P Rico		116	22	4	1	0	0	0	.190	c
1946	Grays		119	43	7	5	18*	83	0	.361@	c

Boldface entries indicate Negro League teams
*Led league
*Negro league record
@Slugging average in 1937 was 1.190; in 1939, 1.033; in 1946, .958.

Recap:

League	G	AB	H	2B	3B	HR	HR/550 AB	SB	BA
Negro Lg		**1820**	**644**	**110**	**70**	**141**	**44**	**32**	**.354**
Latin America		1139	426	72	22	79	38	15	.374
Post Season	35	110	33	2	2	7	35	0	.300
White Majors	15	61	26	1	1	5	45	0	.426
East-West	9	28	15	3	0	0	0	1	.453
Denver Post	7	30	13			4	125		.433
Totals		3189	1157	188	70	236	40	32	.362

Josh Gibson vs. White Big Leaguers

Year	AB	H	2B	3B	HR	Pitcher
1931	6	4	0	0	2	Uhle (11–12)
1932	3	0	0	0	0	Swift (14–10)
	5	3	0	0	0	Swift, French (18–16)
	5	0	0	0	0	French, Frankhouse (4–6)
	(4)	4	0	0	0	Parmelee (0–3)
1934	1	0	0	0	0	D Dean (29–7)
	3	2	0	0	1	D Dean, P Dean (19–11), Kline (7–2)
1935	(4)	3	0	0	0	D Dean, Swift (15–8), Ryba (1–1)
	(4)	3			1	D Dean, Winford (0–0), (Thevenow)
	4	0	0	0	0	D Dean, Winford, Ryba
	5	1	0	0	1	Winford, Ryba, (Herman)
1936	6	1	0	0	0	Whitehill (14–11), Kennedy (21–9)
	4	2	0	0	0	Knott (9–17), Kennedy
1943	4	2	1	1	0	Hughes (in Service; 12–18 in '42)
1946	3	1	0	0	0	VanderMeer (10–12)
15 G	61	26	1	1	5	.426

(Numbers in parentheses are presumed at bats)
(Pitchers in parentheses were not major leaguers)

Index